Internet Society

Internet Society

The Internet in Everyday Life

Maria Bakardjieva

SAGE Publications
London ● Thousand Oaks ● New Delhi

First published 2005

SAGE Publications Ltd
1 Oliver's Yard
55 City Road
London EC1Y 1SP

SAGE Publications Inc.
2455 Teller Road
Thousand Oaks, California 91320

SAGE Publications India Pvt Ltd
B-42, Panchsheel Enclave
Post Box 4109
New Delhi 110 017

British Library Cataloguing in Publication data

A catalogue record for this book is available
from the British Library

ISBN 0 7619 4338 2
ISBN 0 7619 4339 0

Library of Congress Control Number available

Typeset by C&M Digitals (P) Ltd., Chennai, India
Printed in India by Gopsons Papers Ltd, Noida

For my parents Deshka and Peter Bakardjiev
with love and gratitude.

Contents

Acknowledgements

At each step of my work towards the completion of this book I have benefited from the generous help of people with whom I have shared smaller or bigger sectors of everyday life. Ultimately, this project materialized thanks to my respondents – the 23 Internet users who let me into their homes and computers and trusted me with their stories. I am deeply grateful to them all for their generosity and candour. I wish to acknowledge the assistance in recruiting participants for my study that I received from the Board of Directors of the Vancouver Community Net.

My colleagues at Simon Fraser University and the University of Calgary provided a nurturing intellectual environment, direct or indirect advice and example to learn from. I am particularly indebted to Richard Smith, Ellen Balka, William Richards and Linda Harasim at Simon Fraser University, as well as David Mitchell, Liza McCoy, Janice Dickin, Edna Einsiedel, Doug Brent and David Taras at the University of Calgary. Yvonne Pratt provided technical assistance with the printing of my files.

Kathleen Scherf's trust in me and her unwavering support contributed significantly to the realization of this project. Gail Faurschou acted as a sounding board for my ideas at a critical point of my work. My friend David Smith stood by me through difficult times and stimulated my thinking with his suggestions and feedback. Richard Pinet, Ian Chunn, Debra Pentecost, Diana Ambrozas, Susan Bryant, Kwan Ramasoota and James Compton assisted with countless smaller and bigger things, and most importantly, with their friendship and solidarity.

This book owes a huge debt to Andrew Feenberg from whose fascinating work I drew and whose encouragement and comments kept me on track. Steve Woolgar showed me the joy of playing with ideas in unconventional, and often provocative, ways. Elizabeth Cass was involved in this project in more than one way. Her observations and wisdom informed my understanding of Internet use. Her subtle language sense and remarkable empathy helped translate my sometimes enigmatic expressions into proper English.

My parents and my sister Antonina were there for me each and every time I needed a helping hand, understanding or a confidence boost. My bright teenager, Peter, solved my computer problems and never missed a chance to remind me that I should have finished this work long ago. My little boy, Victor, was a wonderful distraction and helped me learn from fairy tales. My husband, Dobromir Rizov, took care of the necessities of everyday life while I was theorizing about it.

I wish to thank Chris Rojek and Kay Bridger for finding great (anonymous) reviewers for my text, and these reviewers themselves for their open-minded reading and interesting suggestions.

The Killam Residential Fellowship awarded to me by the University of Calgary in 2003 was instrumental to the completion of this book. Part of the research work benefited from NSF Award # 0004243. Earlier versions of Chapters 5 and 7 have been published, in the journals *New Media and Society* and *Media, Culture and Society*, respectively.

Introduction

The thousands of people who buy a health magazine, the customers in a supermarket, the practitioners of urban space, the consumers of newspaper stories and legends – what do they make of what they 'absorb', receive and pay for? What do they do with it?

(Michel de Certeau, 1984, *The practice of everyday life*, p. 31)

Among the Natives of the Internet Islands

When I came to North America in the early 1990s and first heard the words 'Internet' and 'cyberspace', they were already the key icons of a new mythology. Making my way through the ample stock of media and academic texts detailing the phenomena denoted by these words, I encountered imaginative accounts of what computer networking was going to do for individuals and society. For some reason, however, I found the natives' enchantment with this mythology hard to understand. My incredulous outsider's mind could not stop wondering who would be interested in experimenting with these new technical marvels and why.

In the early 1990s this sounded like a sensible question. It seemed to me that both the media and the academic discourses regarding the Internet demonstrated a curious inconsistency. They swarmed with sweeping predictions of how computer-mediated communication would transform every facet of society. At the same time, the image of the Internet user lurking behind those predictions was quite specific. In mass media accounts, this was the 'computer geek', the young, dynamic, middle-class North American male or, more rarely, female, excited by everything concerning computers. In academic discussions, the implied user was typically a university student or professor, a computer professional or a semi-professional hobbyist. Sure enough, these images did represent the first wave of Internet adopters. The problem for me stemmed from the fact that the projected future of the medium and its social definitions were based exclusively on the practices of these early user groups. The emphasis on surfing, game-playing, and inventing alternative personae in Multi-user domains/dimensions (MUDs)[1] along with more 'serious' applications enacted by professors, students and other knowledge workers characterized the emergent public understanding of the Internet. It was tacitly assumed that the rest of society would follow suit, captivated by the new possibilities and unconcerned by the costs.

Something in these projections rang false to me. Not having grown up with computers, and balancing a fragile budget, I was experiencing the burden of the time, money and effort needed to acquire a computer, software, and Internet equipment and skills. I was also quite doubtful that the average person juggling work, family and the scarce social life that remains possible in between would find time or be willing to sit in front of the computer to play Dungeons and Dragons, or even to surf the newly emerging World Wide Web. After all, the general population did not hold jobs where processing information was so essential as to justify the investment in computer networking. In short, I could see the utility of the Internet as a working tool and a somewhat eccentric pastime, but I found it difficult to envisage its wide applicability as a household object and mass medium. If such a development ever occurred, I thought, the interests and goals behind it would be different from those pursued by professionals and techno-geeks.

Towards the end of the 1990s, North American statistics were showing a growing rate of Internet adoption. Even with the prevalence of educated and higher-income users factored in (see Industry Canada, 1999; US Department of Commerce, 1999), this still meant that many non-professionals and non-geeks were going online, buying computers, and paying subscriptions to Internet Service Providers (ISPs). The economic viability of ISPs as a new kind of enterprise was itself evidence that the general population was buying into computer networking in both a figurative and a literal sense. Unconvinced by technological determinism, I saw nothing natural in this enthusiastic acceptance of the new technology. I kept wondering why people were going for it. Were they lured by the media hype or brainwashed by advertising? Were they alarmed by the alleged consequences of computer and Internet illiteracy for their children's future? Were the flashy pages of the booming World Wide Web attracting them beyond reasonable cost-benefit consideration?

I could not accept that the thousands of people bringing an Internet connection into their homes were merely dupes driven by promotional rhetoric. British cultural studies notwithstanding, my East European familiarity with brainwashing endeavours (albeit less subtle ones than the marketing of the Internet) had taught me the power of popular resistance and sheer common sense. So, if the masses of new Internet subscribers were not dupes, they should be putting the network to some uses of their own. I wanted to know what these uses were and whether the social institutionalization of the Internet as a communication medium was taking them into account.

Thus the idea of this study was born. It was going to be an ethnography of everyday Internet use. It was intended to approach the question of the Internet's implications for society from the bottom up, that is, starting with the daily experiences of ordinary users. It was to be performed by an outsider seeking to understand the meanings and practices pertaining to this culture.

A few more words regarding my 'outsider status' are in order here. As the 1990s were unfolding, Canada was becoming my actual home, despite the fact that I would seize every opportunity to go 'back home' to Bulgaria to visit. I was living in the gravity field between two homes and two cultures, dissimilar in countless features, but not the least in their degree of computerization. During my undergraduate years in Bulgaria, the computer had been an almost fictional character from a future that my generation contemplated with awe, but did not expect to taste for real. The typewriter had been my working tool as a journalist. I had used a computer for the first time in early 1992, against the passionate discouragement streaming from my computer-knowledgeable friends. Computers belonged categorically within the professional precincts of the technological elite and it was none of my business to venture there. I encountered exactly the opposite expectations when I moved to Vancouver to work on my doctoral degree. The university environment was saturated with computers. My lack of skill around them made me feel immensely inferior to anybody who knew how to cut and paste, as well as continually at the mercy of the technical support staff. Thankfully, the young men running the computer labs were much more helpful and less scornful towards dummies than their Bulgarian counterparts.

Then the Internet came out of nowhere to further complicate my life. Now I was expected not only to write my papers on a computer, but also (the horror, the horror!) to e-mail my professors. As time went by, however, what was initially experienced as severe pressure and an endless source of frustration was turning into a fact of my professional life. Moreover, I brought a computer into my home and found myself staring at its screen not only in the process of writing and editing papers, but also for the purpose of maintaining contacts, reading the news or watching my son play

3

games. Thus, on second thoughts, I have to admit that my study was more than an effort to learn about what other people did with the Internet. It was also an attempt to make sense of my own 'technobiography' (Henwood et al., 2001) by testing it against the stories of my fellow men and women. At the same time, I wanted to go beyond the academic context that defined my own experiences with the Internet. If the new medium was to be a factor in social life at large, I reasoned, it should be of use to people who did not earn their livelihood on and around computer networks and who were therefore not obliged to embrace them the way I was.

I specified the type of Internet user I wanted to meet and come to know as the 'simple customer' (Latour, 1987, p. 137): the man or woman without expertise or vested economic interest in the Internet. This user had to be someone who had tapped into his or her own resources to acquire a computer and had paid for the Internet connection to a commercial (or non-profit) provider.[2] I was aware that this category was pretty broad, but it served my purpose at the time: to exclude the early adopters – computer professionals, academics and hobbyists – and to see who the rest were and why they were there.

Why the Home?

The place where I wanted to meet this 'simple' user was at his or her home. In contrast to computerization and networking at the workplace, the penetration of computers and modems into individual homes was a relatively recent development in the late 1990s. The Internet industry in most western countries had just started taking a decisively domestic orientation. Marketing was beginning to target the family home as the ultimate recipient of Internet services and products. As an overspill of tele-work and tele-education (taking educational courses at different levels over the Internet), an Internet connection was being installed in more and more households,[3] thus increasing the exposure of spouses, children and other family members. In the process, driven by the powerful push from the telecommunications and computer hardware and software industries, the Internet was gradually being assimilated into the home and the daily routines of its inhabitants along with the telephone, the television, and audio and video equipment.

My effort to document the entry of the Internet into the homes of ordinary users was also motivated by the desire to capture an important aspect of this medium's social history. As had happened with earlier technologies and media (see Spigel, 1992), invention, production and regulation formed the focus of interest for Internet historians,[4] while the practices of everyday users remained largely invisible. The time to write this unglamorous, but nonetheless important, history was ripe, I believed, as the 1990s drew to a close.

Communication researchers, for their part, were keenly interested in looking closely at online social phenomena, recognizing in the Internet a radically new environment for social action and interaction (representative of this approach are Corell, 1995; Jones, 1995, 1997; Reid, 1991; Smith and Kollock, 1999). Hine (2000) has pointed out that while these studies produced many valuable insights, they tended to treat the Internet as a culture in its own right and stopped short of making it clear how online activities fit into the offline lives of participants. Cyberspace, following Gibson's (1984) evocative image, was perceived as transcending spatial limitations, conducive to free-floating disembodiment, displacement and the playful engagement with disembodied others in virtual worlds. The home, on the other hand, is the epitome of anchorage, of place, of locale, of materiality and routine. To examine the Internet in the home seemed almost antithetical to the bias of the new medium and everything that fascinated communication and cultural analysts.

Why Qualitative Research?

The HomeNet project carried out by a research team at Carnegie Mellon University (HomeNet, 1999, see also Kraut et al., 1998) represented a different trend in the emergent Internet research. This study did raise the logical and long overdue question of what happens when the Internet enters the home. The social-psychological agenda of the team, however, centred the investigation predominantly on the Internet's *impact* on domestic users. Consequently, HomeNet could not offer the much needed in-depth look at the symbolic processes unfolding in the domestic context. In recent years, qualitative research approaches aimed at revealing the meaning-making work that accompanies the adoption of information and communication technology in various spheres of life has been steadily gaining ground. The European Media Technologies in Everyday Life Network has produced a series of insightful papers focusing on the 'domestication' of information technologies (see www.emtel2.org/). Lally (2002) has examined in detail the consumption of computers as domestic objects in Australian households. Miller and Slater (2000) have documented the diverse meanings and applications that the Internet finds at the hands of users in Trinidadian homes. Yet those seemingly simple questions raised by de Certeau: 'What do they make of what they "absorb", receive and pay for? What do they do with it?' (1984, p. 31) have only just begun to be addressed with regard to home-based Internet users.

I believe the examination of domestic Internet use with these questions in mind is important for several reasons. In the home, the physical entry point to the network, we observe the user as a socially situated individual and can interpret his or her Internet-related behaviour against the backdrop of his or her everyday life. How is Internet use integrated with the practices that constitute family and community? Does it help establish meaningful relationships between the individual and the entities of the larger social world? The social and cultural role of the Internet that many have pondered can be evaluated correctly only by a careful examination of this immediate level of engagement of people with the medium.

Another reason why the domestic context calls for qualitative investigation is the fact that it represents the basis for the appropriation of the new communication system by self-motivated users. What is the relationship between acceptance of and resistance to existing technological and cultural forms? Do users themselves initiate new technical and cultural forms based on the medium? The invention of functions and meanings on the part of ordinary users is particularly vibrant at the early stage of the social shaping of a new technology and communication medium. Later in the process, the interpretations preferred by powerful business and political interests tend to prevail. Alternative possibilities initially evolved by users die out if they do not fit into the dominant mould. Thus, identifying and documenting such possibilities in the case of Internet development might prove to be of historical and political importance. The study of what I will call 'use genres' invented by ordinary users can provide the basis for a political critique of the medium, a critique of the real by the possible (Lefebvre, 1991). What should the Internet be like? What features should it have if the applications and meanings discovered by ordinary users are to be taken seriously and on an equal basis with the visions and interests of engineers, managers and marketers? Such reflections can contribute to a democratic process of building the new communication medium from the bottom up as a sociotechnical system.

Some Tools of the Trade

Several theoretical perspectives on media and technology proved helpful in offering productive concepts for my inquiry. These include, but are not limited to, social construction of technology, critical theory of technology, cultural studies of media and phenomenological sociology. The model of domestication of commodities developed by Silverstone et al. (1992) and further elaborated by Silverstone and Haddon (1996), provided a useful middle-level theory that guided my empirical study of Internet use in the home. While I have endeavoured to remain true to the original content of these theories, I have also appropriated them substantively for my own interests and goals in this project.

My primary theoretical goal has been to elaborate a conception of the user as an agent in the field of technological development and new media shaping. In order to achieve this, I weave together four conceptual strands. The first is the constructivist notion of interpretative flexibility of artefacts (Pinch and Bijker, 1987). The second is Feenberg's (1991) theory of subversive rationalization and democratic transformation of technology. Third, I adopt the concept of alternative reading of texts from cultural studies and extend it into a perspective on technology as language.

Next, I move on to develop an understanding of everyday life, and the place of the home in it, that combines the insights of phenomenological sociology (Schutz and Luckmann, 1973) and critical theory (Lefebvre, 1971, 1991). Phenomenological sociology offers valuable insights into how people experience their everyday lifeworld and how human action is constituted with regard to the structures of the lifeworld. In this way, phenomenological sociology provides access to the standpoint of the subject manipulating her physical and social environment in pursuit of her own projects.

Critical theory, conversely, sets itself the explicit goal of identifying social relations that remain beyond the everyday horizon of the thinking and acting subject, but are nevertheless crucial in determining the limits and possibilities in her thinking and acting. Drawing on ideas from these distinct schools of thought, I expose the dual life of technology as an object in the everyday lifeworld on the one hand, and as an embodiment of social relations on the other. Against this backdrop, technology in the home can be seen as both invader and captive, as colonizer and colonized.

The empirical study of Internet use by non-professional domestic users that I design on the basis of this theoretical framework has an ethnographic character in that it attempts to understand technological practices from the standpoint of users. It draws on users' narratives and examines the arrangements of their personal Internet-related spaces.[5] The exploration of the electronic 'interiors' carved by my respondents in the memory of their computers adds a new technique to the toolbox employed by earlier ethnographies of media consumption (see Moores, 1993).

7

Ultimately, the goal of my study has been to bring to the fore the creative work involved in being a domestic user of the Internet. I want to capture the numerous subtle ways in which people dealing with the medium in everyday life make choices and strike a balance between autonomy and subordination. I want to counter the grand narratives of computer networking with a host of personal stories like the ones people tell each other every day. Grand narratives present us with what is happening beyond our reach. Personal stories give us ideas about what to do in particular circumstances. In this lies their empowering potential.

Notes

[1]Multi-user domain or dimension (MUDs); a text-based virtual environment where users can talk and interact with each other.

[2]This was another aspect that distinguished academics and professionals who, most typically, had access to Internet services provided by their universities or companies free of charge.

[3]According to Statistics Canada, in 1994, 25% of Canadian households had home computers; one third of those had modems. Statistics Canada's Household Internet Use Survey for 1997 and 1998 reported that 39.8% of Canadian households had computers in 1997, and 45.1% had them in 1998. The penetration of the Internet in Canadian homes for these years was respectively 17.2% and 24.8% (Statistics, Canada, 1999). In the US, a survey by the Department of Commerce registered an increase in household Internet availability from 18.6% of all US households in 1997 to 26.2% in 1998 (quoted in Kraut and Cummings, 2002). In the UK, 10% of households had access to the Internet from home in 1998, but the number grew exponentially in the following years (see National Statistics Online, 2004).

[4]See Rosenzweig (1998) for a critical review of various Internet histories.

[5]Altogether, 23 domestic users from the Vancouver area contributed to my study. In some cases, household members of my main informants also took part in the interviews.

ONE Conceptualizing User Agency

Enter the User

Before heading into my empirical study of home Internet use, let me introduce the main character of this book – the Internet User – and explicate her or his part in the interplay between technology and society. By the user I mean the 'ordinary man'[1] (de Certeau, 1984) and woman who is not involved as a professional (engineer, programmer, designer, etc.) or decision-maker in the industrial, commercial or service sectors developing computer-networking technology.

Analysts have seen this ordinary user as the person for whom technological innovation arrives last, but who nevertheless represents the ultimate target of innovation's products. Paradoxically, the user is a marginal figure to the technological project as a subject, but has a central place in it as an object. Many will recognize her as the 'adopter' of innovation studies. She is identical with Latour's 'simple customer' (1987, p. 137) who receives the technological artefact packaged as a 'black box' and is often actively discouraged from examining its contents. Critical studies of technology typically define her as the powerless victim of technological domination. Finally, but tellingly, she is the proverbial fool of 'foolproof' design.

In contrast with most of these patronizing representations of the user, I will attempt to conceive of her as an active contributor to the shaping of technology. To achieve this, I will have to identify sources of influence available to the user, that is, to discern the 'power of the powerless', if I may borrow a phrase coined by Václav Havel[2] (Havel and Keane, 1985) in a different context and in relation to a different object. I will turn to several influential schools of thought to look for concepts potentially helpful in my search for user agency. The place to start, I believe, is the social construction of technology approach (SCOT), as its theoretical framework places human agency at the centre of technological development.

The Social Construction of Technology:
Insights and Controversies

The theory and research of social constructivists has demonstrated convincingly that new technological systems emerge through a process of negotiation and struggle over meanings and material shapes involving a myriad of social actors (see Bijker and Law, 1992; Hughes, 1987; Latour, 1987; Pinch and Bijker, 1987). The central premise of the SCOT approach, which represents one particular stream within the broader constructivist movement (Bijker, 2001), is that all technological artefacts exhibit 'interpretative flexibility' (Pinch and Bijker, 1987, p. 27). This concept expresses the constructivist belief that there is not just one possible way or one best way to design an artefact. Different 'relevant social groups' can come up with widely divergent meanings of the same technology. This circumstance gives rise to technological controversies: different interpretations, problems and solutions concerning the technical shape of the artefact contend for universal acceptance. In time, certain interpretations achieve wide acceptance, which leads to closure of debate – the interpretative flexibility of the artefact diminishes. The artefact itself 'stabilizes' in terms of shape and function (Bijker, 1995, p. 86; Pinch and Bijker, 1987, p. 44).

Therefore, so the argument goes, technical artefacts represent contingent products of the activities of social actors rather than inevitable consequences of scientific achievements or autonomous technological development. Their established forms have not been the only possible ones. Contingency and human choice rather than forces of technical necessity, such as natural laws, shape the course of technological history. By advancing this conclusion, constructivists contribute to the demystification of the social and political character of allegedly technologically rational choices (see Feenberg, 1993a).

The main tool for deconstructing technical design back to the logic of social interaction, out of which it originally emerged, is the notion of 'relevant social groups' (Pinch and Bijker, 1987). It draws attention to the perceptions, goals and strategies of the social actors participating in the process of selection among numerous technical possibilities. Relevant social groups, by definition, are:

> institutions and organizations (such as the military or some specific industrial company), as well as organized or unorganized groups of individuals. The key requirement is that all members of a certain social group share the same set of meanings, attached to a specific artefact. (Pinch and Bijker, 1987, p. 30)

Although this notion offers a useful insight into the historical process through which some enduring technical structures have come into being, it has attracted criticism from various quarters. 'What about groups that have no voice but that nevertheless will be affected by the results of technological change? What about groups that have been suppressed or deliberately excluded? How does one account for potentially important choices that never surface as matters for debate and choice?' Winner has asked (1993, p. 369). For him, the concept of relevant social groups is dangerously pluralist and gives the false impression that all social groups can be equally active and equally influential in making technical decisions.

Another problem critics find with the constructivist theory model of technical change is its inadequate account of structure and agency. Constructivists, in Winner's view, disregard 'the possibility that there may be dynamics evident in technological change beyond those revealed by studying the immediate needs, interests, problems and solutions of specific groups and social actors' (1993, p. 370). The point is that constructivist theory pays no heed to the enduring features of the social system and the deep-seated political biases that can underlie the spectrum of technological choices, or in other words, to the constraining dimensions of social structure. In a similar vein, feminist scholars (see Berg and Lie, 1995; Cockburn, 1992, 1993; Gill and Grint, 1995) have accused constructivism of rendering women invisible and gender irrelevant in the technology-shaping process. By focusing exclusively on networks of social actors immediately involved in the development of a particular technology, constructivist analysis posits women as non-actors because they are, most of the time, empirically absent from research labs and engineering teams. Thus, male domination and patriarchy remain out of the field of vision of the constructivist analyst.

The need to explicate the structural constraints on technical development has been recognized by Bijker in his later work as a key element of the constructivist approach (1993). To this end, Bijker introduces the concept of 'technological frame', 'the cultural system in which an artefact is set, including exemplary artefacts, as well as cultural values, goals, as well as scientific theories, etc.' (1993, p. 123). The technological frame is constructed and sustained by interactions in the relevant social group. 'It provides the goals, and thoughts and tools for action. It is both enabling and constraining' (1993, p. 123). Even after the introduction of this more comprehensive category, however, it remains unexplained whether and how a technological frame, for its part, is grounded in any continuous socio-economic and political conditions of existence of relevant social groups.

The social-interactionist perspective (see Bijker, 1995, p. 191) apparent in these definitions sets limitations on the 'relevant social group' and 'technological frame' concepts. Implicitly, these concepts presuppose direct interactions among the members of relevant social groups as well as among these groups as collective actors. Such a model works well when the historical process of development of a particular artefact is to be captured in its factual detail. It broadens the technical historian's scope compared to the earlier tradition that focused exclusively on the lonely inventor and the research lab. At the same time, this model silently substitutes the interactional for the social. There are social relationships that never get actualized in the interaction process in which a technology is shaped. Nevertheless, such relationships form the cultural horizon delimiting who is considered an actor in a particular situation and who is not, and what it is possible for actors to think, say and do in the process of negotiating and selecting technical solutions.

The interactionist perspective is also responsible for the inadequate representation of the role of users in technology shaping. Consumers and users are obvious candidates for inclusion in a relevant social group, or groups, because the technology or artefact they are using has a meaning for them. At the same time, the fact that this meaning is not necessarily shared among clearly distinguishable aggregations of interacting individuals complicates the picture. The application of Bijker's (1995) conceptual apparatus to grasp the role of users produces confusing results. According to his definition, the technological frame:

> structures the interactions among actors of a relevant social group ... technological frames are located between actors, not in actors or above actors. A technological frame is built up when the interaction 'around' an artefact begins. ... If existing interactions move members of an emerging relevant social group in the same direction, a technological frame will build up; if not, there will be no frame, no relevant social group, no future interaction. (p. 123)

Such a constitution of technological frames and, with them, of relevant social groups can easily be seen to crop up within the communities of photo chemists, electro chemists, celluloid chemists and other professionals considered in the empirical case of the invention of Bakelite, out of which Bijker derives his concepts. The opposite is true of users. How exactly a technological frame forms among them is difficult to imagine given that user interactions around an artefact do not always take place, or elude registration. In fact, it is more plausible to suggest that users become enrolled into the technological frames built up by the different participating professional groups in the capacity of either a cognitive element (the image of the user), or as peripheral participants (buyers). For peripheral participants ('actors with low inclusion') in Bijker's model, the artefact is not particularly flexible; on the contrary, it typically has a 'relatively undifferentiated, monolithic meaning' (1995, p. 284). Consequently, such actors are faced with a 'take it or leave it' choice. 'This is the obduracy of technology that most people know best, and this is what gives rise to technological determinism', Bijker explains (p. 284). So, one may conclude, there is indeed ample room for human agency in the technical sphere, but it is the agency of the 'princes' having the power of knowledge and/or economic, administrative, and political networks and resources. As far as the agency of users is concerned, we come full circle back to obduracy and technological determinism.

Users are hard to perceive as a social group that shares a common technological frame because of their dispersed state of existence, as well as their diverse cognitive and material resources, interests and ideologies. Users inhabit numerous invisible everyday settings. They have no established forums or channels for interaction either with each other or with the designers of the technologies they employ. In contrast, researchers, engineers, managers and government representatives form distinct professional networks. They share cognitive frames of reference acquired in the course of their training and subsequent participation in a community of practice. Their proposals, negotiations and overall involvement in technology formation leave a palpable trail on paper and in technical prototypes. That is why their activities can easily be captured by the interactionist optic, while the activities of consumers or users escape it.

This is not to say that the paradigmatic constructivist studies have ignored users. In his book *Of bicycles, bakelites, and bulbs*, Bijker (1995) diligently traces users' responses to the three technologies whose history he recounts. With Bakelite and bulbs (fluorescent lighting), the picture he presents of the public's involvement is quite sketchy, reconstructed by professional actors or through industrial survey results. In contrast, his captivating tale of bicycles is profusely populated by users. Various categories of them – 'young men of means and nerve', daring aristocratic women, militant moralists and others – take front of stage in the drama of technology construction. The problems they experience, be it with mounting a bike, racing on it or riding it safely across the city and countryside, drive engineers and mechanics to fabricate alternative versions of the machine. Gradually, the (irrational?) resistance of traditionalists and sceptics is slowly but surely overwhelmed. Technologists build the bicycle and users inevitably come flocking. What remains unexplained is why all these people are so eager to jump onto the jerky contrivance, even running the considerable risk of tumbling down head-over-heels, bruising their legs and sometimes worse. Where does the user's fascination with the technology come from? Failing to consider the process from the standpoint, or rather different standpoints of users, Bijker's account presents users as a standing reserve waiting to be swept along by technical development. In this way, ironically, the myth of technological progress enters his historical narrative through the back door.

The marked difference in the treatment of users demonstrated in Bijker's three case studies suggests that the character of the technologies chosen for investigation can also affect the degree to which users' participation will be considered in constructivist research with its 'follow the actors' (1995, p. 46) maxim. Some technologies are employed exclusively in highly structured organizational contexts (e.g., nuclear missiles, blast furnaces). Typically, their use is strictly regulated by formal and vocational rules of production and exploitation. In contrast, technologies intended for mass consumption (the microwave, the Sony Walkman) penetrate everyday life and enter diverse, less structured settings. A second, though admittedly more problematic, distinction can be made between technologies with a high degree of openness to interpretation (the automobile, the computer) versus technologies allowing for fewer alternatives with regard to function and application (the microscope, the vacuum cleaner). On the one hand, it is logical to suppose that technologies employed in formally organized settings and those relatively low in openness are less conducive to user involvement and hence user-oriented research. On the other hand, technologies that penetrate everyday life and invite diverse interpretations more often become an object of user creativity. The Internet is a paradigmatic case of an open and ubiquitous technology. It calls for a broadening of the research scope beyond the traditional innovation agencies, the examination of which would have satisfied our curiosity in the case of a more rigid and specialized technology.

To sum up, two main deficiencies of the constructivist approach prevent it from becoming the sole framework for conceptualizing user agency in the case of the Internet. The first shortcoming lies in its lack of sensitivity to the power and resource differentials among relevant social groups and its consequent inability to problematize the macro-dimensions of technological change. The second problem lies in the fact that the interactionist lens misses the forms of involvement in technology construction characteristic of less organized and less culturally uniform groups such as users. In order to overcome these limitations, the helpful concepts proposed by social constructivists need to be incorporated into a different analytical framework – one equipped to both appreciate and transcend the level of immediate interaction among actors.

Critical Theory of Technology

Another perspective on the problem of human agency in the technological sphere that builds on the main insights of social constructivism, but points a way beyond its recognized limitations, is the critical theory of technology proposed by Feenberg (1991). Over the years, Feenberg's theory evolved into an approach that can be characterized as *critical constructivism* (Feenberg, 1995, 1999). The most intriguing quality of this approach is that it upholds the non-determinist and non-essentialist tenets of the constructivist project while addressing head-on questions of agency and structure, inequality and domination. Furthermore, Feenberg's theory has a clear political agenda. It sets itself the task of conceiving ways in which the process of technological development can be made more inclusive and permeable to democratic values.

Critical theory of technology rests on the basic premise, shared with social constructivism, that natural laws and purely technical principles by themselves do not determine the shape of technology. Social forces drive technological development right down to the level of concrete design choices. Feenberg (1991) makes this claim the focal point of his examination of the character of technological rationality. Notably, the social forces he has in mind are much less contingent and transient than Pinch and Bijker's (1987) relevant social groups. Not fleeting technological frames, but the long-term interests and priorities of dominant social agents live, according to Feenberg, under the allegedly neutral surface of technological rationality. This makes technology one of the instruments that insure the systematic domination of certain social groups over others.

Modern forms of domination, Feenberg (1991) argues, are based on a variety of social activities including those that are technologically mediated. Hence, the democratization of society requires radical technical as well as political change. The main task of a critical theory of technology is to explain how modern technology can be redesigned to adapt to the needs of a freer society. Thus, envisaging non-traditional agencies and discovering new possibilities for wider involvement in the social shaping of technology becomes an integral part of the project of social democratization.

Feenberg draws on Marx, Marcuse and Foucault to challenge the purported neutrality of technical rationality. Technological progress, he maintains, may indeed achieve advances of general utility such as ease, convenience and speed, but the concrete form in which these advances are realized is determined by the social power under which they are made, and serves the interests of that power (see 1991, pp. 34–35). Technology, therefore, is not neutral. As far as particular interests have shaped it, it carries a class bias and helps to entrench capitalist power. It does not follow, however, that critical theory denounces technology and suggests irrationalism as an alternative to technical rationality. The thinkers in this school sought to discover alternative forms of rationality which could oppose the dominant oppressive form. Marcuse saw the possibility of a qualitative change in society in the reconstruction of its technical base, with a view to achieving different ends (1964, p. 232). Foucault (1980), for his part, maintained that the imposition of a particular form of rationality gives rise to a multitude of 'subjugated knowledges' (quoted in Feenberg, 1991, p. 77), which could become the basis for challenging and changing the dominant order. In Marcuse's and Foucault's notions of alternative rationalities lie the roots of Feenberg's own concept of 'subversive rationalization' (1991, p. 92), later re-defined as 'democratic rationalization' (1999, p. 76), one of the main pillars of his critical constructivism.

Constructivism in the sociology of science and technology informs Feenberg's (1991) theory by providing numerous concrete examples demonstrating the flexibility of new technical designs and the extent to which their final shape is determined by the cultural logic of particular human actors. The design problems and solutions championed by different relevant social groups represent instances of alternative rationalizations contending for materialization in the new technical device. The struggle among these rationalizations, and not a neutral technical criterion, determines the final outcome. Yet the end result of this contest is not completely open to contingency, as the constructivist model may suggest. It is delimited by the hegemonic technical code at any given historical moment. The technical code is the widely accepted set of technical principles and procedures guiding the creation of technical objects, which is congruent with the interests of the dominant social forces.[3] The technical code translates the values of a dominant order into technical terms. Thus it delineates the moral and cognitive horizon under which technical choices are conceived and made (see Feenberg, 1991, pp. 78–83). By introducing the notion of the hegemonic technical code, Feenberg effectively draws boundaries around the 'interpretative flexibility' of any given artefact socially constructed at a given time. He also marshalls the varied meanings generated by relevant social groups into a more or less clear-cut hierarchy. Some of these meanings happen to be more in line with the dominant technical code, thus they appear more rational, and are more likely to become part of the winning definition of an emergent artefact.

Feenberg, unlike other critical analysts of technological development (e.g. Robins and Webster, 1999; Winston, 1998[4]) does not see this as the whole story. Following Foucault, Feenberg recognizes the perpetual resistance to dominant rationality that goes on in the numerous micro-scenes where modern individuals come in contact with technological systems. At such points, diverse technical micropolitical practices challenging the dominant technical code emerge: 'Technical micropolitics involves forms of concrete political protest that aim to transform particular technologies through pressure from the grassroots activities of users, clients, victims' (Feenberg, 1995, p. 37). That is how contingency enters the picture once again and the possibility for constructivist involvement in technological shaping on the part of non-traditional actors is opened up.

Thus in Feenberg's critical constructivist model, technology exhibits a fundamental ambivalence summarized in two principles: the principle of conservation of hierarchy, and the principle of subversive (or democratic) rationalization. The principle of conservation of hierarchy is realized through the 'operational autonomy' of the powerful,[5] that is, through their capacity to make technical choices that reinforce their dominant position and guarantee them technical initiative in the future. The hegemonic technical code serves to make these choices seem natural and indisputable. The principle of 'democratic rationalization', on the other hand, holds that new technology can often be used to destabilize or circumvent the existing social hierarchy, or to force it to respond to needs it has ignored (see Feenberg, 1999, p. 76).

It follows that the basis for alternatives to technocratic domination need not be sought in any non-technological realm and its technologically innocent inhabitants. These alternatives are generated by the practices of questioning the technical choices made by the powerful, and pushing for solutions that correspond to alternative value systems and a broader spectrum of needs. The capacity for democratic rationalization lies in the hands of individuals who inhabit a technical system. Such individuals are 'immediately engaged in technically-mediated activities and able to actualize ambivalent potentialities previously suppressed by the prevailing technological rationality' (Feenberg, 1996, p. 45).

There are different ways in which the dominant technological system may react to alternative rationalizations originating from the margins. In some instances these initiatives may be reincorporated into strategies that restructure domination at a higher level. On other occasions, they may affect the system in ways that weaken the grip of the dominant rationality (see Feenberg, 1996, p. 48). Playing on Marx's 'expropriation of the expropriators', I will call the first type of response to the practices and definitions developed at the margins, 'appropriation of the appropriators'. This response represents an adaptive and exploitative strategy employed by the powerful in order to appropriate the fruits of the creativity at the margins and dissolve the tensions that threaten to undermine the system's hierarchical order. An example of this approach can be found in the successful co-optation by corporate enterprise of ideas generated by the alternative technology movement in the 1970s (see Slack, 1984). We are witnessing many similar attempts on the terrain of the Internet – for example, the appropriation of the practice of virtual community-building initiated by users for the purposes of product marketing and customer loyalty (see Werry, 1999).

Reincorporations of marginal rationality that weaken domination remain the hope for democratizing technology. When, how and why do such reincorporations occur? Feenberg (1999) points to three mechanisms constituting contemporary 'technical micropolitics': technological controversy, innovative dialogue and creative appropriation (pp. 120–129). Technological controversies draw attention to violations of the rights and health of those affected by a technological enterprise. The resulting public pressure calls forth new technical solutions, which take into account the demands of the victims. Innovative dialogue brings together the lay person and the expert, and initiates a process of continuous revision of technology in which technological design incorporates different values and comes to reflect a broader range of interests. An exemplary practice is participatory design.[6] With creative appropriation, new dimensions of a technology are opened up and widely recognized, thanks to the spontaneous inventiveness of its users. Such was the case when computer networks were turned into media for human communication, as opposed to their original, rationally envisaged function restricted to exchange of files and resources by military researchers (Leinier et al., 1997).

Feenberg's (1991, 1999) theory firmly links democratic rationalizations to technology use and to the variety of human contexts in which a working technology becomes implicated:

> ordinary people are constantly involved in technical activity, the more so as technology advances. It is true that they may be objects rather than subjects of the technologies that affect them, but in any case their closeness offers them a unique vantage point. Situated knowledges arising from that vantage point can become the basis for public interventions even in a mature technological system. (1999, p. 90)

Dominant rationality under the conditions of capitalism is organized around a value system grounded in the principles of capitalist production. Maximization of profit disguised as 'efficiency' takes the leading position in this value system. Consequently, technological objects are furnished with features that support and reinforce this normative orientation. Other features corresponding to values characterizing different contexts of existence are either eliminated or suppressed in capitalist technological design. However, when a technology is put into practice, it re-enters actual living systems of relationships and must be integrated with the natural, technical and social settings in which it is supposed to work. This opens the way for other social interests and values to re-define the features of any technology from the perspective of an alternative, locally grounded rationality.

The concept of affordances used in studies of technological design can serve as an appropriate illustration of this idea. The concept refers to what a technical environment offers relative to the person or group perceiving or recognizing that quality of the environment (Gibson, 1979, p. 127). This suggests that people and groups situated in different activity contexts may be able to recognize different affordances in a technical system or device. Thus the employment of technologies in particular local projects by particular actors could bring to the fore new, sometimes unforeseen, potentialities of this technology.

To sum up, the simple customers or ordinary users whose agency I am trying to conceptualize are significant players in Feenberg's scheme by virtue of their contact with and participation in technological systems. These systems can never exhaustively define the conditions of existence of the subjects involved with them. People generate interpretations and applications that often diverge from the ones originally envisioned by designers. These are not irrational modifications as the dominant ideology may see them. Rather, they reflect a practice of rationalization rooted in alternative sets of values and interests. On this basis, users, clients and victims of technological systems engage in technological controversies, innovative dialogues and creative appropriations directed towards reforming technology with more humane and democratic aims in mind. Note that these are not practices of negation, of avoiding engagement with technology, but practices that attempt to draw on unaccentuated or dormant technological potentialities in order to address the needs ignored by mainstream technological development.

British cultural theorist Raymond Williams was an early predecessor of the critical constructivist approach to technology in the area of communication studies. In his book, *Television: technology and cultural form*, Williams (1974) discusses in detail the social shaping of the paradigmatic communication technology of his time – television. Williams is aware of the inherited inequalities in terms of power and resources available to the social actors involved in the process. At the same time, he leaves open the possibility of alternative uses initiated by subordinate social groups. Williams maintains 'Technology opens new dimensions for those perceived as objects, public, market; ... they are exposed to certain uncontrollable opportunities' (1974, p. 74). The viability of these alternative uses and cultural forms is decided in continually renewable social action and struggle.

An important distinction Williams (1974) makes in his discussion of television's social history is the one between a communication technology, and its institutions and cultural forms. While this distinction escapes accounts originating from the sociology of technology and much philosophy of technology, it is very useful for the analysis of communication technologies because it underlines their social complexity. It also points to more levels of variability, which means more arenas of struggle and possible change.

Giving this distinction a contemporary reading, 'social institutions' can be taken to signify the structures of rules, resources and recurrent practices (see Giddens, 1984) surrounding technologies that have acquired an enduring presence in society. 'Cultural form' refers not only to the new genres of television content, but also to the new forms of television viewing. These two related aspects of the notion of cultural form characterize the production-consumption relation. In this sense, television cartoons produced to entertain children represent a cultural form, but so does the domestic practice of using television for babysitting. Computer games constitute a cultural form anchored in computer technology, and so does the computer-game talk practised by schoolboys (see Haddon, 1991). Thus, Williams's formulation makes user activity visible at the level of cultural form. At the level of the institution, user activity manifests itself in regulative controversies and user interventions in political processes related to media's operation in society. The events taking place in these additional arenas of user activity – institution and cultural form – reflect back on the technical problems and solutions that experts perceive and tackle.

Semiotic Approaches: Technology-as-Text

It will be noticed that Feenberg has taken the idea of interpretative flexibility of artefacts into deep political waters. He has turned it into the keystone of a project of technology democratization driven by the inventiveness and techno-political action of users. In this section, I will track a different line of argument anchored in the concept of 'interpretative flexibility'. In this case, the goal is to understand the relationships between producers and users of technologies by examining the emergence, meeting, clash and negotiation of meanings. To make the most of the semiotic potential of the concept, this approach extends it into the metaphor of 'technology as text', or more concretely, 'the machine as text'.

The machine text, Grint and Woolgar argue, 'is organized in such a way that its "purpose" is available as a reading to the user' (1997, p. 73). That said, the model of text-authoring and text-interpretation can be taken as a guide in the examination of technology design and use. Following this method, Woolgar (1991, 1996) identifies designers' strategies for inscribing certain 'preferred readings' into technological artefacts. Designers, he contends, deliberately grant centrality to certain 'characters' or components of the machine text and relegate others to marginal positions; for example, through the conspicuous or inconspicuous placement of buttons and icons. By the same token, the reader/user is invited to identify herself with certain groups and their respective practices and to dissociate herself from others. In textual examples this can take the form of expressions suggesting various degrees of affiliation or distancing between author and reader, such as the royal 'we' or the alienating 'some people believe ...'. In designing artefacts, analogous techniques include the sorting of menu items under the category 'advanced' or marking particular parts and functions of a machine as off-limits or dangerous (see Grint and Woolgar, 1997; Woolgar, 1991). Taken together, the application of such techniques constitutes the process that Woolgar dubs 'configuring the user' (1991). The end result is that dominant producer preconceptions of the user become embodied in the machine. In the subsequent stage of technology deployment, the actual users are confronted by the preconceptions of themselves reflected in the design of the machine (see Woolgar, 1996).

The machine as text metaphor serves also to address the general question of agency versus determinism, both technological and social. Does the reading–interpretation–use of an entity such as a text or machine arise from the inherent (or inscribed) characteristics of the entity itself, or does it derive from the circumstances of its reception and use? (see Grint and Woolgar, 1997, pp. 68–69.) The answer to this question hinges on the reaction of users to the 'configured' version of themselves. Will they accept and follow through with the preferred readings of the machine text imposed by producers? Woolgar admits that while the reader/user is not absolutely forced to act in a particular way, non-preferred readings or uses are more costly, that is, they require more effort and resources than the preferred ones. At the same time, to claim that readers/users will immediately recognize and enact the preferred reading/use of technology amounts to replacing one form of determinism (technological) with another (social). Despite the existence of a preferred reading/use, there remains an 'irremediable ambiguity' about what the technology is and can do.

Woolgar leaves us with the insight that both the process of construing preferred readings of technologies and that of performing actual readings/ uses are imbued with contingency and ambiguity. His handling of the technology-as-text metaphor succeeds in dispelling technological essentialism by demonstrating the work of human agency on the production side of technical development, namely in bestowing machines with selected characteristics and preferred readings. Users are the inextricable obverse side of the 'writing' process. They are present in it from the very beginning as a factor to be predicted and controlled. Users are cast as deciding the ultimate impact, value and success of technologies inasmuch as they conform to, resist or challenge the preferred readings/uses configured by producers. By virtue of all this, user agency figures as an important variable in the technology-as-text formula Woolgar employs to capture the dynamic of technical development. This variable, however, remains cloaked in much more uncertainty and ambiguity when compared to its counterpart – producer agency. While the power of designers, engineers and marketers to configure users is clearly demonstrated in Woolgar's account, user agency is readily proclaimed, but largely unsubstantiated. While it leaves the possibilities open, Woolgar's model falls short of offering any clues as to why users may react in ways different from those prescribed by producers. As I will argue in later chapters, this question can only begin to be answered when the detailed analysis of the process of configuring the user is complemented by an analysis of its dialectical obverse, that is, the process of becoming a user.

Very similar to Woolgar's technology-as-text approach is the method of 'script analysis' proposed by Akrich (1992) and Akrich and Latour (1992). Technology here is seen as one particular and rather categorical type of text – film script. Just as the script determines the plot of a movie, technologies act as determinants of human action. They prescribe the characters of the actors, the space in which they are supposed to act and the concrete actions to be performed. Scripts take shape along the lines sketched by Woolgar in his account of configuring users. Designers inscribe in the technical artefact their own conceptions of users and appropriate uses. When materialized, technologies themselves become actors in the show exerting their influence on human actors. In their 'convenient vocabulary for the semiotics of human and nonhuman assemblies' Akrich and Latour (1992) introduce terms that capture the relationships between human and nonhuman actors: designers, technologies and users. The concepts intended to reflect the agency of users are 'subscription', 'de-inscription' and 'antiprogram' (see Oudshoorn and Pinch, 2003). Subscription and de-inscription are the possible responses of users to the prescriptions embodied in artefacts. 'Subscription' refers to the acceptance of the preferred readings or courses of action embodied in the technology. 'De-inscription' occurs when users resist and/or try to renegotiate the scenario. An 'antiprogram' is a course of action users themselves want to pursue that appears deviant from the designers' perspective. Accordingly, the 'programs' of action designers inscribe in technologies often attempt to anticipate and block the prospective users' antiprograms (see Latour, 1992). Thus Akrich and Latour's 'convenient vocabulary' starts differentiating the various possible fates that a technology may have at the hands of users. The user agency that this vocabulary recognizes, however, remains largely reactive, that is, delimited in its structure by the designer's agenda. Users may put up a resistance to the script, but they can take no initiative outside it.

A significant breakthrough with regard to the conceptualization of user agency within the technology-as-text paradigm takes place in works associated with the tradition of British Cultural Studies. From their very inception, the studies of mass media audiences carried out by members of the Media Group at Birmingham University's Centre for Contemporary Cultural Studies recognized the power of readers as active decoders of media texts. At the same time, readers were conceptualized as sociologically grounded subjects whose semiotic involvement in a dialogue with the media is shaped by their socioeconomic and cultural position. British Cultural Studies researchers were committed to establishing a careful balance between readers' freedom and media power. They were aware that the range of alternative readings available to audience members was limited by social and ideological forces: 'Polysemy must not ... be confused with pluralism. Connotative codes are not equal among themselves. Any society tends ... to impose its segmentations, its classifications of the cultural and political world upon its members. There remains a dominant cultural order,' Hall (1973, p. 13) insisted. Thus, while there is a clear correspondence between the idea of different decodings of media texts developed by the school of British Cultural Studies, and the social constructivists' notion of interpretative flexibility of artefacts, cultural studies researchers were explicitly oriented towards the structurally produced inequalities between groups of readers.

In empirical reception studies undertaken by Morley (1986) and other members of the Birmingham Media Group, the importance of the contexts in which media content is consumed came to the fore (see Moores, 1993). Researchers focused their attention on the everyday microsettings in which media reception took place, directing their efforts towards understanding the connection between actions performed and meanings generated within these microsettings and the wider structural formations of society. Projects like these gave birth to a trend of reception ethnography within the cultural studies paradigm. The stated aim of this research was to see things 'from the virtual standpoint of actual audiences' (Ang, 1991, quoted in Moores, 1993, p. 35).

As noted by Mackay and Gillespie (1992), it does not take a great leap of imagination to extend this approach to the consumption of technologies. Rather than media messages, technological artefacts came to be perceived as polysemic texts encoded by designers, developers and advertisers and calling for active decoding on the part of users. Here too, striking a balance between freedom and constraint was believed to be critical to the analysis (see Mackay, 1997, p. 270).

Informed by the cultural studies paradigm, authors have analyzed communication technologies such as radio (Moores, 1993), television (Silverstone, 1994), satellite television (Moores, 1996) and home computers (Haddon, 1992), identifying divergent interpretations generated by users. One of the most elaborate constructs developed in this tradition is the model of domestication of media and communication technologies proposed by Silverstone and his colleagues (Silverstone et al., 1992; Silverstone, 1994; Silverstone and Haddon, 1996.) It is intended to capture the appropriation of new technologies and their adaptation to the spaces and rhythms of everyday settings, most typically the home. The domestication model decisively sets its focus on users and their everyday world. It qualifies as the counterpart of Woolgar's (1991) 'configuration' model in the sense that it examines in depth the strategies employed by users in their efforts to re-define and re-configure domestic technologies to make them fit into the meaningful activities of the household.

Along with its numerous helpful components which will be discussed and drawn upon in more detail in the following chapters, Silverstone et al.'s (1992) model shows a number of limitations as far as the analysis of Internet use is concerned. True to the legacy of British Cultural Studies with their interest in the cycle of production and consumption of media texts, these scholars view the processes that are set into motion after a new technology enters the home as a specific instance of consumption. The kind of consumption they have in mind is indeed active and creative, but it still ties the analysis to a dualism which renders consumption as the opposite of production. This is problematic at two levels. First, portraying the home predominantly as a centre of consumption fails to recognize the changing functions of this unit in a post-industrial society. Increasingly, the home is being charged with productive functions, such as work and education, and most recently, tele-work and tele-education, activities representing moments of the social process of production in the classical sense. Thus, new communication technology, and the Internet in particular, is often adopted with specific productive applications in mind. It enters the home as a working tool, rather than as a recreational item or a conduit for commodities to be consumed.

Second, the experience of using interactive communication technologies in the home differs substantively from that brought about by broadcasting media. Unlike broadcasting media, interactive communication technologies have demonstrated their potential to serve as tools in a symbolic productive process involving an active exchange between the household and the outside world. This exchange is, in effect, a weaving and sustaining of social networks and meaningful relationships, in which individuals participate as active creators of public value. In the case of the Internet, users often become providers of content not just for a closed group of friends, but also for the public at large, as exemplified by the proliferation of personal websites serving various purposes. De Certeau's (1984, pp. 30–31) charge that the notion of consumption obfuscates the idea of the active and productive role of the user, of the inventiveness with which she draws the commercially offered product into operations of her own, applies to the Internet with a vengeance. That is why I will follow de Certeau's example, choosing to work with the concept of 'use' rather than 'consumption'.

The cycle of consumption, understood in its conventional sense, inevitably reproduces the 'operational autonomy' (Feenberg, 1991) of the economically powerful, that is, their privileged position in choosing the shape of technology most profitable to themselves and imposing it on the rest of society (with minor compromises eventually brought about by marketing studies of consumer preferences). Consumer creativity is taken into consideration only in so far as it maximizes profit. In order to envision potential sources for a democratic transformation of technology, the cycle of consumption should be, at least theoretically, transcended. Users should be perceived in their threefold capacity of consumers, producers and citizens. For that matter, such a view would be in accord with the way people normally see themselves. The use of technology in everyday life involves not only consumption, but also an array of creative activities constituting the reproduction of the social actor with her relationships, knowledge and emotional well-being.

To reiterate, I believe that in order to reveal how users play a role in the formative process of a new communication technology, its pertaining institutions and set of cultural forms, the overarching concept of 'consumption' should be replaced by the more open notion of 'use'. Use subsumes consumption of both technology and content, but it also encompasses a wide set of significant productive practices that remain invisible from the perspective of the standard production-consumption dualism.

A Pragmatic Approach: Technology-as-Language

At this point, I feel compelled to generalize my objection to all the dualisms reviewed so far that construe use as the subordinate, passive or reactive member of a relationship: that between production and consumption, writing and reading, generation and interpretation, or inscribing and subscribing. To break the repressive bond, I will take the metaphor of 'technology-as-text' one step further. I will propose a conception of the user-technology relation that goes beyond the 'semiotic approaches' as Oudshoorn and Pinch (2003) have characterized the suite of technology-as-text models. I will lay out a *pragmatic approach* to user agency, where technology use is defined as a formative strand of meaningful action in specific contexts. To begin with, I will explore the idea of what it would be like if technology and, in particular, a complex communication system like the Internet, is conceptualized as language. By this I mean that users will not be seen only as readers, interpreting the technical text. They will be construed as speakers performing speech acts in which they appropriate the technical medium to achieve their own objectives.[7]

Like Woolgar (1991), who engages the metaphor of technology-as-text in an experimental way, I am not saying that technology actually *is* language. I would like to explore the potential of the metaphor of technology-as-language for the discussion of user agency in the technological sphere. Are there any insights to be gained by employing this metaphor? How far can it go? In short, what are the advantages and the limits of 'talking in this bizarre way' (see Woolgar, 1991, p. 61)? Let us consider the grounds for drawing an analogy between technology and language.

Despite obvious differences in the nature of their materiality and internal organization, both language and technological systems are culturally established, formal structures of means and rules, or as de Certeau puts it, 'ensembles of possibilities ... and interdictions' (1984, p. 98) that the user actualizes in his or her individual concrete operations. Complex technological systems exhibit the same *double-level agency* as language (see de Certeau, 1984): The forms and functions of the system, invented and established by a knowledge elite or an anonymous cultural producer, become an object of manipulation by practitioners who have not produced them. The practitioner actualizes only some of the possibilities inscribed in the system. She moves them about and invents others – as in new, unexpected figures of speech. Thus, de Certeau observes, 'Charlie Chaplin multiplies the possibilities of his cane: he does other things with the same thing and he goes beyond the limits that the determinants of the object set on its utilization' (1984, p. 98).

De Certeau insists that the notion of the 'speech act' is applicable in a sphere much broader than that of verbal communication because it suggests a general distinction between 'the *forms used* in a system and the *ways of using* a system' (1984, p. 98). He provides an example of applying the model of language to the analysis of a domain of non-linguistic operations, such as the city maintaining that 'The act of walking is to the urban system what the speech act is to language or to the statements uttered' (p. 97). Following this line of analysis, I propose that *the act of use is to the technological system what the speech act is to language*. For the purposes of my investigation, the distinction between 'forms used' and 'ways of using' can be gainfully applied to the sphere of technological practice. Unlike standard forms, acts of use and the ways of using the system they give substance to are characterized by an 'everyday historicity' (de Certeau, 1984, p. 20). They cannot be dissociated from the existence of the subjects who are their agents and authors. Finally, acts of use, like speech acts are at the same time, both a utilization of the system and an operation performed on it. This circumstance implies that the system, linguistic or technological, may be prone to change originating in the everyday acts of use performed by practitioners.

Technical tools and 'psychological tools'[8] such as signs and language, have been jointly considered as mediators of all human action and human mental functioning by a school of socio-cultural psychology drawing upon the work of Vygotsky (see Wertsch, 1991, p. 28). The socio-cultural school subsumes language and technology under the notion of 'mediational means' and its equivalent 'cultural tools'. Wertsch (1998) argues that mediational means and human agency are in a constant irreducible tension and jointly shape action. In order to act, individuals have to master and appropriate the mediational means offered by their surrounding environment. The studies of socio-cultural psychologists have drawn on both technological and linguistic examples to demonstrate how the dynamic between agent and mediational means plays out in concrete historical, cultural and institutional contexts (Wertsch, 1991, 1998; Wertsch et al., 1995). Due to the psychological framework in which this school operates, the focus of its interest is on how the use of objects and linguistic or other signs results in changes in the agent and her actions, including her cognitive functioning. The question of how mediational means or cultural tools themselves evolve is given some limited consideration that takes into account the influence of cultural and institutional power and authority. The capacity of the agent to appropriate and resist cultural tools in concrete contexts of action is also acknowledged, but no effort is made to relate these appropriations back to the evolution of cultural tools. The agent's practical definition of a cultural tool is revealed in the isolated acts of use, but does not necessarily lead to the re-writing of that tool's authoritative dictionary definition.

In the remainder of this chapter, I will mobilize the conceptual resources developed by predecessors of the socio-cultural school such as Voloshinov and Bakhtin[9] to steer the discussion of user agency with respect to cultural tools beyond resistance and subversion. I will draw on this stock of ideas in my attempt to envisage more dramatic consequences flowing from users' appropriation of linguistic and technical systems. The metaphor of technology-as-language will direct my reading of Voloshinov's work which explicitly addresses the problem of language evolution and relates it closely to the process of everyday speaking or use. My goal in this investigation will come as no surprise: I will be trying to discover how Voloshinov's linguistic insights could shed light on techno-logical evolution and enhance our understanding of user agency.

In his book *Marxism and the philosophy of language*, first published in Russian in 1929, Voloshinov (1929/1986) criticizes the Saussurian approach to language, which he terms 'abstract objectivism', for creating a false dichotomy between language as a system (*langue*) and its imple-mentation (*parole*), or in other words, between statics and dynamics in language. Perceiving language as an abstract system of stable norms dutifully applied by speakers in daily verbal practice is an approach, Voloshinov charges, that fails to account for the multiplicity of meanings carried by the word and the constantly changing and socially conditioned nature of these meanings.

At the same time, Voloshinov objects to the antithesis of Saussurian lin-guistics – the Humboldtian tradition that postulates the individual psyche as the prime source of linguistic activity. The flaw of this tradition, according to Voloshinov, lies in its 'individual subjectivism' which assumes that the inner world of the speaker has an independent existence and plays the role of the prime mover in language evolution. This view of linguistic activity, Voloshinov argues, is fundamentally untenable, first, because 'there is no such thing as experience outside of embodiment in signs' (1929/1986, p. 85), and second, because the motive force of linguistic expres-sion, does not lie in the individual psyche, but in the social world.

For Voloshinov, 'the actual reality of language-speech is not the abstract system of linguistic forms, not the isolated monological utterance, and not the psycho-physiological act of its implementation, but the social event of verbal interaction implemented in an utterance or utterances' (p. 94).

This event, for its part, is a moment in the continuous process of verbal communication accompanying the all-inclusive social reproduction of a given human collective. Thus it is inextricably interwoven with the 'extraverbal situation' (p. 95) in which it occurs:

> Verbal communication can never be understood and explained outside of this connection with a concrete situation ... In its concrete connection with a situation, verbal communication is always accompanied by social acts of a non verbal character (the performance of labor, the symbolic acts of a ritual, a ceremony, etc.) and is often an accessory of these acts. (p. 95)

The connection between verbal performance and its forms on the one hand, and the extraverbal situation – the concrete social conditions in which verbal interaction occurs – on the other, becomes the key to understanding language evolution. Voloshinov analyzes this connection through the concept of 'little behaviour genres'. While innumerable unique situations of social life may elicit a variety of forms of utterances, in any concrete society and culture there exist some typical situations with their corresponding forms of interaction and verbal exchange:

> Each situation, fixed and sustained by social custom, commands a particular kind of organization of audience and hence, a particular repertoire of little behavioral genres. The behavioral genre fits everywhere into the channel of social intercourse assigned to it and functions as an ideological reflection of its type, structure, goal and social composition. The behavioral genre is a fact of the social milieu: of holiday, leisure time, and of social contact in the parlor, the workshop, etc. It meshes with that milieu and is delimited and defined by it in all its internal aspects. (Voloshinov, 1929/1986, p. 97)

Specific patterns of verbal forms will comprise the genre of the light casual conversation of the drawing room where everyone feels at home. These structures will be markedly different among a random aggregation of people waiting in line, in a village sewing circle, workers' lunchtime chats, conversations between husband and wife, etc. (see p. 97). In all such instances, specific relations among speakers and the practices in which they jointly participate invoke specific forms of verbal expression. As changing circumstances of social life generate and sustain new situations with their characteristic sets of relations and activities, new genres of verbal communications, new word meanings and new linguistic forms emerge:

> *Language acquires life and historically evolves precisely here, in concrete verbal communication, and not in the abstract linguistic system of language forms, nor in the individual psyche of speakers.* (p. 95 [emphasis mine])

Voloshinov's (1929/1986) model is specifically focused on explaining the process of language change as a sociological process involving countless socially situated speakers, practitioners or users. In Voloshinov's interpretation, language evolution exhibits a dual character. On one hand it is determined by 'the basis' (p. 96) of social life including relations of production with their inherent power inequality. But on the other, it is driven by the verbal activity of variously situated language practitioners. Note that while in de Certeau's (1984) terms the activity of users is expressed in subversions of the system that, for its part, remains by and large the same, in Voloshinov's (1929/1986) model practitioners' actions in the numerous situations of concrete verbal communication results in pressures on the linguistic system leading to its gradual change. This is because Voloshinov understands language not as a reified system, but as a 'generative process of signification' (p. 106) that unfolds in actual situations of use.

How is this analytical model to be employed in the study of technology? What relevance can it have for a system (or systems) whose substantive nature, social function and historical evolution are so different from the system of language?

Applying Voloshinov's (1929/1986) model to technology, the actual reality of technology will be found in the concrete acts of its use and, more precisely, in the social events of technologically mediated interaction between the user and her environment. Such events are not isolated and random but, on the contrary, inseparably embedded in the 'continuous, all-inclusive generative process of a given social collective' (p. 95). This leads us to the connection between technology use and the social situation in which it occurs, or in other words, to the phenomenon of 'little behaviour genres'. The element of little behaviour genres of technology use, *use genres*, would augment a model of technology development with an adequate representation of user agency. This notion allows user agency to be understood not as absolute freedom or voluntaristic whim, but as a product of the specific encounter between technology and typical human projects arising in typical social situations. In such instances, reflexive actors come up with ways of using technology that have the potential to expand its meaning, form and function beyond producer 'scripts'.

It is my contention that such use genres can indeed be observed in all spheres of activity involving technology. In their everyday life, socially situated subjects put technologies into use in the course of their interaction with their environment, both physical and social. With time, social custom and circumstances contribute to the stabilization of certain forms of technology use to some appreciable degree. Thus, diverse practitioners initiate genres of technology use delimited and defined by their immediate social milieu. The meanings that different social groups assign to a technology emanate from these emergent use genres rather than from dictionary definitions or through abstract reflection.[10] The stabilization of some use genres, and the fading of others, is intertwined with the processes of invention, selection, stabilization and re-consideration of concrete technological forms on the production side of the generative process of technology.

What else can the study of *speech genres* teach the emergent inquiry into technological use genres? In his definitive articulation of speech genre theory, Bakhtin (1986) demonstrates that genre represents a blend between the individual and the typical, between verbal form and extraverbal activity. As he defines it 'Each separate utterance is individual, of course, but each sphere in which language is used develops its own relatively stable types of these utterances. These we may call *speech genres*' (p. 60).

Due to their function of shaping verbal expression in accordance with the dynamic of specific spheres of social life and activity, speech genres are for Bakhtin '*the drive belts from the history of society to the history of language*' (p. 65). This is an echo of Voloshinov's insight that language evolves in the very concrete situations in which it is put to use by speakers. Use genres associated with technologies articulate technological change and social practice in a similar fashion. Certainly, there is much more intentionality, expert involvement and interested agency behind technological developments than linguistic ones. Nevertheless, any new technology originates from existing practices, including use genres anchored in predecessor technologies, and becomes socialized through the medium of newly emergent use genres. Thus, conceptually, the notion of use genre becomes a helpful stepping stone for overcoming the duality between the technical and the social.

Like Voloshinov, Bakhtin insists on the essential connection between genre and situation. Genres, he argues, 'correspond to typical situations of speech communication, typical themes, and, consequently also to particular contacts between the meaning of words and actual concrete reality under certain typical circumstances' (1986, p. 87). Miller (1994) argues that typicality and recurrence should not be understood in a purely objective or subjective sense: 'Situations are social constructs that are the result, not of "perception", but of "definition"', (p. 29). What recurs is not a material configuration of circumstances, participants and events, but social actors' construal of a type of situation which draws on their cultural stock of knowledge. Thus the study of the typical uses of language in speech genres opens a perspective on the character of a culture or a historic period (see p. 31). Here lies the value of the concept of use genre for the study of the social construction of technology as well. Typical uses of technology, along with the recurrent situations in which they arise, make up the fabric of a society and culture. As in the case of language, agents' definitions of the situation and their choices of technologies and use genres are inter-connected. New genres of technology use stem from the specific encounter between the functionality of a technology and the characteristics of typical situations of social life as defined by different categories of actors.

Examining the staggering diversity of speech genres, Bakhtin (1986) notes that some of them are fixed and rather rigid in form and content, while others are flexible and open to modification. In general, however, speech genres are much more elastic and free compared to language forms, that is, forms regulated by grammar. The latter are typically stable and compulsory for the speaker. Speech genres, on the other hand, are adaptable and flexible, allowing much more room for personal preference and creativity. Applied to technology, this observation evokes a parallel distinction between use genres and manipulation rules. The computer interface stipulates a set of operations that the user is bound to perform, if she wants to get her machine to work. These rules are not open to negotiation, they are compulsory and rigid. At the same time, the use genres in which the same machine gets implicated can be quite diverse, depending on the situational configuration and the user's goals. The computer can be used to do accounting, to keep a diary, to maintain databases of technical information, to play games, and so on.

Certainly, speech genres themselves exhibit a substantial degree of normativity. Bakhtin (1986) traces the complex dialectic of agency and compulsion involved in the enactment of speech genres. Each utterance is characterized by the speaker's *speech plan* or *speech will* (p. 77). This plan determines the choice of generic form in which the utterance will be cast. The choice of genre is also determined by the specific nature of the sphere of speech communication, as well as thematic and other considerations, and the concrete communicative situation, including the composition of participants. Once an appropriate generic form is identi-fied, the speaker's speech plan, with all its individuality and subjectivity, is adapted to its requirements. Speech genres are 'given' to the speaker in the inherited verbal experience of the community to which she belongs. They are mobilized by the individual in the pursuit of her own intentions in particular situations:

> Our speech, that is, all our utterances (including creative works), is filled with others' words, varying degrees of otherness or varying degrees of 'our-own-ness', varying degrees of awareness and detachment. These words of others carry with them their own expression, their own evaluative tone, which we assimilate, re-work, and re-accentuate. (Bakhtin, 1986, p. 89)

Speakers, Bakhtin observes, do not take their words and expressions out of dictionaries, but rather out of other people's mouths, out of other utterances that are kindred to theirs in genre. Yet words and genres become our own 'only when the speaker populates it with his own intention, his own accent, when he appropriates the word, adapting it to his own semantic and expressive intention' (1981, p. 294). By engaging in this appropriation and adaptation of the word or genre to her particular situation, the speaker expands the verbal experience of the community with new shades of meaning, accents and patterns, and thus contributes to what others will be able to say further down the road.

In a comparable way, users of technology find tools and machines already steeped in earlier uses, charged with the intentions, accents and achievements of previous users. New users, children for example, learn when and how to use everyday utensils in the same fashion that they learn how to speak their native language. New technologies reach ordinary users after some considerable degree of experience in their application has already been accumulated in various quarters of society. Then there are always the 'dictionary definitions', the guides and manuals prepared by the gurus who, like grammarians, understand the inner workings of the technical system. These are the 'authoritative utterances' (Bakhtin, 1986, p. 88) that emanate from the 'masters of thought' (p. 89). They are cited, imitated and followed. Consequently, varying degrees of otherness and our-own-ness fill individual acts of technology use. Each of these acts is an exercise in assimilation, re-working and re-accentuating of previous ways of using with respect to our personal circumstances and agendas. Unsurprisingly, the most meaningful and easily acceptable are the uses kindred to ours in situation and genre. Operating in the tension zone between otherness and our-own-ness, practitioners become involved in two important developments. First, they select, expand and perpetuate use genres corresponding to typical situations, activities and plans. Second, they give technology a new, possibly peculiar, spin or accent that others may assimilate at a later point.

Let me now go back to the technology-as-language metaphor and review the gains from applying it to the analysis of the user-technology relation. Thanks to this metaphor, I was able to focus on technology use as an integral moment of situated action. This action emerged as a complex entity encompassing the agent's definition of the situation, her intent and received cultural means. In it, I was able to distinguish analytically the components of the individual act of technology use, the use genre, and the typical situation, which, for its part, represents an instance of and a link to the broader social and cultural context. By thinking about technology use in this way, it is possible to avoid determinism associated with the driving force of technology but at the same time stay away from naïve subjectivism attributing unlimited freedom of choice to the agent. Positing users as doers, and not simply as consumers, interpreters, adopters and so on, makes it logical to go on looking for the effects of their action on the tools they select, appropriate and implement. Recognizing the situated character of users' doings opens up a perspective on how the technical, the social and the subjective interpenetrate, delimit, and facilitate each other. The notion of use genre comes to the fore as a focal point in which these different forces meet. It promises help in balancing out the uniqueness and recurrence, the freedom and constraint, the originality and replication that transpire in each individual act of technology use.

Summary

To develop an adequate account of the user-technology relation proved to be a complex task which could not be accomplished solely by drawing on existing approaches. It necessitated a radical re-thinking of the received notion of technology as self-contained physical artefacts, machines, or equipment conceived, designed and produced by experts and expert organizations. To start comprehending the part of users in this relation as active, reflexive and consequential, I had to join the physical objects known as machines, instruments or equipment with the living, generative process of their use. As a second step, following Voloshinov, I had to recognize the inseparable unity between use and social situation. Use is neither a prescribed, or 'configured' (Woolgar, 1991) course of actions nor a subjectively voluntaristic project. In use, a human agent mobilizes available cultural tools to respond to a social situation. By doing this, she either enacts or invents use genres, or both. Thus the phenomenon I am addressing in the rest of this book can be characterized as technology-in-use-in-social-situations. An awkward species, to be sure. But cut its hyphenated tail off, and you have expelled the user from the generative process of technology.

Three central points for a research programme follow from my conception of technology extended to include the acts of use in social situations. The first stage is an exploration of the variety of use genres emerging around a particular technology. The second stage includes examining the course of selective stabilization of some of these genres, their normalization and their reinforcement by supporting technical forms, as a course determined by social structures, culture and the typical, everyday situations that constitute them. The third stage aims at identifying possibilities for retaining a richer spectrum of use genres, or in more ambitious political terms, for technological democratization. Returned to ordinary users, the products of this research would encourage their informed participation in the generative process of technology.

In the following chapters I will start implementing this research programme by surveying the territory in which the engagement of ordinary users with technology takes place – everyday life – and specifically, one of its central loci: the home. First, I will develop a detailed conception of everyday life and the place and role of the home within it. Then, I will enter this territory in order to meet some of the common heroes who bring the new Internet technology into their homes and engage in the complex process of ascribing it place and function, meaning and value. I will try to understand the choices of these users against the backdrop of their specific social situations. In this way, I hope to grasp the rationality of the emergent Internet-use genres and to uncover their implications for the generative process of technology.

Notes

[1] In the dedication of his book *The practice of everyday life,* de Certeau (1984) wrote: 'To the ordinary man. To a common hero, a ubiquitous character walking in countless thousands on the streets. In invoking here at the outset of my narratives the absent figure who provides both their beginning and their necessity, I inquire into the desire whose impossible object he represents'.

[2] *The power of the powerless: citizens against the state in Central-Eastern Europe.*

[3] Feenberg explains: 'Capitalist social and technical requirements are thus condensed in a "technological rationality" or a "regime of truth" which brings the construction and interpretation of technical systems into conformity with the requirements of a system of domination. I will call this phenomenon the social code of technology or, more briefly, the *technical code* of capitalism. Capitalist hegemony, on this account, is an effect of its code' (1991, p. 79).

[4] Winston (1998) offers a number of historical examples of how the radical potential of new technologies of communication has been contained within the boundaries of the established social hierarchies through selective technical configurations and regulatory measures. In Winston's story, however, there is little hope of ever turning this tendency around toward democratic rationalization.

[5] Speaking about the 'powerful' in this context, I do not understand the concept to signify any general and fixed positions held by social groups, but the temporary constellations of knowledge and resources that differentiate the participants in technological development. In this particular context and its pertaining set of relations, experts, managers, granting agencies, venture capitalists, corporate decision-makers and others stand out as significantly more influential than lay users. For their part, lay users may hold very diverse assets, and hence positions of influence, in other contexts, but they typically remain a marginalized category with respect to the technological establishment.

[6]In participatory design, workers and engineers collaborate in teams to design technologies for particular work settings. It represents a user-centred approach to information system development that originated in the Nordic countries with the idea of empowering workers in technology-rich environments both individually and collectively (see Schuler and Namioka, 1993).

[7]Benston (1988) proposes such a view of technology, observing: 'The technology available at any specific time provides a range of options for acting on the world … these options function rather like words in a language' (p. 18). Benston goes on to argue that contemporary technology represents a language created by men, which limits the action options available to women.

[8]This notion stems from Vygotsky (1978), *Mind in society*.

[9]Despite the widespread belief that it was Bakhtin who wrote some of the works published under the name of his friend and disciple Voloshinov including *Marxism and the philosophy of language* (see Clark and Holquist, 1984), I prefer to go by bibliographical authorship. The possibility remains that Voloshinov did in fact write, or contributed significantly to these works. Moreover, the controversy around the authorship has no implications for my use of the ideas articulated in the book.

[10]The Wittgensteinian slogan 'meaning is use' (1958, para. 43) is clearly at work in the case of technology.

TWO Technology in Everyday Life

Introduction: What is Everyday Life?

In this chapter, my goal is to develop an approach to studying technology users that breaks away from viewing them as a partner in an asymmetrical relationship where most, if not all, initiative and power rests with either technology itself or its producers. I invoke and examine the concept of everyday life in an effort to distinguish the position of the user of technology and, specifically, the Internet, from the organizational contexts in which development, design and production of technology takes place. These contexts are, to a large degree, centred on the technology itself, while everyday life presupposes a focus on the human being who lives it. Everyday life cannot be reduced to the private sphere and the processes of consumption. The analytical power of the concept lies in its capacity to embrace diverse activities in multiple settings (Lie and Sorensen, 1996).

People living their everyday lives, of course, populate the design, development and production settings where technology is created. However, it is not the designers' and constructors' experience of new technology in their everyday lives that will occupy me here. My aim is to analyze the place of the Internet in the everyday lives of 'simple customers'[1] and the ways in which it both affects these lives and is affected by them.

Among the multiple sites of everyday life where simple customers can be found, the home holds a particular significance. This is especially so in the case of the Internet. In its most recent incarnation, the medium presupposes the home as the physical entry point to a global network of computers, content and people. At this entry point, we can observe the user as a socially situated individual and interpret his or her Internet-related behaviour in relation to the larger picture of his or her life. Both 'home' and 'everyday life' are intricate empirical and conceptual constructs. I will survey their multiple dimensions in order to be able to start unravelling the distinctive relationships between users and technology that these entities harbour.

As noted by Waites (1989), the commonplace phrase 'everyday life' has had a complex history in social science and has taken on different meanings in different social theories. It would be an excruciating task to follow all the lines of reasoning drawn through and around everyday life and attempt to resolve the debates still raging. I will limit my excursion into the studies of everyday life to two main schools of thought – phenomenological sociology represented by the work of Schutz (Schutz and Luckmann, 1973) and critical theory represented by Lefebvre (1971, 1991). Secondly, I will discuss two attempts at synthesis of the valuable tenets of both the phenomenological and the critical tradition undertaken respectively by Habermas (1984) and Smith (1987). In these two theoretical frameworks, the phenomenological tradition serves as a means for conceptualizing a thinking and acting subject, situated locally in an immediately experienced world, while the critical tradition supplies the means for transcending the observable individual world and grasping the higher-order social relations that organize it. The upshot of this theoretical survey will be a conceptual map of everyday life directing me where to look and what to pay attention to when I investigate concrete cases of Internet use.

Users shape technology by way of their everyday living with it (and here the analogy with language intrudes again) and not through participation in a specialized scientific-technological practice, or conscious attention to scientific and technical principles. In Schutzian terms this means that most users appropriate technology without stepping out of their everyday lifeworld into a different 'finite province of meaning' (Schutz and Luckmann, 1973, p. 23) such as the 'scientific-theoretical attitude' (p. 24). At the same time, technology alters the structure of users' everyday lifeworlds, including their horizon for action. By saying all this, I am already invoking Schutzian vocabulary, which needs to be understood as part and parcel of his system of phenomenological sociology.

The Schutzian Everyday Lifeworld

The sociological work of Alfred Schutz provides a rich and meticulously developed conceptual vocabulary with which to discuss what he called 'the everyday life-world' (Schutz and Luckmann, 1973, p. 3).[2] Schutz defines the everyday lifeworld[3] as 'the region of reality in which man [*sic*][4] can engage himself and which he can change while he operates in it by means of his animate organism' (Schutz and Luckmann, 1973, p. 3). This is the region in which man experiences other people (his fellow men) with whom he constructs a shared world. These two features taken together make the everyday lifeworld 'man's fundamental and para- mount reality' (p. 3). In the attitude of common sense, or in Schutz's term, the 'natural attitude', the everyday lifeworld is taken for granted. Everything man experiences within its limits is 'unproblematic until further notice' (Schutz and Luckmann, 1973, p. 4).

Of particular importance to my project is the fact that the everyday lifeworld in Schutz's definition is the arena, as well as what sets the limits, of human action. Hence, as Schutz himself states: 'The problems of action and choice must, therefore, have a central place in the analysis of the life-world' (Schutz and Luckmann, 1973, p. 18). The lifeworld is a reality which we modify through our acts and which also shapes our actions.

Our actions in and upon the everyday lifeworld are guided by our understanding of it ('to the degree necessary') given to us in our 'stock of knowledge'. This stock of knowledge is comprised of all our previous experiences, including our immediate experiences as well as those trans- mitted to us by our 'fellow men' (above all parents, teachers, mentors). Our stock of knowledge provides us with the reference schema necessary for our organization of the surrounding world. Objects and events that confront us in the lifeworld are mapped onto a set of typifications: we experience them as mountains and stones, trees and animals, houses and machines, etc. (see Schutz and Luckmann, 1973, pp. 6–7).

Several of Schutz's concepts regarding the everyday lifeworld prove to be useful for the purposes of this study. First, Schutz's discussion of the spatial, temporal and social arrangements of the everyday lifeworld prompt the Internet researcher to look for transformations in these arrangements related to Internet use. Second, his notions of situation and relevance structures provide a basis for gaining a systematic understand- ing of local action contexts as they present themselves to the acting subject. The relevance that the Internet acquires for users in their particular situations lends itself to a thorough examination thanks to this conceptual apparatus.

Spatial and temporal arrangement of the lifeworld

Schutz distinguishes between two main spatial dimensions of the everyday lifeworld: the world within actual reach and the world within potential

39

reach. The 'world within actual reach' is the sector of the world which is accessible to the subject's immediate experience (Schutz and Luckmann, 1973, p. 37). It embraces actually perceived objects as well as objects that can be perceived through re-focusing the attention. This is the place where the person finds herself – the actual 'here' and starting point of her orientation in space, the 'zero' point of her coordination system.

Sectors of the world that were once in the subject's actual reach form the province of her 'restorable reach' (Schutz and Luckmann, 1973, p. 37). It is experienced as such due to the belief (idealization) that what was once within the subject's action limits, can always be brought back there. Thus, this province transcends the world 'within actual reach' and represents a dimension of the world 'within potential reach', constituted by the experiences of the past. Another dimension of the world of potential reach is characterized by orientation toward the future. This is the province of the lifeworld that has never been in the subject's reach but can be brought within it, if the need or desire arises. Therefore, it constitutes the 'world within attainable reach' (p. 38). This province, or zone, of the lifeworld is particularly suggestive to my analysis because it is delimited on the one hand by the 'grades of ability' (p. 39) at the subject's disposal that are physical, technical, socio-cultural, and on the other, by her own biographical situation and the hierarchies of plans for action derived from it.

Applied to the subject's fellow men, this system of spatial arrangements becomes an important aspect of social relations. As Schutz points out, it 'enters into the differentiation of intimacy and anonymity, of strangeness and familiarity, of social proximity and distance' (Schutz and Luckmann, 1973, p. 41).

With regard to action, these dimensions of the spatial arrangement of the lifeworld take the shape of differentiated 'zones of operation' (p. 41). Within the world of actual reach and as a subsection of it there exists a zone which the subject can influence through direct action – the zone of operation. Schutz draws a distinction between the 'primary zone of operation', where action is tied to the physical body of the actor, and the 'secondary zone of operation' (and its corresponding 'secondary reach'), in which action can be performed only with the help of various media (see p. 44). The province of mediated action meets its limits in the prevailing technological conditions of a society, and is being dramatically enlarged with the advance of technology and its penetration into the everyday lifeworld. Schutz clearly recognizes the broad variation of subjective secondary zones of operation among the members of a single society. Social structures and the position a subject occupies within them determine differential access to what is technologically possible.

The three most important aspects of the temporality of the lifeworld in the Schutzian framework are 'permanence/finitude', the 'fixed course of temporality/first things first', and 'historicality/situation' (Schutz and Luckmann, 1973, p. 50). These aspects derive from the permanence of the world and the subject's finitude within it:

> I know that there are limits to my duration. The relevance system of the natural attitude is derived from this: the manifold, mutually interwoven systems of hope and fear, wants and satisfactions, chances and risks that induce men to master their life-world, to overcome obstacles, to project plans and to carry them out. (Schutz and Luckmann, 1973, p. 47)

Thus the knowledge of one's finitude is the foundation of the subject's projects within the framework of her life-plan.

The second aspect – fixed course of temporality – derives from the intersection of subjective time (stream of consciousness), biological time (the rhythm of the body), world time (the seasons) and social time (the calendar). The incongruity of events in these different dimensions imposes on the subject a time structure within which she has to arrange the temporal course of her affairs according to degrees of urgency, that is, postpone one thing and concentrate on another in each particular moment.

> The succession of events in the outer world is imposed on me in my corporeal rhythm and in the social calendar. ... All of the 'unimportant' interludes, partial acts, etc. which for example I can pass over in my daydreams, are necessarily elements of my life in everyday situations in which nature and society, including their temporal structure, give me 'resistance'. ... The imposed, fixed course of the temporal structure affords a plan for the day alongside the life-plan determined by my finitude ... it depends importantly upon the principle of 'first things first', the fixed courses of events in everyday existence. (Schutz and Luckmann, 1973, p. 48–49)

Finally, historicality/situation refers to the realization that one is born into a particular historical situation which is only a moment of the history of the social world, but which one cannot exchange for another.

These three aspects define the 'unalterable limits' determining the timetable of one's dealings (Schutz and Luckmann, 1973, p. 49). They intersect with the spatial aspects of the lifeworld to define the 'province of the practicable' (p. 50), that is, the subjective representation of the zone in which one feels capable of acting. Importantly, this province is limited both by the ontologically unmodifiable structures of the lifeworld and by the 'technologically practical' (p. 50).

The social arrangement of the lifeworld: zones of anonymity

I experience other men in various perspectives and my relation to them is arranged according to various levels of proximity, depth and anonymity in lived experience. The breadth of variations in my experience of the social world extends from the encounter with another man to vague attitudes, institutions, cultural structures and humanity in general. (Schutz and Luckmann, 1973, p. 61)

Schutz describes the social structures of the lifeworld, our experience of other human beings, starting from the most immediate experience of an Other with whom one shares a sector of the lifeworld at a particular moment. The people falling into the zone of one's actual reach are termed 'fellow-men' (Schutz and Luckmann, 1973, p. 62). These are the people with whom I (the generic human being) am in a face-to-face encounter. When I turn my attention to the Other and grasp his existence before me in spatial and temporal immediacy, a 'thou-orientation' (p. 62) is established. When the thou-orientation is reciprocal, that is, I turn to you as you do to me, a 'we-relation' takes hold.

We-relations are established at different levels of nearness, depth, engagement, coordination, mutuality or, in sum, immediacy. Tracking further these different 'gradations of immediacy' (p. 69), Schutz moves into the zones of the social world populated by 'contemporaries'. This term refers to 'those other men with whom I do not actually have a we-relation, but whose life falls in the same present span of world time as mine' (p. 69). Our experience of contemporaries is qualitatively different from that of our fellow men. This difference lies in the dramatic decrease in the 'abundance of symptoms through which the conscious life of the other is accessible to me' (p. 69). Therefore, contemporaries are experienced as 'types' (p. 75) to which certain attributes, certain functions and behaviour are ascribed. These types display various degrees of anonymity on the basis of which the world of contemporaries is stratified into personal types, functionary types, and typifications of social collectivities. The anonymity of a typification is inversely proportional to its fullness of content, which is determined by the origin of the typification – was it inferred from immediate experience of an earlier fellow-man, or was it a learned generalization of social reality?

The degree of anonymity of an individual social type depends, in the end, on how easily the relation constituted through it can be changed into a we-relation. 'The sooner I can immediately experience the typical characteristics of someone as properties of a fellow-man, as components of his conscious life, the less anonymous is the typification in question'

(Schutz and Luckmann, 1973, p. 81). Thus the immediate encounter with a fellow-man and the mediate experience of a highly anonymous social type represent two poles between which many intermediate forms can be found. At this point, an isomorphism between the spatial and the social structures of the everyday lifeworld becomes obvious. The structures of attainability and restorability characterizing the spatial arrangement of the lifeworld can be recognized in the subjective experience of the social world as well. Based on the complex graduation of immediacy constituted by the various degrees of restorability and attainability of a once-existent or achievable we-relation, the structure of the social relationships between contemporaries emerges.

Schutz's structures of the social world present the key to understanding the unique character of *communication* technologies compared to all other technologies and artefacts. Communication technologies and devices mediate subjects' perceptions of and actions onto the social world, while the effects of all other technologies are realized first and foremost in the physical world. It is clear from the outset that media are implicated in a re-charting of the zones of anonymity of the experienced social world. Mass media, for example, enlarge the number of types of contemporaries of whose existence I know in general, that is, whose existence I can infer on the basis of my knowledge of the social world as reference points of typical social functions. Thus, a question to be addressed in the analysis of the experiences of Internet users would be: How does this medium restructure the social worlds of users? What changes does it induce in the structures of immediacy and anonymity? In Chapter 7, I will also employ Schutz's arrangement of the social world to reformulate some of the intractable problems generated by the public-private dichotomy. Analysts have attributed to the Internet a potential to overcome social distances and barriers very much along the same lines that led McLuhan (1964) to envision a 'global village' (p. 93) brought into existence by the broadcasting media. Looking at the actual experiences of users in later chapters, I will test and, possibly, qualify the validity of such claims.

Situation and relevance: imposed and intrinsic relevances

In every moment of conscious life, I find myself in a situation. In its concrete contents this situation is indeed endlessly variable: on one hand because it is biologically articulated, so to speak as a 'product' of all prior situations; on the other hand, because it is relatively 'open', that is it can be defined and mastered on the basis of an actual stock of knowledge. (Schutz and Luckmann, 1973, p. 100)

In his fine-grained analysis of the microscenes within which human action unfolds, the 'situations' of everyday life, Schutz lays out a complex relationship between individual freedom and constraint. This is the interplay between the 'imposed' and 'open' elements of each situation. Similarly to the observations regarding speech situations outlined in Chapter 1, in the action situations discussed by Schutz, individual interests and goals are formulated and pursued against the backdrop of a culturally inherited stock of knowledge and through the utilization of culturally provided means. Schutz lays particular emphasis on the pragmatic motive that organizes action in each situation. Situations and their pertaining elements are given meaning (determined) depending on the practical interest the subject is pursuing. This interest itself is a product and expression of a complex structure of subjective plans spanning the life-course. It is subjectively experienced as a task or goal with a certain level of urgency derived from the hierarchy of priorities in the course of life, the course of the day, for work and leisure, etc. The plan-determined interest is included in the situation and is to a certain extent 'swept along' (p. 115) and modified by it.

This qualifying circumstance seems to remain unnoticed by critics who consider Schutz's concept of action to be overly individualistic and assuming 'the power to act and coordinate in a planned and rational manner and to exercise control as an individual over conditions and means' (Smith, 1987, p. 64). This model, Smith maintains, represents the life-world of the bureaucratic man, which is organized by the formal rationality structuring his work role. My interpretation of Schutz's notion, however, emphasizes the human capacity for projecting, planning and striving despite, and often times against, the formal rationality of bureaucratic institutions structuring subjective existence. Subjective plans can be a product of emotion and desire as much as of pragmatic interests in control of the surrounding environment. They can be ill-considered, tentative or unviable. But to take away from the subject, even though only conceptually, the capacity to plan her next step or day amid the limitations and possibilities present in her situation would mean to surrender the everyday world to nothing other than formal rationality.

While most situations in our lives are routine and we only need to apply habitual recipes in order to master them successfully, other situations are 'problematic'. Schutz's concept of action recipes, internalized prescriptions for 'how to bring forth in typical situations typical results by typical means' (Schutz, 1970, pp. 239–240), can be compared to Bakhtin's concept of speech genres arising in typical situations. While in Bakhtin's case these habitual patterns capture verbal action and forms of utterances, in Schutz's framework recipes refer to patterns of action that are deemed appropriate for mastering recurring situations. More often than not, in their routine daily activities people draw on genres and recipes provided to them in the stock of knowledge acquired throughout their enculturation. This changes when they are confronted by a problematic situation. In these instances typical means do not guarantee the desired results. Personal ingenuity and new knowledge have to be mobilized, and new ways of speaking and acting have to be cooked up on the fly. In case of positive results, the cultural stock of knowledge absorbs the novel solutions and is extended.

The plan-determined interest organizing each situation is also responsible for determining relevance structures, the totality of those objects, features or concepts which are experienced as relevant in a particular situation (Schutz and Luckmann, 1973). The plan-determined interest at hand orients the subject's attention towards different aspects of the situation with a view to its 'mastering' (p. 116).[5] Thus, different areas of the subject's knowledge as well as objects and properties of her material and social environment come to the fore as relevant depending on the nature of the interest organizing each situation. Schutz distinguishes four regions of decreasing relevance, or 'zones of relevance' (Schutz, 1970, p. 111).

First, this is the part of the world within our reach which can be immediately observed by us and also, at least partly changed and rearranged by our actions. This is the 'zone of primary relevance' (Schutz, 1970, p. 112) that requires an optimum of clear and distinct understanding of its structure. Second, there are the fields indirectly connected to the zone of primary relevance but, unlike it, not open to our control. These fields or 'zones of minor relevance' can provide 'ready-made tools' (p. 112) for the accomplishment of our goal, or establish conditions affecting the implementation of our plans. Third, there are the zones which for the time being have no connection with our interest at hand. These are the irrelevant zones that we can take for granted and ignore unless significant changes that create risks or new opportunities with regard to our interests and plans occur in them. The fourth zone is the field(s) of 'absolute irrelevance' (p. 112). No possible change occurring in these fields can, so we believe, influence our objective at hand. These relevance zones, Schutz emphasizes, are not separated from each other with clear-cut borders. On the contrary, they penetrate each other and overlap, creating intermediate transitional areas.

Characterized from a different perspective, relevances can be subdivided into systems of 'imposed' relevances and systems of 'intrinsic' or 'volitional', relevances (Schutz, 1970, p. 113), which again, in daily life, are intermingled with one another and never found in a pure state. The intrinsic, or volitional, relevances are the outcome of our spontaneously chosen interests and goals, those that are within our control. In contrast, imposed relevances are those imposed on us by events and situations over which we have no control (p. 114).

An example of a system of imposed relevances is the relevance structure prevailing in the social group or culture of which the individual is a member. Given its cultural hierarchy of values, every social community establishes its own hierarchically ordered 'domains of relevance' (p. 115). These domains of relevance are culturally transmitted from one generation to another and are often institutionalized. While it is true that the content of these socially constituted domains of relevance is in continuous flux, the individual, at every moment, acts in a social world providing a particular structure of domains of relevance and has to orient herself according to them.

The notion of relevance will be employed in my further analysis of Internet use to address questions concerning situations and plan-determined interests that draw the Internet into the zones of primary relevance of subjects. How does the Internet emerge out of the zone of the absolutely irrelevant gradually to traverse its course through the zones of minor relevance and into the zone of primary relevance? What types of situations and what pragmatic interests organizing them underlie this movement? It will also be important to determine the type of relevance – intrinsic (volitional) or imposed – that this medium attains for residential users. I expect that creative appropriation of the Internet occurs in problematic situations, in which users have to come up with new understanding of its relevance and involve it in novel patterns of action with a view to mastering their situation. Furthermore, I see in Schutz's notion of intrinsic and imposed relevance, an analytical tool that could be useful in the investigation of the micro-dimensions of power in everyday life. Is the Internet, along with certain ways to use it, imposed on subjects by powerful institutions and discourses? Do users, by accepting it, fall prey to dominant interests and lose part of their freedom and humanity? Clearly, whether the relevance of an object, piece of knowledge or action recipe is imposed on the subject or intrinsic to her will be difficult to establish unequivocally. That is why, I will consider the two types of relevance as the poles of a continuum along which particular cases can be located. Thus, subjective relevances and choices will be a mix of various degrees of imposition and free volition. How, then, does this dynamic play out in the daily practice of Internet use?

Another question to be investigated refers to the Internet's potential to affect the interplay between imposed and open elements of the situation and intrinsic and imposed relevances in a more general sense, at the level of situation definition and action plans. Does the medium open new possibilities for formulating and pursuing goals of intrinsic relevance to subjects? Or, on the contrary, is it functioning as yet another vehicle for imposing on them socially established relevances, most likely aligned with the interests of the powerful? Sorting through the collected empirical data, I will use the concepts of imposed and intrinsic relevance to analyze the adoption process and the different relationships that users establish with the Internet.

Social-biographical situation and its pertaining structure of relevances

Schutz used the concept of 'situation' to designate the immediate here and now of the acting subject. The situation is the unit of time and space that the subject inhabits and defines on the basis of the prioritized plan-determined interest at any given moment: 'it is the province of what is open to me now to control' (Schutz and Luckmann, 1973, p. 111). In this micro sense, my situation at this moment is determined by the prioritized goal of producing a piece of text which paves the way towards completing my book and thus represents a minuscule component of my hierarchy of plans for the day, the year, and my life as a whole. This situation is biographically articulated because of my past actions (performed in prior situations). Completing an academic programme, selecting an area of specialization, studying the literature in this area, choosing a topic for investigation, are all actions that have brought me to this point. Elements of the situation that are imposed on me include the nature of a piece of text (it has to be conceived as a set of ideas by its author and objectified, in writing as opposed to growing out of a seed the author buries in the soil or some other mode of creation involving other materials and procedures), the language in which I am writing, the standards of the scholarly community, and the character of the literature on which I am drawing.

Open elements of this situation, or elements that are feasible for me to determine, are those particular ideas and links between them that I will choose to consider and/or express in my text; the exact words I will use, the breaks I will decide to take; the possibility of discussing this text with my colleagues and so on. My computer is drawn into this situation, gaining what Schutz (1970) calls 'minor' (p. 111), but I would rather refer to as 'secondary', relevance. The computer is not a focal element of the situation at hand. My plans and, subsequently, my attention, are not centred on the computer or computer technology itself. At the same time, I find in it a useful, ready-made tool for accomplishing my primary goal. In this case, I don't need to know how my computer works. I need only the skills of typing, formatting and saving text which I have acquired at some previous point and which make the computer (in its word-processing function) a 'transparent' technology to me. My computer as experienced in this situation belongs also to the system of relevances imposed on me. In the social group of actual and aspiring academics, with which I identify, producing text on a computer is a matter of convention. By the same token, the computer is construed by this group – with regard to its typical plans and derivative relevances – primarily, although not exclusively, as a word-processing machine.

This situation is quite different from the situation in which I found myself half an hour ago, when I experimented with an Internet-based conferencing system while trying to create a forum, a virtual club, where I could meet with my group of high-school friends. My priority at that moment was the goal of maintaining my membership in a dispersed community. That situation also had its cluster of imposed elements such as the geographical distance between my friends and me and my socially and biographically articulated need to be in touch with them. My computer and my Internet connection then represented a situational aspect of volitional, intrinsic relevance. I was orienting myself to it willingly and consciously in my search for a means of mastering the situation. By doing this I was creating a minuscule precedent of constructing the computer as an emotional, community-sustaining, social machine.

With a view to the following analysis of Internet use, I would like to propose a second concept of situation rising above the microscopic to a higher level of generalization. I feel I need a concept that refers to larger units of space/time and a correspondingly higher level in the hierarchy of subjective plans and interests. Schutz himself distinguishes between 'the basic temporal structures of inner duration in which the meaning of ... experiences becomes constituted' (i.e. the immediate micro-situation) on one hand, and on the other 'a superimposed signification level of temporal articulation' with a broader scope (see Schutz and Luckmann, 1973, p. 56). I would like to reserve Schutz's notion of 'social-biographical situation' for these broader temporal spans of everyday life. The terms in which such situations are subjectively defined are given to the individual in the form of 'historical formations of meaning-bestowing categories experienced in the natural attitude as taken for granted articulations of the course of life' (Schutz and Luckmann, 1973, pp. 56–57). Examples of such categories are the variants of age: childhood, youth, maturity, old age; work: unemployed, unskilled worker, skilled worker, professional; material prosperity: poor, economically comfortable, rich; health: disabled, in poor health, healthy; and all the variations of married life and family. These categories are, Schutz maintains, socially imposed on the subject and interiorized by her.

This notion of social-biographical situation will represent the backdrop against which I will try to make sense of the individual Internet-related experiences of the respondents in my study. Different aspects of these situations (which in principle can be explicated without limit) will be drawn into the foreground when determining the relevance of the Internet to users' lives. Thus, I will not be confined to the predetermined demographic and social categories that analysts typically hold responsible for Internet adoption such as level of education, occupation, income and gender. Rather, I will be able to gain insight into a wider variety of situational characteristics, as experienced and defined by subjects themselves, that make the new medium relevant and attractive to users.

Transposing the logic of Schutz's exposition concerning the immediate situation, which I will call 'the situation at hand', I will posit that at any time of her life, a person finds herself in a social-biographical situation. This situation can be described in conventional social categories such as the ones listed above that refer to economic, occupational, family, and health status and role. At the same time, this situation is relatively open and can be explicated without limit, or indeed within the limit of the plan-determined interest for the moment.

To sum up, taking up an existing ambiguity in Schutz's notion of situation, I have introduced a distinction between the situation at hand, the micro-level of pragmatic orientation at this particular moment in the person's immediate zone of operation, and her social-biographical situation. The latter represents a signification unit with a broader scope, a higher-level juncture in the hierarchy of plans determined vis-à-vis the socially available types of biographies on one hand, and the individually constructed plan for one's life on the other. In my immediate situation, I am composing and typing a text on a computer keyboard. In my social-biographical situation, I am a professional striving to make a contribution to her field, a working mother struggling to master her tough portfolio, an immigrant to Canada who refuses to let go of her old culture and relationships while building new ones.

By defining social-biographical situation in this way, I make a few assumptions that are at odds with action theories contrasting plans to situated action as, for example, Suchman's (1987). I acknowledge the individual's capacity for conscious reflection and planning of a life-course that, to me, is synonymous with personal efforts (no matter how effective or viable) to be in control of one's own life. However, this capacity also exhibits a fundamental situatedness. Plans that individuals make for the course of their lives at any particular moment are rooted in their specific, socially and individually articulated, social-biographical situation and are often swept along with it and modified.

Like situations at hand, social-biographical situations obtain their specific systems of relevance that can be analytically divided into zones of primary and secondary relevance or irrelevance. The two types of relevance – intrinsic and imposed – are of particular importance here as they represent temporarily more stable structures compared with the systems of relevance deriving from the situation at hand. If I were to investigate the relevance of the computer and the Internet with regard to the immediate situation at hand, I would be looking closely at the particular actions that they are drawn into – writing a book, chatting with a friend, ordering a product. I will necessarily do some of that in my research. Locating the Internet within the social-biographical situation of a user, however, will allow me to get access to a more stable cluster of meanings and relevances that the medium acquires for a person. Consequently, use genres identified against the background of typical social-biographical situations will act as indicators of the significance the medium has acquired in society and culture at large.

Before getting to that point, however, another perspective on everyday life needs to be considered. While Schutz's project was idealist, in the sense that he aimed at charting the everyday lifeworld as it is constituted and experienced by the subjective consciousness 'from within', materialist philosophers employed the concept of everyday life in an attempt to ground their critical theory in the most immediate exchange between a person and her material environment.

From the 'Head World' to the Material World: The Misery and Power of Everyday Life

Lefebvre (1991) started his inquiry into the quotidian (everyday life) with the conviction that he was developing a Marxist sociology. He distinguished his approach from the preoccupation of Marxist philosophers and thinking people of his time[6] with the political dramas acted out in 'higher spheres' (p. 6), such as the State, parliament, or party policies. Lefebvre's interest focused on the 'humble everyday base' (p. 6) of politics; in matters related to food, housing, rationing, wages, the organization and reorganization of labour. He was at pains to grasp and articulate in a definition the 'difficult to define and yet essential and concrete "something" that "just a quarter-of-an-hour alone" with a man from a distant or extinct culture would reveal to us' (p. 7). In contrast to descriptive historians and ethnographers, Lefebvre's goal was to develop a transformative *critique* of this elusive something. Lefebvre, Highmore argues, was both a Marxist and a romantic. As a Marxist, he saw everyday life as organized by the logic of commodity and relentlessly run according to the code of capital. As a romantic, he saw forces and potentialities within everyday life that could be mobilized toward its transformation (see Highmore, 2002, p. 115).

In his critique of everyday life, Lefebvre (1991) explicitly focused his attention on phenomena that his contemporaries greeted as 'technological progress'. He was not satisfied with the proliferating celebratory descriptions of the application of modern techniques in daily life. He wanted to discover 'the real social process beneath an accumulation of technological detail' (p. 9). Thus, his critique of technological development under capitalist modernity set off with the proposition that the continual introduction of new gadgets eventually deprives everyday life of some of its previously valued characteristics. Something had to be given up (especially by peasants and working-class families) in exchange for the gadgets of technical 'progress'. At the same time, Lefebvre insisted, technical progress realizes a critique of the everyday 'from within', rather than through dreams, poetry or art. This is the critique of 'the real by the possible' (p. 9) which reveals the existence of a wide range of alternative possibilities and directions for technical development. In reality, however, much of 'what is humanly possible' (p. 233) to achieve through technical progress is precluded by the choices made by the powerful.[7]

But first of all, what is everyday life for Lefebvre (1991)? Where is it to be found? The obscurity of this notion, Lefebvre claims, stems from the fact that modern capitalist society differentiates and separates from each other previously blended elements of human life – work and leisure, individual and community, public and private consciousness and spheres of activity. This is exactly the reason why the concept is of a special sociological value: everyday life involves all these discrete elements; it is their unity and their totality, and 'it determines the concrete individual' (p. 31). Everyday life stands for:

'what is left over' after all distinct, superior, specialized, structured activities have been singled out by the analysis, and must be defined as a totality. ... Everyday life is profoundly related to all activities, and encompasses them with all their differences and their conflicts; it is their meeting place, their bond, their common ground. And it is in everyday life that the sum of total relations which make the human – and every human being – a whole takes its shape and its form. In it are expressed and fulfilled those relations which bring into play the totality of the real, albeit in a certain manner which is always partial and incomplete: friendship, comradeship, love, the need to communicate, play, etc. ... The substance of everyday life – 'human raw material' in its simplicity and richness – pierces through all alienation and establishes 'disalienation'. (Lefebvre, 1991, p. 97)

The critical study of everyday life, then, becomes a vast inquiry, looking at professional life, family life and leisure, public and private activities, in terms of their many-sided interactions. The goal is to extract 'what is living, new, positive – the worthwhile needs and fulfillments – from the negative elements: the alienations' (Lefebvre, 1991, p. 42).

The central notion serving as a tool for performing a critique (as opposed to mere description) of everyday life for Lefebvre (1991) is the Marxian concept of alienation. The source of alienation is the commodity relation in which the product of the worker's labour acquires independent existence and comes back to confront the worker as an alien power. Productive labour, the essential activity in which human powers are realized, becomes external, alienated from the worker, governed by an autonomous external agency which he, the worker, cannot even know. This results in a relation-ship of the worker to his own activity as something which is alien and does not belong to him, a relationship of self-estrangement, of loss of active human will and spontaneous creativity. Thus, estranged labour reduces man's conscious being to a mere means for his physical existence, depriving his life of what is essentially human (see pp. 59–63).

Lefebvre (1991) extends Marx's analysis by discovering additional forms of alienation that take over areas of life other than production (see Shields, 2001). He discusses the specific character of alienation in politi-cal life, where the State takes on a power superior to the life of society. Leisure and recreational activity can also be alienated to the degree to which they are constituted as distraction, compensation for work, and escape. Social organization takes over allegedly spontaneous human needs and their related activities, and directs, shifts and modifies them into alienating forms.

No form of life or activity, however, can be touted as inherently alien-ating, Lefebvre (1991) claims. Complexes of heterogeneous activities making up people's everyday lives have to be examined in their historical concreteness. The notion of alienation has to be applied to concrete situ-ations in everyday life. Only on this basis the distinction between what is 'life-enhancing' (p. 82) (as opposed to alienated) and what is alienated can be made. This is the task of the 'critique of everyday life' (p. 83) – to promote a critical and self-critical consciousness, higher than 'the consciousness exerted when we make the occasional uncomplicated choice' (p. 83) of action in everyday life.

The result of such an investigation is, Lefebvre (1971) concludes, a 'sort of contrasting diptych' (p. 35), where the first panel represents the misery of everyday life and the second panel portrays its power (see p. 35). This idea of double-sidedness, or bifurcation, of everyday life will persist in further critical studies and deserves a closer look. Lefebvre provides a long list of illustrations for both sides of the quotidian. Its negative content revolves around the tedious tasks and humiliations to which the working class is subject by virtue of capitalist social relations – preoccupation with bare necessities, abstinence, hardship and suppressed desire. The positive content stems from the ability to create 'from the solids and spaces of everyday life, to make something lasting for the individual, the community, the class, the reproduction of essential social relations' (p. 35).

At the heart of this distinction between the positive and the negative content of everyday life is Lefebvre's (1971) extended notion of production, which represents one of his most important insights. He draws on the early work of Marx to challenge the narrowly economist notion of production and to endow it with a 'more forceful and wider significance' (p. 30). In Lefebvre's interpretation, production is not merely the making of products for the market:

> the term signifies on the one hand 'spiritual' production, that is to say creations (including social time and space); and on the other material production or the making of things; it also signifies the self-production of a 'human being' in the process of historical self-development, which involves the production of social relations. Finally, taken in its fullest sense, the term embraces re-production, not only biological (which is the province of demography), but the material reproduction of the tools of production, of technical instruments and the social relations into the bargain ... (1971, pp. 30–31)

The notion of production thus acquires its fullest significance as the production by a human being of her own existence. Everyday life emerges as the sociological point of interaction and feedback between all different types of production. From this perspective, then, even if an individual's involvement in the process of social production taken in its economic sense is marked by alienation, a whole range of diverse productive activities still remain open at the level of everyday life for her free and creative engagement. Forms of alienation may have encroached on some of these activities (for example, leisure) as well, but that is exactly where the 'critique of everyday life' enters the picture as a method for critical evaluation of social and individual practices and a search of directions and sources for change.

To compare the Schutzian concept of the everyday lifeworld with Lefebvre's (1971, 1991) materialistic critical concept is not a straightforward task. In the first case, the everyday lifeworld is an ideal construct, an attitude, a standpoint from which the subject perceives and acts. Its structures are ontologically unalterable, no matter that they can adopt different content in different historical times. In this sense, the Schutzian concept of the everyday lifeworld makes no claim to suggesting directions for change at the individual or social level. Its very essence is its taken-for-grantedness.

In Lefebvre's (1991) version, everyday life represents the palpable dynamics of matter and energy, and most importantly, of 'human raw material' (p. 97). It is one definite section of the material, social world seen from the perspective of and chosen as a focus by a critical observer – the section which represents 'the meeting place of all human activities, their bond, their common ground' (p. 97). In Schutzian terms, this can be recognized as the zone of 'working'.[8] Here we reach a point where the phenomenological and the critical studies of everyday life strike an implicit agreement – everyday life is the terrain in which the individual is an actor physically and mentally involved in producing, in its widest sense, the social world and her own self. Schutz is interested in how this terrain is experienced from within the acting individual's head, while the critical materialist scrutinizes this terrain from outside, after having abstracted it from all 'distinct, superior, specialized, structured activities' (p. 97). The phenomenological perspective is geared towards understanding and description, while the critical materialist perspective is geared toward evaluation and change. The phenomenological account gives primacy to the active symbolic construction performed by the individual and defines social reality as its outcome. The critical materialist recognizes an outer and typically anonymous force – social relations such as the commodity relation – as organizing and dominating the living process of everyday life. Notably, part of what in Schutz's framework figures as 'imposed elements' of situations and 'imposed relevances' borne by ontological and social factors, the critical approach to everyday life construes as alienations stemming from a well-known source – the exploitative class relations under capitalist modernity.

I argue that both these perspectives are necessary for understanding the complexity of everyday life. In examining users' experiences with the Internet, I will apply the phenomenological approach in order to discover how the new medium is constructed as an element of subjects' everyday lifeworlds. I will attempt to establish its relevance in particular social-biographical situations. I will also look for the transformations in the content of users' everyday lifeworlds brought about by the medium. In addition, I will employ Lefebvre's (1971, 1991) critical method in order to identify the characteristic alienations to which Internet users are exposed. I will examine in depth the productive work, taken in Lefebvre's extended sense, performed by users through and around the Internet. In the process of this work, I contend, users create meanings, spaces, and social relations. They express their human potential in new ways and in the process shape the Internet as a medium of social communication. On the basis of the version of this medium that I find in users' everyday lives, I hope to be able to advance a critique of the real with the possible along the lines suggested by Lefebvre.

Towards a Synthesis: Lifeworld and System

Several attempts at synthesis of the insights of Schutz's phenomenology and critical theory have striven to elaborate a multi-focal optic combining the analytical powers of both perspectives. Habermas (1984) has identified the limitations of the Schutzian everyday lifeworld in its 'culturalistic abridgment' (p. 138) of social reality. According to Habermas, Schutz's interpretation of society commits the fallacy of 'hermeneutic idealism' (p. 148). This internal perspective, through the eyes of the actor, 'screens out everything that inconspicuously affects a sociocultural lifeworld from the outside. ... From the perspective of subjects who are acting communicatively, no alien authority can be hidden behind cultural symbolism' (pp. 148–149).

However, as authors in the Marxist critical tradition have argued, there is more to society than what acting subjects directly perceive, interpret, communicatively negotiate with each other and pursue through their intentional actions. A subject's goal-directed actions are also shaped and coordinated through 'functional interconnections that are not intended by them [the subjects] and are usually not even perceived within the horizon of everyday practice' (Habermas, 1984, p. 152). Lefebvre's (1971) diptych of the power and the misery of everyday life is brought about exactly by this state of affairs. It is the diverse wilful activities of individual people in everyday life that constitutes social organization, material and spiritual culture. At the same time, the imperatives of social organization come to overpower individual wills and enslave human beings in relationships unintended, unwanted, and often incomprehensible to them.

Different thinkers take different avenues toward representing the relationship between the two components of the emerging conceptual dichotomy. For Habermas (1984), these are the notions of System and Lifeworld and the process of progressive colonization of the latter by the former. Smith (1987) matches the Habermasian uncoupling of System and Lifeworld with a 'bifurcation' (p. 84) of her own – on one hand, a world directly experienced from oneself as centre, and on the other, an external organization of social relations – 'concerted sequences or courses of social action implicating more than one individual whose participants are not necessarily present or known to one another' (p. 155).

There is, however, an important difference in how Habermas (1984) and Smith (1987) interpret the relationship between System (external organization) and Lifeworld. Habermas perceives the two entities as embodiments of qualitatively different types of rationality with the forms of system aggressively invading the lifeworld and seizing its traditional territories. For Smith, although (abstract) social relations cannot be immediately discerned by actors in the everyday world, they are constituted through the activities and rationalities operating within it. For her part, she finds the paradigm of the reciprocal constitution between everyday actions and social relations in Marx's analysis of the commodity relation and his theory of alienation:

> It takes only a little imagination to see that all such [social] relations are present in and produced in the organization of activities at the everyday level as well as entering the everyday into relations that pass beyond the control of individuals (1987, p. 134).

Smith's project calls upon sociological inquiry to take on the task of making the everyday world problematic to actors, which represents a turning around of the Schutzian definition of the lifeworld. The problematization of the everyday world, as performed by Smith, represents an effort to bridge conceptually and practically the split between the immediately experienced local, subjective world and the social relations that organize it behind the subject's back:

> The problematic of the everyday world organizes inquiry into the social relations in back of the everyday worlds in which people's existence is embedded. It opens up the possibility of exploring these relations as they really are, of discovering how they work and how they enter into the organization of the local historical settings of our work and experience and of our encounters with others. (Smith, 1987, p. 134)

The goal of Smith's sociology is thus to create 'a knowledge that is "for us", that will explicate the social determinations of our own lives and experience' (p. 153). These social determinations can be fully disclosed only by a specialized investigation such as sociology. But the inquiry, although involving the special skills of the sociologist, must be understood as a cooperation between her and those who want to understand the social matrices of their experience. It is a form of 'consciousness-raising' (p. 154), aimed at finding the objective correlates to what, from a subjective perspective, had seemed a private experience. Smith insists scientific-theoretical investigation should appreciate, involve and build on the existing stocks of knowledge held by everyday actors when addressing their condition from the perspective of sociology.

Smith's (1987) conception integrates many of the strengths of the approaches considered in this chapter. At the beginning of her story of everyday life is the infinitely rich subjectively centred and locally experienced (Schutzian) lifeworld of the thinking and acting individual. This lifeworld is articulated to a structure of social relations (System, in the Habermasian sense), orchestrating the actions of multiple individuals from a position external to their lifeworlds and thus organizing their subjective experiences in accordance with the imperatives of the 'abstract mode of ruling' (Smith, 1987, p. 81). This mode of ruling is itself produced not in some specialized distinct compartment of society, but in the everyday practices of numerous thinking actors.

The way towards liberation from the imperatives robbing human actors of their autonomous will requires joining a specialized reflective practice (sociology) with the local competency of the inhabitants of subjective lifeworlds. The result of this union will be a 'sociology for' a particular type of human actors sharing similar experiences and subjected to similar forms of oppression. It will help these actors understand their own particular situations in light of new knowledge of the abstract principles (relations of ruling) that organize them. In this scheme, coming to consciousness through critical reflection is crucial. It involves taking a theoretical attitude and construing the concrete lifeworld(s) as problematic.

Taking an example from Smith's (1987) sociology *from the standpoint of* and *for* women, I set out to study the Internet *from the standpoint of* and *for* ordinary users. Like women in a patriarchal social order, ordinary users are marginalized subjects in a technocratic society. They are excluded from the governing of a society steeped in technology because they have no voice in the process of designing and implementing technical systems. Like women in a patriarchal order, ordinary users represent objects of seduction and control in the name of and through technologies. Their marginal position at the interface between the technological establishment and the everyday practices into which technologies are drawn and put to work, however, gives them a unique vantage point. This is precisely the vantage point from which my investigation will start. The insights it generates will be a joint product of my informants' situated knowledges and my own theoretically informed epistemology. The goal will be to discern both the forms of empowerment and the alienations brought about by the penetration of the Internet into everyday life as well as to identify the possibilities and the limits of critical choice in Internet use.

A Critical Phenomenology

In this section, I will examine the place ascribed to technology in the different conceptions of everyday life that I have reviewed so far. What kind of relationship exists between technology and everyday life according to the authors discussed here? From a causative perspective, I would like to know whether everyday life changes to accommodate the various technologies penetrating it from the specialized spheres of science and engineering. Or, rather, does everyday life itself induce transformations in technological systems and artefacts, and how do such transformations take place?

From a normative perspective, the question is how the effects of such changes can be evaluated vis-à-vis the normative dichotomies discerned by Marxist critiques of everyday life: when are these effects alienating and when are they life-enhancing and empowering? By raising this series of questions, I continue my inquiry into user agency. If everyday life is the scene of non-specialized activity of human beings, then it is also the scene where the *users* of technology perform. It is a terrain where human actors objectify themselves drawing upon and appropriating socially given means with a view to their own situated plans and motives. It will be logical then to expect that technology, being one of these means, is both formative to users' actions and transformed by them to a certain extent.

Will we be able to see in this terrain how users make 'innumerable and infinitesimal' (de Certeau, 1984, p. xiv) transformations geared towards adaptation of technological systems to their lifeworlds? Or, will we observe how System (or the social relations of ruling) embodied into technical devices organizes the innumerable and infinitesimal acts of everyday life and subordinates them to the dominant rationality, further alienating human actors from their products of all kinds? In other words, the task of this section will be to elaborate an account of the technology-everyday life relationship that is both phenomenologically and critically informed.

Technology in the phenomenological lifeworld

As noted earlier in this chapter, Schutz saw technology as a crucial factor in determining the boundaries of the different provinces of the lifeworld – the world within actual and potential reach, the province of the practicable, subjects' levels of ability, but also, to some extent, social relations of proximity and distance. From another perspective, it can be deduced that technology represents an element of the various situations constituting the course of life and can obtain different degrees of relevance with respect to the plan-determined interest driving individual action. It is also an ingredient of the recipes for mastering situations that are part of the stock of knowledge a person receives from her culture. Hence, technology can be either an imposed or an open element of subjective situations. Its relevance can be a matter of free volition, or externally imposed. It can be drawn into routine or problematic situations with their specific dynamic.

Schutz himself did not discuss these various dimensions of technology's involvement in the everyday lifeworld in any detail. That is why I will turn to Ihde's (1990) *Technology and the lifeworld* for help where the different ways in which technology becomes drawn into the subjective everyday lifeworld are carefully considered.

Ihde distinguishes four types of human-technology relations. The first type, which he calls 'embodiment relations' (p. 73), refers to the situation where technology is taken into subjective experience as a means of perceiving the world thus transforming the subject's perceptual and bodily sense: 'In Galileo's use of the telescope, he embodies his seeing through the telescope thusly: Galileo – telescope – Moon. Equivalently, the wearer of glasses embodies eyeglasses technology: I – eyeglasses – World' (p. 73). The technology is between the seer and the seen in a position of mediation. But the referent of the seeing – that toward which the sight is directed – is on the other side of the optics. If the technology possesses technical characteristics allowing the user to see through it in the literal and figurative sense, it becomes a part of the perceptual apparatus through which the user ordinarily experiences her surroundings. As a result, an embodiment relation between technology and user is established: My glasses are 'taken into my own perceptual-bodily self-experience thus: (I–glasses) – World' (p. 73). Ihde draws attention to an essential ambiguity existing in this relation: it has a necessary 'magnification/reduction structure' (p. 74). Embodiment relations simultaneously magnify and amplify or reduce and place aside (screen out) what is experienced through them. The moon observed through a telescope is a different entity from the moon crowning the night sky as perceived by the naked eye. The person experienced through the telephone is brought to me across a great distance at the expense of being reduced to a voice.

Ihde terms the second type of human-technology relations 'hermeneutic relations' (p. 80). In these types of relations the technology is a carrier of a representation of some entity lying outside the subject's sensory scope. When focusing her attention on the technical artefact, be it a written text, screen or map, the subject sees not the artefact itself, but rather a reference to something beyond it, for example, a landscape described in words or cartographic symbols. In Ihde's words: 'the chart itself becomes the object of perception while simultaneously referring beyond itself to what is not immediately seen' (Ihde, 1990, p. 82). In this case the transparency of the technology is hermeneutic rather than perceptual. The subject needs knowledge (code) of how to read the instrument, the text or other kinds of technological representation. The formula with which Ihde describes this relation is: 'I – (technology–world)' (p. 86).

The third type of human-technology relations Ihde (1990) identifies are the 'alterity relations' (p. 97) in which technology is experienced as an Other or quasi-Other, i.e., an animated being different from myself. Examples of these types of relations are the idolization of artefacts in religious practice and, more recently, involvements characteristic of human-computer interaction such as playing a game *against* the machine, and perhaps even blaming the machine for failing you. The formalization employed to describe this relation is: 'I-technology-(world)' (p. 107), indicating that the world, in this case, remains in the background and technology emerges as a focal entity with which I momentarily engage.

Finally, Ihde (1990) recognizes a fourth type of human-technology relation which differs from the previous three in that it does not implicate technology directly in a conscious process of engagement on the part of the human. Ihde refers to this type as 'background relations' (p. 108). Technologies falling into these types of relations function within the context of daily practice without being drawn into the foreground of action. Automatic and semi-automatic technological systems such as lighting, heating and cooling systems exemplify this type of relation. We live in their midst without consciously attending to them and often without realizing to what extent our existence is conditioned by them.

I will use this taxonomy of human-technology relations to go back and re-examine the structures of the everyday lifeworld laid out by Schutz and reflect on how technologies are involved in the constant transformation of the concrete lifeworlds of the subjects who use them. Let us start with the world within actual reach of a technologically equipped subject living in the contemporary technology-rich society. What is now accessible to our immediate experience from the point Zero position of our corporeal body includes multiple technological objects with which we stand in a hermeneutic relation, that is, objects representing something beyond themselves. Typical examples would be the books on my shelf, the photographs in my album, the thermometer on the balcony, the computer printout I received from the insurance office and, of course, the image on my television set. Through these technical representations we can perceive things that are distant or past from within the zone of our actual reach. The implications of this ability are equally important in the formation of our stock of knowledge and our action plans.

Nowadays, in our zone of actual reach we also find a growing number of technologies allowing not just the perception of remote natural and social objects and relations, but also the manipulation of such objects and relations. That is, our secondary zones of operation are extended tremendously by new technological means that enter our primary zones of direct action. The embodiment relation (I–technology)–world identified by Ihde (1990) at the perceptual level acquires a practical sense. Things that I do within my primary zone of operation – dialling a number, talking into a microphone, typing on a keyboard and so on – translate into actions having a bearing on the world far beyond my doorstep, affecting distant objects and people. Thus over the telephone, I can pay a bill, get a loan, break off a relationship, and help my child with his homework. My networked computer allows me to download a file from a remote server, request a book from the library and give advice to my friend overseas. More and more, our zone of actual reach comes to resemble a control tower from where we can perceive distant objects and social entities by reading them off technical representations – I–(technology–world), which extends our zones of actual and potential reach. We can also exert action upon distant objects and people through technological levers – (I–technology)–world, which extends our secondary zone of operation and our province of possible operation.

If we recall the amplification/reduction structure of the human-technology relations Ihde (1990) proposed, we will have to qualify what seems to be an unquestionable increase in our powers of action. First, our mediated actions are shaped to a great degree by the technologies involved; and second, the structure of these technologies determines the specifics of the occurring amplification/reduction. I am able to order a library book from my place of residence or work (amplification of scope of action) but I will have to adopt the categories of classification imposed by the library database and forfeit the chance to receive guidance by a human assistant through an interactive exchange (reduction). I am able to give support to my distant friend (amplification) but I can do it only in the form of electronic text. She will not receive comfort from my voice and encouragement from my touch (reduction).

Missing from Ihde's (1990) account is an important issue concerning the structure of amplification/reduction implicit in the technological mediation of perception and action: how, exactly, is the trade-off between amplification and reduction achieved? It is true that I am interested in amplifying my scope of action by paying my bills online, but the reduction I incur – the lack of contact and guidance from a human bank clerk, loss of privacy with respect to my financial activities which can now be stored in a database – is far from being an objective necessity imposed by technical possibilities alone. It is inscribed in the technological system by a set of design choices. These choices are guided by the objective of reducing the human work force involved in banking services and increasing surveillance. The reduction I suffered in supporting my friend is brought forth by the limited capacity for human emotional contact built into a system whose primary function is the exchange of information.

Technology intervenes powerfully in the temporal arrangements of the everyday lifeworld most notably with regards to what Schutz has called fixed course of temporality – the principle of first things first. Although the search for life-prolonging medical treatments is ongoing, the fact of human finitude vis-à-vis the permanence of world time remains unchanged. So, in principle, does the historical situation in which one is born – time-machines remain a fantasy. The fixed course of temporality, however, is an aspect of the lifeworld effectively addressed by technological invention and perfection. The phenomenon of waiting, in which Schutz finds a typical expression of the incongruence between subjective time on one hand and biological time, world time and social time on the other, is undergoing substantive transformations. I do not need to wait any more for my sugar to dissolve in the glass of water if I want to drink sugar water – an example Schutz used about 40 years ago. I can simply use instantly dissolving sweetener, a technological product eliminating the waiting time. If I want to ski, I do not need to wait for the snow to fall but can get on a plane and go to a part of the world where it is snowing now. I no longer need to comply with the rhythms of social time: my colleague is asleep at 2 a.m. (social time), and I cannot immediately share with him the brilliant idea that dawned on me or ask the question that arose in my mind, but I can send him an e-mail message reflecting my spontaneous impulse and stream of consciousness as they unfold in my subjective time. I can take work from my company home in a computer file and do it on my computer at any moment I choose (subjective time) after the office is closed (social time).

In all these cases, I use technology to bring biological time, world time, and social time into closer conformity with my subjective time. In a sense, this can be interpreted and experienced by the actor as an increase in personal freedom, spontaneity and control, or in other words as empowerment and disalienation.[9] These new technologically created possibilities seem to address the pressing need for democratization of everyday life. Alberto Melucci (1989) characterizes this need – in matters of time – thus:

> the need to escape from external constraints and to achieve a level of self-determination of both complete life cycle and daily life. The need to establish a new rapport between inner time and social time creates a demand for reversible time, for autonomously chosen and regulated units of duration unburdened from the rhythms of clocks and calendars. (p. 178)

Let's take the example of information technologies introduced with the promise of delivering education and training at any time, independently of the stage of life. You may no longer be young and mobile (traditional social expectations related to enrolment in a university or training course); you may be doing something else in the course of your day; but you still can take distant education programmes supported by various information technologies.

The feeling of freedom and empowerment that stems from these enlargements of one's action zone in terms of space and time drowns technological criticism and renders us oblivious to the reductions entailed. We lose the immediate sensory experience of objects, deprive ourselves of face-to-face contact with people, and get caught up in sequences of operations and waiting time periods imposed by the technical equipment. Ironically, overwhelmed by the new possibilities inscribed in this equipment as preferred readings,[10] we readily agree to be 'configured' (Woolgar, 1991) and often fail to exercise our imagination in envisioning possibilities of our own. This is a subtle form of reduction that, as I will argue later, can be brought to light through the critique of what is real, versus what is possible, proposed by Lefebvre (1991).

Importantly, we should heed a remark Schutz himself felt it necessary to make in his discussion of the variations of technical possibility given to members of every particular society: A distinction should be made between the degree of extension of operation (and of reach) that is possible due to the condition of technological knowledge in society, and the one that is typically accessible and employable by persons in daily life.

Social structures demonstrate typical distribution of the prospects of access to what Schutz called 'extensional factors' (Schutz and Luckmann, 1973, p. 44). This state of affairs must be considered 'in the empirical analysis of the life-world of the Eskimo, of the modern American, etc. even if it need not be considered in the formal analysis of the structure of the life-world in general' (p. 44). In critical terms, this is the problem of unequal access to technology. In the Schutzian analytical system, unequal access is related to differences in the everyday lifeworld experienced by people occupying different positions in society. Thus, the horizons of potential reach and the limits of zones of operation and provinces of the practicable vary according to social position. However, it will be noticed immediately that the social categories of people excluded from the benefits (amplifications) that come with technology do not become subjected to the reductions involved.

Technological mediation, and particularly information and communication technologies, similarly rearranges the structures of anonymity stretching from the most intimate we-relations to the most distant they-relations. Communication media contribute to the restorability of old, and attainability of new, we-relations by allowing me to access the conscious life of an Other even if only in a curtailed fashion. Similarly, they-relations, or relations with types of people I have never met, can be filled with additional content with the help of communication media. For instance, I experience the previously anonymous type of the striking Ontario teachers or Bosnian war victims, for instance, in more concrete human detail by reading a newspaper article or watching a television programme about them, which remotely mimics a we-relation. The anonymous type of the 'computer expert', for example, can become more real for me if I post a question in a computer-oriented newsgroup and receive an answer from the programmer Joe Doe written in his own words, in his own subjective time. In this imaginable quasi we-relation, Joe Doe would also have experienced the anonymous type of the computer dummy through my individual characteristics – my language, my problems and my frustration.

Applying Ihde's (1990) typology of human–technology–world relations to the social world, we can explore the amplifications and reductions involved in mediated communication. We will notice an interesting merger between the embodiment relation and the hermeneutic relation in acts of mediated interactive communication. When I relay to an Other my state of mind using a technology, I enter an embodiment relation with the technology: (I–technology)–social world. This can take the form of writing, speaking into a telephone, shooting a video and so on. The response of the

Other comes to me through a hermeneutic relation: I–(technology–social world). The end result is that from my here and now, that is, from within my zone of actual reach, I can initiate social contact and become the addressee of response, or of somebody else's initiation. The resulting amplification of sociability represents a qualitative leap. The restorability of we-relations, attainability of new relations, access to richer content regarding social types, and the possibility for transforming functionary types into individual types grow exponentially. I can penetrate further into the social world and in a wider variety of ways. That is, my means of social production, understood in the wide sense suggested by Lefebvre (1991), grows in diversity and power. I can express myself in new forms and for new purposes.

Along with it, however, I have to suffer multiple reductions – of intensity and spontaneity, of reciprocity and tangibility. Technology becomes an extension of my social self and a representation of the social world to me. Hence, both my means of self-expression and the codes in which the social is represented to me have to be adapted to the structure of the mediating technology (and the social institutions and practices growing upon it). Thus, I have to express my love for my distant mother through the sole medium of my voice amplified by the telephone/telecommunication system, over a period of time constricted by the high cost of the long distance call. The human detail that adheres to the type of the striking teachers through the newspaper report is, I realize, sifted through the institutional discourse and organization of news production and dissemination. These reductions can and do become sources of technologically produced alienation: oppressive and manipulative practices can grow out of them, overshadowing the possibility for empowerment. Along with old-style media manipulation, new alienations arise from new media. One example is the use of personal information produced by technologically mediated interactions and transactions for purposes other than the ones intended by the person from whom it originated and to whom it refers. In this case, analogously to what happens in the commodity relation, the product of human activity, captured as a bundle of data, stored in databases and manipulated for unknown purposes, returns to confront its creator as an external alien force. Very clearly, such reductions are related to the dominant technical code of 'informational capitalism' (Castells, 1996) dictating that human beings should be made profitable (see Lefebvre, 1991, p. 230).

Up to this point, technology has been examined in its capacity to contribute to the formation of subjective everyday lifeworlds in principle. The question of whether technology remained a constant, an ontological given, throughout its interaction with subjective lifeworlds was not raised. Will users accept the structure of amplifications and reductions inscribed in a given technology as is, or will they attempt to re-configure it? To find answers to these questions, we have to recall that technology is always encountered by acting subjects as an element of their specific social-biographical situation and immediate situation at hand. The degree to which it acquires relevance to subjects is determined by each subject's pragmatic interest with a view to mastering her situation. It can be expected that, depending on the definitions of the situations they attempt to master, users will recognize and enact different amplification possibilities present in a particular technology. This means they will perceive different affordances (Gibson, 1979 and Chapter 1) in that technology. Some of these affordances will be accentuated in the 'preferred reading' suggested by designers. Others will be spontaneously discovered by users in light of their distinct situations, pragmatic interests and intrinsic relevances. As for reductions, the awakening of critical consciousness with regard to the dominant definitions of technologies would lead users to try to renegotiate the configuration of amplifications and reductions (though some reductions will always have to be endured) etched in a particular technology.

Thus, drawn into diverse social-biographical situations, technology acquires new practical definitions in accordance with the various locally meaningful projects comprising the infinitely rich lifeworlds of subjects. It becomes implicated in new 'behavioural genres' (Voloshinov, 1929/1986) relative to the status quo at the moment preceding the innovation. The subjective relevance the technology has obtained for the individual at the centre of a particular social-biographical situation can potentially expand the spectrum of meaningful applications of that technology and hence, new use genres. New use genres are related to new affordances – newly recognized qualities of the technical environment. When or whether these new affordances will become part of the culturally acknowledged definition of the technology will depend on the degree of typicality of the social-biographical situations in which they have arisen and on the social prominence and power associated with them.

Technology as system

Analyzing everyday life in modern capitalist society, which he dubbed 'the bureaucratic society of controlled consumption', Lefebvre (1971, p. 68) recognized the 'programming' function of technology in everyday life. For him, the automobile, a paradigmatic technology in that society, 'directs behaviour' in various spheres from economics to speech. It imposes laws and fosters hierarchies in everyday life, produces social forms and institutions that use it and that it uses (see pp. 101–103). To the extent that human agents unreflectively accept and submit to the laws imposed by objects like the automobile, their relations with objects and with each other via those objects are alienated.

A whole critical tradition of technology studies led by Marcuse (1964) and including labour process theorists such as Braverman (1975) and Noble (1984) and philosophers of technology – Winner (1977), Leiss (1990) and Feenberg (1991, 1999) among others – has demonstrated the disciplinary, action-directing function of technology. These theorists have seen technology as an instrument for organizing human action under the imperative of capitalist class relations. That is, technology is a medium translating the abstract social relations of capitalism into concrete human relations and actions. Coming from a different perspective, the sociologist of technology, Latour has found 'the missing masses' (1992, p. 225), the previously lacking account of how social practice gets coordinated, in the compulsions produced by technology.

Joining this line of argument in technology studies with Habermas's (1984) model of System and Lifeworld, Feenberg has proposed that tech- nology be recognized as a 'coordination medium'[11] (1999, p. 169) in the sense in which Habermas (1984) describes money and power. Technical control exerted through and by devices, Feenberg (1999) asserts, introduces instrumental rationality characteristic for System into the Lifeworld of acting subjects. Technical rationality operationalized as productivity and effectiveness becomes reified and organizes local action, eliminating the necessity for linguistic negotiation (which is constitutive of the Habermasian lifeworld). Feenberg goes on to insist that even if there are good reasons for thinking about it as a medium of systematic coordina- tion of social action, technology still has to be critically questioned on its own grounds – something that is missing from the Habermasian treat- ment of coordination media. Technology does not embody universal rational principles. Its socially shaped design determines, in the final account, what kind of social relations technology, as a coordination medium, will help to establish and sustain.

I argue that technological design is coterminous with the structure of the amplifications and reductions that a particular technology introduces into the lifeworld of the subjects using it. The decisions made in the process of design about what should be foregrounded (amplified) and what can be left out (reduced) are a matter of systems of relevances.

Some of these relevances are socially established in the relative-natural attitude manifested in the technological sphere by the dominant technical code. In the encounter between a technology and users' lifeworlds, the amplifications and reductions inbuilt in the technology are actively renegotiated with respect to the situational definitions, plan-determined interests and systems of relevances organizing users' actions. The product of this negotiation are innovative use genres, giving technology a different spin and, consequently, some unexpected effects.

This analysis of the interaction between technology and the everyday lifeworlds of thinking and acting subjects suggests that, in order to grasp the generative process of technology in its entirety, the Habermasian uncoupling of System and Lifeworld has to be dialectically negated. System and Lifeworld, abstract social relations and local action have to be re-coupled. Smith's (1987) work points to an elegant way to implement this re-coupling:

> The very ordinary presence of the objects of our daily lives, chairs, tables, are ... socially organized in our everyday practices and organize their concerting. The terms for socially constituted objects are anchored in and anchor a social organization of actual practices in and through which table becomes table ... (p. 124)

If this is so, if objects, technology included, are constantly reconstituted by the practices they organize, then different or changing situations of human action represent a source of object/artefact/technology mutation and change. Subjects in different social-biographical and action situations reconstitute the structures of amplification/reduction properties of a technology. What ensues is a different locally experienced and actualized technology and a different brand of use genres anchored in it. With time, this variability in accentuation and application induces changes in the technology as an object. Once this is recognized, the analogy with the evolution of language intrudes with a new power. What escaped the Habermasian (1984) interpretation of the interaction between System and Lifeworld was the phenomenon recognized by de Certeau (1984), Voloshinov (1929/1986) and Bakhtin (1984). If it is true that System continuously colonizes the Lifeworld, the opposite is also taking place – the Lifeworld encroaches on System, undermines and changes it.

History of technology has shown that new technical inventions have sometimes travelled a long way before they could meet the system of relevances that would resonate with the potentialities of their design. Initial designs have been transformed under the pressure of originally excluded or ignored typical interests and action plans. As critical examiners of technological innovation have demonstrated, however, the structures of power in a particular historical social formation have given preference to designs suiting the dominant systems of relevance.

How often has technological design responded to the relevances of powerless social groups? Not very often, for sure. But even though such avenues in the evolution of technology may not have been followed, they have been there, and are still – in the case of the Internet – able to offer a basis for a critique of what is real against what is, or has been, possible.

The task of identifying alternative possibilities in the evolution of the Internet necessitates focusing observation on spaces and instances in everyday life where creative appropriation of technology by users is most likely to happen. Among the various backstages of human behaviour (see Goffman, 1959), that is, settings or situations where the social actor can forgo formal rules and ready-made, socially sanctioned recipes for action, the home emerges as a particularly good candidate for closer investigation. Home is that place in everyday life which the individual experiences as her own. It is a 'protected place at one's disposal where the pressure of the social body on the individual does not prevail, where the plurality of stimuli is filtered, or, in any case, ought to be' (de Certeau et al., 1998, p. 146). Hence, taking technology home means endowing it with personal significance. Home, I will argue in the next section, can be viewed as the base of the powerless, where rationalizations of technology alternative to those imposed by the dominant technical code emerge.

The Home as a Site of Everyday Life

Everyday space, as Heller (1984) notes, is anthropocentric. It is organized from the spatial perspective of the subject at its centre. The categories of left and right, near and far, up and down, represent the relative dimensions of everyday space. Among these relative categories organizing everyday space for us is the concept of home. Everyday life is not synonymous with life at home. Like 'everyday life', 'home' is a complex construct that has taken different meanings as a component of various social theories. My task in the following pages will not be to present an exhaustive account of these theories and their take on 'home'.[12] I turn to the notion of home with the objective of capturing its specifics as a site of everyday life. Heller defines the relation between home and everyday life thus:

> Integral to the average everyday life is awareness of a fixed point in space, a firm position from which we 'proceed' ... and to which we return in due course. This firm position is what we call 'home' ... . 'Going home' should mean

returning to that firm position which we know, to which we are accustomed, where we feel safe, and where our emotional relationships are at their most intense. (1984, p. 239)

In Schutzian terms, home can be described as a familiar zone of operation, a stage where recurrent unproblematic situations occur. The fellow-men and women with whom I share the home are in an intimate we relation with me, a relation constantly reproduced, easily restorable and attainable. With these people I share common intrinsic relevances and we recurrently confirm for each other the validity of our grasp of the surrounding world (see Schutz's, 1964, 'The Homecomer').

Czikszentmihaly and Rochberg-Halton (1981) suggest a definition of home that emphasizes its role as a site of identity-formation. For them, the home is a 'space for action and interaction in which one can develop, maintain and change one's identity ... . The home is a shelter for those persons and objects that define the self; thus it becomes, for most people, an indispensable symbolic environment' (p. 144).

Related to the critical understanding of everyday life as the terrain of the reproduction of the person as a whole (Heller, 1984; Lefebvre, 1991), is an interpretation of home as an economic unit and resource system. In this sense, Silverstone (1994) speaks of the 'domestic'. The domestic, he claims, is 'the site and source of our activities as consumers and also as citizens ... and through consumption, paradoxically but plausibly, it is becoming increasingly significant in the modern public life' (pp. 50–51).

Thus, the domestic is the sphere of immediate we-relations and communicative interaction, making up what is often called 'private life', as opposed to the public realm of Gesellschaft – the market and bureaucratically administered formal organizations akin to the notion of System. In this capacity, the domestic emerges as a small realm of freedom, spontaneity and authenticity, a 'kind of balancing mechanism providing meanings and meaningful activities to compensate for the discontents brought about by the large structures of modern society' (Berger et al., 1974, quoted in Weintraub, 1997, p. 21).

Along an alternative axis of distinction between public and private, the private realm, and by implication the domestic, can be characterized as the atomized capsule of self-centred existence and particularistic interest, physically isolated and alienated from the political community. From this perspective the idea of the private is tied to the development of the home as an autonomous consumer unit and to the retreat from the public realm of community (see Tomlinson, 1990).

The atomic unit of the 'home-centered society' bewailed by critics such as Kumar (1995, p. 155) and the emotionally intense domain of non-instrumental relationships and refuge from the constraints and pressures of formal institutions (see Morley, 1994, p. 105; Weintraub, 1997, p. 20) are thus two alternative images and, actually, two of the multiple sides of the home. It can be noted that these distinctions follow principally the same fault lines as the System-Lifeworld and alienation-disalienation dichotomies that emerged in theories of everyday life in general. Which one of these sides would be reinforced by the arrival of a new technology, in our case the Internet connection, into the home? Will the lifeworld of the home be invaded by the systems of market and bureaucracy through the conduit opened by the new communication technology? Or, will the narrow capsule of self-centred alienated existence in the home be cracked open to allow for higher concerns and involvement in public life? These are open questions for empirical investigation and topical issues for political debate to which academic research should be adequately oriented.

In her study of computerization of industrial organizations Zuboff (1988) argued that information technology is characterized by a 'fundamental duality'[13] (p. 9). It has the capacity to 'automate' and to 'informate' (p. 10). To automate means to replace the human body and the human mind with a machine and thus disempower the worker. To informate, in contrast, is the capacity of computers to 'introduce an additional dimension of reflexivity', to produce 'a voice that symbolically renders events, objects and processes so that they become visible, knowable and shareable in a new way' (p. 9). With the penetration of the smart machine and the smart network into the home, a similar dilemma emerges. Computer-network technology has the potential to *isolate* the home – to reinforce bad privateness as discussed above. But it can also *associate*, or connect, the home with the public worlds of citizenship and community in new ways by giving these worlds a new symbolic visibility and accessibility. My empirical study has the task of uncovering the manifestations of this dual potential in their 'historical concreteness' (Lefebvre, 1991), in the daily lives of particular people. I will attempt to find out how home Internet users perceive and perform the choices available to them in assigning the smart network a place and a role in their homes.

In this connection, I find it necessary to examine also the potential and the actual role of the home as a place of resistance and creative appropriation. Relative to the human actor, home represents an interior as opposed to an exterior, or environment. The life stories collected and analyzed by Bruner (1987) offer a vivid illustration of this perception of the home. Bruner notices a common figure in the 'psychic geography' constructed by his narrators: for each of them home is 'a place that is inside, private, forgiving, intimate, predictably safe. The "real world" is outside, demanding, anonymous, open, unpredictable, and consequently dangerous' (in Mackay, 1997, p. 108). The movement from home into the outside world is marked by a struggle to create for oneself 'homelike' special places – allowing, permitting and teaching. Bruner says of one of his storytellers: 'It is as if Carl manages the "real world" by colonizing it with "special places" that provide some of the privileges of home'[14] (p. 109).

Discussing the interplay between the powerful and the powerless, de Certeau (1984) acknowledges the capacity to create 'an "interior", a place that can be delimited as its own and serve as a base from which relations with an exteriority ... can be managed' only to subjects with will and power – 'a business, an army, a city; a scientific institution' (see pp. 35–36). From a phenomenological perspective, however, the thinking and acting subject, regardless of her actual social position of power, always constructs a base of her own, no matter how physically ephemeral it could be. I contend that this base is identical with what in the natural attitude we call 'home'. Home is the locus into which the powerless can withdraw and elaborate a strategy vis-à-vis her environment.

bell hooks (1990) forcefully confirms this role of the home in her analysis of the symbolic production and self-reproduction of segregated black people, particularly women. Houses, she writes, were women's special domain 'as places where all that truly mattered in life took place – the warmth, the comfort of shelter, the feeding of our bodies, the nurturing of our souls. There we learned dignity, integrity of being, there we learned to have faith' (p. 42). These homes were sustained by black women who made their living outside the home serving white people – an oppressive Other, a system of domination. However, after a hard day of work in the terrain of the Other (to evoke de Certeau's vocabulary), these women came back home 'to make life happen there'. hooks goes on:

> Historically, African-American people believed that the construction of a homeplace, however fragile and tenuous (the slave hut, the wooden shack), had a radical political dimension. Despite the brutal reality of racial apartheid, of domination, one's homeplace was the one site where one could freely confront the issue of humanization, where one could resist. Black women resisted by making homes where all black people could strive to be subjects, not objects, where we could be affirmed to our minds and hearts despite poverty, hardship and deprivation, where we could restore to ourselves the dignity denied us on the outside in the public world. (1990, p. 42)

Throughout their history, therefore, African-Americans have recognized the subversive value of homeplace and the importance of having access to such a place. Domestic space has been a crucial site for organizing, and for forming political solidarity in the context of the black liberation struggle. The structure of homeplace as a site of resistance has been defined by the black people's effort to 'uplift themselves' as a people and resist racist oppression and domination (see hooks, 1990, p. 47).

Abstracted from this concrete historical experience is a general understanding of resistance as 'opposition to being invaded, occupied, assaulted and destroyed by the system' (hooks, 1990, p. 42). In exactly the same way, home was experienced as a site of resistance amid the totalitarian systems of East European societies where public spaces were inescapably dominated by state ideology and command. Home was the place that nurtured alternative moral values and critical thinking in the face of an outside world constructed as an all-embracing brainwashing and disciplining apparatus.[15]

These extreme social contexts illuminate a side of the home which, I believe, is important to appreciate also with regard to less brutal forms of system domination such as market rationality and cultural hegemony. In the final account, home is 'that place which enables and promotes varied and ever changing perspectives, a place where one discovers new ways of seeing reality, frontiers of difference' (hooks, 1990, p. 148).

As one of the sites of everyday life, home is the place where objects from the exterior – such as products of a market system, messages of political and commercial propagandists, technologies originating from the domains of industry and science – are taken in and used. Within this space, ordinary men and women elaborate their distinct ways of using the macro-order of society reflected in its artefacts. Indeed, one can agree with de Certeau (1984) that these creative ways of operating remain dispersed and fleeting, from a macro-perspective, and do not crystallize into a visible product of their own: 'The television viewer cannot write anything on the screen of his set. He has been dislodged from the product; he plays no role in its apparition' (p. 31). But then again, the subjectivity of the user as an autonomous human being resisting assimilation is perhaps the ultimate product of these ways of operating. She may not be producing anything exchangeable or capitalizable in the economic sense of the term and under the rules of the market system, but she is still producing in Lefebvre's (1971) extended sense – a space, an identity, a genre, a culture.

Summary

The examination of home-spun genres of using a new technology (the Internet), the possibility and the reality of their proliferation and socialization, and finally the question concerning the consequences they breed for technological design and institutionalization, represent the focus of the empirical study I will report in the following chapters. I will attempt to make sense of the patterns of Internet use emerging from the empirical material in light of the concepts and normative dichotomies suggested by the theoretical studies of everyday life reviewed in this chapter:

- What kinds of transformations do the everyday lifeworlds of Internet users' undergo?
- What are the 'isolating' and what the 'associating' properties of the medium? Does it contribute to increased alienation and 'bad' privatization of domestic life or does it create new opportunities for socialization and participation in the life of various communities?
- Does Internet use result in subordination of the home to economic, political and cultural domination, or does it present new opportunities for its revitalization and empowerment?
- Do users passively accept technological form and content or do they demonstrate resistance and creativity?
- Are we-relations in the home undermined by the new medium or is the medium involved in new forms of reinforcing these relations?
- Are gender inequalities exacerbated in the domestic practices of Internet use or are gender gaps in technological and communicative competence closing?

Needless to say, looking for answers to these questions, I will also be testing the utility of the very dichotomous thinking out of which they emerge.

Notes

[1]Recall that Latour (1987, p. 137) describes the 'simple customer' as being the user who receives a technological artefact packaged as a 'black box' and is often actively discouraged from examining its contents.

[2]This book represents an anthology of Schutz's thought, prepared and published after his death by Thomas Luckmann.

[3]I use the spelling 'lifeworld' as one word throughout this book. Note that the spelling of the term used in Schutz and Luckmann (1973) is 'life-world.' I have preserved this spelling in direct quotations from the book.

[4]The problem of gender bias in language will recur throughout this chapter as many of the sources I have used predate the awareness that is now the norm in scholarly writing and publishing. I will use the original language of the works from which I draw.

[5]The notion of 'mastering' as I understand and use it in this chapter refers to reflexivity, intentionality and the desire to control one's own life as intrinsic human capabilities. It does not necessarily imply relations of power between human beings. Neither is it intended to signify rational individualistic control over circumstances.

It is clear in Schutz's account that the 'mastering' of a situation can never be fully accomplished and that it involves the navigation of conditions and means not of the subject's own making.

[6] Post-World-War-II French society.

[7] This idea is in fact very similar to Feenberg's (1991) argument in his *Critical theory of technology* (see Chapter 1).

[8] Note that Schutz's definition of working is specific. It includes human actions which gear into the world by bodily movements: 'The wide-awake self integrates in its working and by its working its present, past and future into a specific dimension of time; it realizes itself as a totality in its working acts; it communicates with others through working acts; it organizes the different spatial perspectives of the world of daily life through working acts' (Schutz, 1970, p. 126).

[9] However, I have to wait until the web page I have requested from a remote server downloads onto my computer. Thus it should be noted that while resolving the incongruence between subjective and world, biological or social time, technology creates others.

[10] Recall the section on technology-as-text in Chapter 1.

[11] It seems to me that one extreme example of such a recognition can be found in Manuel Castells's (1996, 1997, 1998) trilogy *The information age*. In this grand narrative of the 'network society' Castells performs a curious fusion between System and Medium in the Habermasian sense. Computer networks become both a medium of social coordination and the System itself as their logic pervasively determines the activities and relations of social actors.

[12] For an excellent survey of this kind see Morley (2000).

[13] This idea is similar to Feenberg's 'ambivalence' of technology (see Feenberg, 1991 and Chapter 1).

[14] This observation points to the possibility suggested earlier in this chapter for a process of two-way colonization between System and Lifeworld.

[15] Nikolchina (2002) discusses the ambiguity of private space under communist regimes in light of the East-West debates about feminism. Part of the argument made by East European feminists, she observes, was that, 'the family was that private area where people could find refuge from the control of the state and as such it was the locus of solidarity, rather than confrontation, of the sexes in their common resistance to the alienating political structure. As one commentator characteristically put it: "political discussions were conducted around the kitchen table, the home represented the only place for open discussion like this; it was here rather than in any public sphere that the possibility for transcendence occurred"' (Sharp, 1996, p. 102, quoted in Nikolchina, p. 107).

THREE Researching the Internet at Home

Grown-ups love figures. When you tell them that you have made a new friend, they never ask you any questions about essential matters. They never say to you, 'What does his voice sound like? What games does he love best? Does he collect butterflies?' Instead, they demand: 'How old is he? How many brothers has he? How much does he weigh? How much money does his father make?' Only from these figures do they think they have learnt anything about him ... . But certainly, for us who understand life, figures are a matter of indifference. I should have liked to begin this story in the fashion of the fairy tales. I should have liked to say: 'Once upon a time there was a little prince who lived on a planet that was scarcely bigger than himself, and who had a need of a sheep ...' (Antoine de Saint-Exupéry, 1943, *The little prince*, p. 20)

The Blueprint in Hand

The charting of my research blueprint began with the choice of the main character of the Internet story I wanted to tell. From the outset, I had defined the type of Internet user that I wanted to investigate as the 'simple customer' (Latour, 1987, p. 137), technology's Other, the man and woman lacking expertise in the ways of the Internet. I further specified my definition of this user as someone who taps into his or her own resources to acquire a computer and pays for the Internet connection to a commercial (or non-profit) provider. This specification of the user I wanted to study aimed at excluding the early adopters and the people for whom the use of the Internet was related mainly to earning income and/or profit.

The stage on which I wanted to meet this character was his or her home. I decided to operationalize the relative phenomenological notion of home as an inside, a territory which the practitioner of everyday life experiences as familiar, safe and manageable, through the actual homeplaces of my respondents. Granted, not everybody's homeplace is equivalent to this relative notion of home. There are people without a home anywhere; people with homeplaces experienced as the direct opposite of the notion I am employing here, and of course people who feel at home somewhere else, not at the place where they sleep, rest and reproduce. Appreciating this complexity, I made a conscious decision to bracket it out in the name of the primary focus of my interest. For the purposes of my research, which aimed at tracing the activity of the user, I was determined to look at cases where home (a safe and familiar terrain, a base where the person feels in control) and homeplace (the place of residence) coincided. The very arrangement of my meeting with respondents presupposed such a correspondence. I was asking Internet users to accept me, a complete stranger, into their home, to show me its interior, to tell me their Internet stories. To be able to accept the role of the host in a situation like this, one needs self-confidence, a feeling of safety and a substantial degree of control over one's domestic time and environment. I am aware that people who did not feel that way in their homes were practically excluded from the study.[1]

The essential third choice, that of method, was the easiest to make. I felt that my commitment to the user's standpoint and my quest for subjective meanings and relevances necessitated the employment of a qualitative methodology. I found a fitting methodological paradigm in the strand of media studies often referred to as 'audience ethnography' (Morley, 1992) or 'reception ethnography' (Moores, 1993). This research tradition originated from British Cultural Studies and represents a strategy for capturing the contextualized activity of audiences as they read, or decode, media texts. Seiter (1999) identifies several distinctive features of this so-called 'ethnographic' research orientation in comparison to the long-established functional tradition reigning in the field of mass communication research. According to her, the researchers who pioneered the ethnographic audience investigation were interested not so much in observable behaviour, but in *structures of meaning* produced by the audience. They found it important to examine the *contexts* of media reception. They sought to establish *rapport* with their respondents and treated language as *discourse* rather than as a means for transmitting unequivocal information as in the case of eliciting clear-cut answers to standardized questionnaires.

The characterization of audience ethnography articulated by Moores (1993, 1996) and Morley (1992) is similar. These authors also stress the importance of natural settings, context, holism and subjects' own viewpoints as the definitive way in which ethnographic audience research projects are framed. Projects of this kind, Moores (1993) explains, took to heart Hobson's (1982) call on media theorists to acknowledge the medium's place as 'a part of the everyday life of viewers' (quoted in Moores, 1993, p. 42) and not to isolate the text from the conditions of its reception.

In short, this tradition adopted the principle of 'simultaneous commitment to "real" situations and grasping the understanding of informants' that, according to Hakken (1999, p. 46), separates anthropological ethnography from Modernist science. However, it did not always live up to the requirements of classical ethnographic methodology. Some of the projects cited as representative of this tradition have been based on brief periods of contact between researcher and subject in the form of an in-depth, open-ended, semi-structured interview (see Gillespie 1995; Seiter, 1999). The lack of long-term participant observation, considered a hallmark of anthropological ethnography, has raised questions about whether this kind of research genuinely deserves to be called ethnography at all. For example, Gillespie (1995), who has provided an exemplary case of long-term participatory ethnographic study of media use by Punjabi youth in Southall, England, insists on reserving the term 'ethnography' for research that involves long-term immersion. For Gillespie 'The "native" view envisioned by classical ethnographers is hardly to be grasped through a series of one-off "in-depth" interviews or brief periods of observation' (p. 55).[2] Nightingale (1989) has gauged the audience ethnography trend against the widely accepted definition of ethnography given by respected anthropologists such as Marcus and Fischer (1986). According to this definition, ethnography is:

A research process in which the anthropologist closely observes, records and engages in the daily life of another culture – an experience labelled as the fieldwork method – and then writes accounts of this culture, emphasizing descriptive detail. These accounts are the primary form in which fieldwork procedures, the other culture and the ethnographer's personal and theoretical reactions are accessible to professionals and other readerships. (p. 18)

Nightingale (1989) finds few of these canonical practices making up the 'ethnographic process' (p. 55) in audience research projects that have been touted as ethnographies: 'Not only do they not set out to provide an account of an "other" culture, but in many of them the only contact with the "other culture" is an interview or the reading of a letter' (p. 54). Commitment to recording and providing descriptive detail is also conspicuously absent from them, Nightingale complains.

Identifying my methodological stance with that of audience ethnography and employing short-term interview and observation techniques (which will become clear later in this chapter), I realize that the genuineness of my 'ethnography' is questionable from this classical anthropological perspective. Yet, I believe ethnography remains the closest conceptual framework against which my methodology can be defined and understood. What is carried over from ethnography into the kind of research design that I have constructed is not so much a canonical set of techniques but rather a specific *engagement* between researcher and respondents. I have been committed to, first, studying a naturally occurring practice,[3] second, interacting with my informants in their natural settings,[4] third, grasping their understanding, and finally, maintaining an open *dialogue* with them. Like Schrøder (1999), I see this latter condition as belonging to the core of media ethnography. Dialogue, Schrøder states, represents an interactive human encounter in which contextualized meanings are exchanged through language. A specific relationship between researcher and research participants obtains in the process of dialogue.

It should be noted also that the situation created through my research design – a home visit – is much more 'real' (and therefore ethnographically valid) than a purportedly 'participant' observation conducted by a researcher on a household's everyday life would have been. Given the private character of domestic life in Western culture, as Moores (1996) has rightly observed, to expect us to 'live alongside our informants "immersed" in the routines of a family or household group, is in most cases unrealistic' (p. 31). Participant observation in domestic settings would be disruptive and distorting to the fabric of family everyday life. This life is closed to outsiders by definition. Or more precisely, outsiders are given one acceptable role in private daily life at home – that of, in the best case, a welcome visitor. This is precisely the role that I chose to play with respect to my respondents.

Do the intrinsic properties of domestic contexts ordain that the home has to remain forever sealed off from ethnographic research? I think this is a rhetorical question, the answer to which depends to a large extent on ethnographers' readiness and potential to expand their research practice beyond canonical principles for the sake of penetrating the numerous non-typical terrains on which modern culture takes shape. I find encouraging signs of a new, more tolerant and exciting conceptualization of ethnography in Marcus's (1995) idea of mobile, multi-site ethnography. This kind of ethnographic practice arises, according to Marcus,[5] 'in response to empirical changes in the world and therefore to transformed locations of cultural production. ... Empirically following the thread of cultural process itself impels the move toward multi-sited ethnography' (p. 97). This ethnography also represents a response to the need to track complex objects of study throughout society.[6]

Following the cultural process of a new medium's social shaping, I found that the home represents an important site of cultural production. The penetration and examination of the multiple domestic sites populated by Internet users, requires ethnographic mobility, re-thinking of old and invention of new ethnographic techniques. I cannot claim that the validity and reliability of such a new set of ethnographic techniques would be beyond questioning. But I am convinced that in order to upgrade these techniques to the status of a trusted method, the research community has to accumulate experience with them in practical research situations. Thus, I see my own project as one such methodological experimentation.

Respondent Recruitment

Already at the stage of recruitment, I had to start imagining and modelling my relationship with respondents. I invested conscious efforts in elaborating an encounter strategy that would ensure reciprocity and some degree of reduction of the characteristic power differential between an academic researcher and a human subject. Although I did not expect my economic and social status to be higher than that of my respondents,[7] I was still going to play the role of the learned person in the relationship. I had the background of my academic education and the potential, no matter how vague, for an academic career in the future. These elements of my social-biographical situation could, presumably, represent a source of inequality. Ultimately, the very game of scholarly research that my respondents and myself were going to play together gave me the power of interpreting their stories in a written document and for a larger audience, while the echo of their judgment of me and their interpretations of my performance was to remain limited to their own personal worlds.[8] It was not in my power to change the macro-rules of this game, but I wanted to do my best to make its micro-procedures as fair and equitable as possible. Thus I took steps to explain myself in a way similar to the one I expected my respondents to explain themselves. For that purpose, I created a web site where I posted the call for participation in my project. In this call I briefly explained my research interest and emphasized that I wished to learn from domestic users how they were using the Internet and what it did for them – a matter in which they themselves were the most knowledgeable experts. I was not going after any 'objective' technical or theoretical knowledge that they might have of the medium. I was asking for simple sharing of their subjective everyday experiences involving the Internet at the pragmatic and the semantic level: What do you do with it and what does it mean to you?

I also found it important to emphasize that by responding to my call people would be teaching me and helping me to learn what I wanted to learn, as well as finish my degree. Upon reflection, I think that this element of my definition of the situation in which my respondents and myself were to be involved offset to a significant degree the power advantage I, in my formal role of a researcher, was supposed to have in the interview process. They were extending their generosity to me, doing me a favour that I was appreciating with gratitude and humility.

I included in the site a page describing myself as a professional, through my academic curriculum vitae, and as a human being. To accomplish the latter, I wrote a short text representing a definition of my own social-biographical situation. I described myself as an East European immigrant to Canada, daughter, mother, and graduate student still battling for ground in my new environment. Although I have not asked the people who responded to my call to share their impressions of my self-description, it is my belief that at least some of them decided to participate because they could relate to my situation – be it as a working mother, a newcomer to the country, someone with a precarious social status or someone in need of assistance. I also made it clear that this project was of a purely academic nature. By implementing it, I was seeking to satisfy my own scholarly interest and not the commercial interest of any Internet business, which could have easily been the case given the seeming similarity between what I was studying and market and audience research. Exposing my actual social position and sincere interest in being informed by the participants in my project, I think I managed to go a long way toward reducing the possible anxiety my respondents could have had if the situation had been perceived differently. By talking to me, they were communicating with a person pursuing meaningful goals rather than an institution seeking to objectify them for a purpose they could not understand.

After I put up my project pages on the university web server, I went on to attract potential participants' attention to my call. My obvious target was Internet users in the Vancouver area as they were within my reach in terms of distance and expense. I posted short announcements with a reference to the project web site in local Internet newsgroups. I came in contact with the board of directors of the Vancouver Community Net (VCN) serving, among its other functions, as a low-priced Internet service provider, and reached an agreement with them that they would put a short announcement of my study on their homepage. I also asked friends and colleagues to search through their social networks and try to recruit participants to my study. I published ads in two local community newspapers.

The return from these attention-attracting tactics was uneven. I received a few responses from people using local newsgroups, but most of them were professionally involved with computers and/or the Internet and thus did not qualify as 'simple' customers. In the end, only one respondent was recruited through this channel. The Vancouver Community Net announcement was much more productive and a total of nine respondents were recruited from among the VCN clients. These people were typically low-tech users in the sense that the Internet features they had access to through the VCN were quite limited and exclusively text based. Most of them had known almost nothing about computers and networking at the beginning of their VCN experience. Typical of these users was also their comparatively low income, a circumstance that had lead them to the VCN services despite some deprivation with regard to quality and convenience they had to incur. Through the mediation of friends and colleagues, I was able to recruit twelve respondents of different levels of computer and network proficiency and equipment. The ads published in the newspapers returned nothing.

Net-Time Stories and the Art of Listening

I prefer to think about what I did as encounters with fellow-men and women in overlapping sectors of our everyday lives. With a view to the scholarly goals of those visits and dialogues, however, I will have to step into the discourse of social science and call them procedures for data collection. These procedures, as I originally planned them, included four complementary and partly overlapping components. Each component was intended to allow for a different view on the same object – the cluster of activities and relations implicating the home Internet connection.

First of all, I wanted to hear the stories of my respondents regarding how and why the Internet connection had arrived in their homes and how its use had gradually taken shape. The model underlying my interview protocol presented the Internet connection as the point of intersection of several heterogeneous networks. The physical network included the household's computer and wiring, plus the other domestic objects to which it had a relationship, the Internet provider and the conditions for access among many other small but crucial technical elements. The information network was constituted by the sources of information available on the Internet to which the users turned. The social network spanned all the people, organizations, real and virtual collectivities and loose formations with which the household was linked via the Internet. The activity network was knitted together by the interrelated actions that the household members performed on and through the Internet (my expectation here was that they would represent components of diverse activity systems such as work, play, learning and socialization). The semantic network included the meanings produced and expressed in relation to the Internet – its perceived role, value and significance. Juxtaposing the structures of these networks at the individual and the family level, I expected to be able to discern patterns of domestic Internet use that would later be interpreted as Internet use genres arising in typical situations.

Second, I wished to see and experience those spaces in the respondents' homes where their computer and Internet use occurred. That was what I called the tour of the computer and Internet-related spaces in the respondents' homes. An important feature of these tours was the fact that the users themselves were my guides explaining how these networked niches in the home were gradually carved, in what relationship they stood to the rest of the domestic space and how they organized activities and relationships in the home.

Third, I asked to be taken on a tour of the 'computer space' constituted by Internet-use practices, that is, the traces of Internet use deliberately saved in the memory of peoples' computers or, as it sometimes turned out to be the case, in their accounts on their provider's server. In the language of networking interface programs, these were bookmarks, favourites, address books and inboxes. This particular procedure allowed me to examine the electronic artefacts created by users as they moved in and consciously manipulated the substance of cyberspace. Note the difference between this approach and the examination of log files, cache files and other traces that users leave unconsciously as they move in and manipulate cyberspace. The electronic artefacts I examined had a meaning for users. They represented tokens of interests, activities and relationships in which people were involved as knowledgeable actors.

Finally, where possible, I carried out short group-interview sessions in which I asked respondents' household members to talk about the Internet use in their home. In practice, finding other family members at home during my visits was rarely the case, no matter that I always asked the main respondents to invite other members of their households to participate in the interview. On the few occasions when that happened, the participation of family members took place on an ad hoc basis: a spouse or a child would join the conversation for a short period of time to contribute comments concerning the main respondent's use practice and to provide a general outline of his or her own Internet experiences. In the remaining cases, information on family members' use practices was usually received indirectly from the main respondent's verbal account and the examination of the household's computer space, when the computer happened to be used by other family members as well.

The conversations (interviews) with main respondents and household members were audio taped. Both audio taping and note taking were performed during the two kinds of tours – of the real and the virtual spaces constituted by Internet use. The audio tapes were later transcribed verbatim and analyzed. Only two interviews were carried out differently. One took place in a cafeteria, as this was the choice of the respondent. The other was conducted through e-mail: the interview protocol was sent to the respondent and she e-mailed her answers back. The two tours were not possible in these two instances, however the respondents were asked to give a verbal description of their homes' Internet-related spaces. My use of the data produced by these two interviews is very limited.

Most of my visits started with an informal exchange in which the main respondent and I negotiated details such as where exactly our conversation was going to happen: in the living room or the kitchen, whether we would have coffee or tea, who else would be present and other details. In many cases we talked about our personal and family histories, how he or she came to live in that location and what the neighbourhood was like. Then, we moved to the more structured conversation starting with the respondent's reading and signing the informed consent form. After the form was completed, I could turn on the tape recorder and begin with the questions of my interview protocol. In most sessions, this structured, researcher-directed format was only followed for the first 10–15 minutes of the conversation. Thereafter, the roles usually changed, with me responding with queries and requesting additional explanations on the basis of what my conversational partner had said. The function of my questions and comments was indeed to direct the flow of his or her talk to topics and issues of interest to my research. I was at the same time careful to ensure enough room for my conversational partners to suggest issues and questions for exploration stemming from their own systems of relevance.

The tapes have captured this complex negotiation in the course of the dialogue. My respondents were aware that I was supposed to sit in the driver's seat, and that it was my goals that the conversation was intended to serve. Yet, they took their chances to initiate changes of direction, or switch into a narrative mode when they felt strongly about something or wanted to present a coherent interpretative account of an experience. I, for my part, struggled to stay on topic while at the same time tolerating and even encouraging digressions that aroused my curiosity and tapped into unanticipated areas and issues. In retrospect, I have to admit I had cut short quite a few potentially revealing digressions. At several points in the transcripts, I caught myself silencing the respondent, unable to recognize what promised to be an insight or an enriching detail of his or her story. Unfortunately, it is impossible to recreate these moments. Even if you can, in principle, phone, e-mail or meet the person again and ask for further explanation, the momentum of the narrative is lost. In the speech genre of the 'active interview' (see Holstein and Gubrium, 1995) that I was invoking, knowledge is not elicited from people, it is discovered in the process of exchange and can also die with it, if not properly handled. These failures notwithstanding, I tried to practise a whole register of voices, from mildly authoritative, directing and demanding where I could sense a need for structure in my partners, to passively accepting and uncritically encouraging back-channel responses where my partners had stories of their own to tell.

After we finished the interview, we usually moved to the computer where the respective basement room, closet or kitchen corner was briefly examined and discussed. Then, we would turn on the computer and start the virtual tour of the computer space of the user. The main benefit of this procedure was that it allowed the respondent's verbal account of his or her Internet use to be confirmed and specified. Secondly, users' technical skills and challenges could be discussed in a hands-on context. Contrary to my expectation that the users would have introduced a personalized order in their computer space, from which I would be able to read their use patterns, this was actually observed only in the cases where the users were, as I initially thought, technically inclined. The rest of the virtual tours revealed a rather disorganized picture of imposed technical features on one hand, and on the other, users' refusal to take these features into account and arrange their computer interior in accordance with them. I was able to make better sense of this difference when I related it to respondents' Internet stories later in my analysis. It turned out to be an indicator of two quite distinct types of relationships that users were forming with Internet technology. I will discuss these relationships at length in the next chapter.

A shortcoming of the procedure of the virtual tour of the user's computer interior was the lack of a technical tool for capturing the successive screens that the user and I were moving through. Although I audio taped their talk as they led me through their computer space, it later proved to be very difficult to interpret the transcripts without access to the visual images (the particular computer screens) referenced by the verbal explanations. I asked some respondents to send me the lists of their bookmarks and address book entries by e-mail, but this did not solve the problem because establishing the link between an indexical verbal comment ('this is', 'as you can see', 'here are') to the concrete item it was pointing to, remained a matter of guessing.

I still believe that, methodologically, the virtual tour was a valuable procedure. It gave respondents the chance to validate and concretize their narratives. Looking at bookmarks and contact addresses they were reminded of significant experiences and could recreate them in remarkably vivid form. Thus the electronic artefacts – obscured, but yet material, traces of past events – served as 'trails of crumbs', as one of the women in my study put it, tracing my respondents' trajectories in cyberspace.[9]

Closing my research design outline, I have to mention the failed pie. In my original plan, I had included a procedure where I would ask the respondents to cut a pie representing their Internet use into slices proportionate to the frequency with which particular types of activities characterized their use, such as (1) work, (2) learning, (3) socializing, social relationship building and maintaining, (4) consumption (ordering products, paying bills) and (5) entertainment. I had hoped to be able to identify types of relevance and corresponding user types with regard to these activities.

Indeed, in some cases, users could methodically slice the pie and assign percentage measures to the frequency of the different activity-contexts of use. More often, however, the different types of activities enlisted above collapsed into one another, leaving the user unable to disentangle learning from entertainment or socializing from work. The puzzlement with which most respondents approached the task of cutting the pie convinced me that the typology of activities I had devised had no personal meaning to users. It was particularly difficult for them to do a quantification of the frequency of their use across the different types of activities. That is why I decided to abandon this procedure and to try to extract categories of use out of respondents' own accounts instead. Indeed, this was a strategy better suited to the phenomenological underpinning of my research. As my later data analysis demonstrated, most of the time people were turning to the Internet in response to specific aspects and problems of their social-biographical situations (isolation, dispersed social networks and communities of interest) and not in pursuit of some highly rationalized goal pertaining to a clearly definable sphere of activity.

The Respondents: Social-Biographical Situations

The group of people who volunteered to take part in the research – the self-selected sample of 'simple' customers of the Internet – was rather diverse. Looking at participants' socio-demographic characteristics, there was only one point of relative convergence – they were mostly people of modest income: the annual income of their families fell between $20,000 and $50,000 (Canadian dollars). The remaining socio-demographic characteristics were widely divergent. The respondent group included eleven women and twelve men of different marital status, both single (six women, three of them raising children; three men) and living with a partner (five women, nine men; all but one of these couples had children); people aged from 22–73; a range of educational levels – from high school to graduate degree; people with different employment situations (see Appendix for a socio-demographic and social-biographical features of respondents). Socio-demographic diversity was a desired feature of this group with a view to the exploratory nature of the research. The goal of this project was not to establish a relationship between a particular socio-demographic position and the medium of the Internet, but rather to uncover what elements of different social-biographical situations make the Internet relevant to people.

Note the distinction between the notion of position and that of situation that is made here. 'Position' refers to the practice of classifying subjects with regard to theoretically pre-established systems and hierarchies of relations in society for specific purposes by social scientists, economists, marketing and government agencies. In contrast, situations are defined by actors themselves. 'Situation' suggests a subject-centred perspective with regard to action. I saw the users of the Internet as interested actors struggling to master particular social-biographical situations and, in the process, facing the need to acquire new knowledge and resort to new means, and media, of action. What are these situations? Are they randomly variable, or do they share certain common features? What aspects of the Internet as a communication medium do they bring to the fore? What kinds of practices involving the Internet originate from them? Are these practices taken into account in the technical development and the social institutionalization of the Internet? These were the concrete questions with which I approached the interpretation of the data.

Data Analysis with a Little Help from Fairy Tales

The verbatim transcripts of the interviews were entered into the qualitative analysis software QSR NUD*IST. This software allows scrutiny of selected elements of a transcript (word, phrase, sentence, or paragraph) and their categorization with regard to a predefined and/or emergent set of concepts (analytical categories). It further supports the comparative examination of excerpts originating from different interviews (or generally, documents) subsumed under the same category, as well as the search for relationships between and among categories.

I used NUD.IST to analyze all individual interview transcripts. I dissected each transcript into excerpts addressing different topics (as intended by the respondent) or related to concepts that interested me. I classified all these excerpts under different 'nodes' or categories derived from their topics. I had a pre-existing taxonomy of topics, the discussion of which I had elicited through my interview questions. I also identified a multitude of new topics initiated by the respondents that emerged from the interviews. Thus at this stage, I performed a qualitative content analysis of the transcripts assigning excerpts to topics: what the respondents talked about. In the end, this analytical procedure left me with an intimidating number of different topics originating from the different interviews that showed very few points of convergence. This was a terrifying moment of my research. I could not figure out what I could find in this body of data other than a number of disparate individual experiences and opinions. The experience of a disabled single woman communicating with a support group via the Internet, the hobbyist-like engagement with the medium of a retired mechanical engineer e-mailing children and friends and the Internet research of a nutrition consultant seemed to have very little in common.

My model of the Internet connection as a point of overlap of several heterogeneous networks – physical, social, informational and semantic – felt too artificial to provide a basis for re-assembling the various subtopics emerging out of respondents' talk into a meaningful structure. My typology of activities underlying the pie-cutting exercise was not supported by respondents' experiences. I felt like an archaeologist in the middle of a rich excavation, surrounded by thousands of small fragments of artefacts, but having no idea which pieces belonged together and what was to be assembled from them. I was in need of a different logic to make sense of the interviews, other than my original model.

After the first wave of panic subsided, I decided to leave my fragmented excavation for the time being and go back to the whole and intact transcripts of the individual interviews. I read each of them carefully, this time looking not for labels that could be attached to selected fragments, but rather for the underlying structure of the narrative. At this stage I had to recall Mishler's (1986) discussion of narrative analysis and the lessons learnt from Propp's (1928/1968) study of the morphology of Russian fairy tales. I focused my attention on the different components of my respondents' Internet narratives and how these components worked together to produce a coherent story. From this perspective then, I could distinguish several recurring turns of the narrative. First, in response to my request to tell me the story of how they came to know about the Internet and how they had brought it into their homes, my respondents were actually producing an account that I later called 'becoming an Internet user'. Common for most of these accounts was the presence of the person who helped my respondents, then new users, to come to grips with the new technology. The accounts typically culminated with a discovery – the discovery of one or two important and personally meaningful applications of the medium that justified its continued employment. An interesting twist of the narrative at this point was the introduction of 'because' clauses that connected the discovery with aspects of the respondent's social-biographical situation at the moment: 'because I was isolated', 'because after my retirement ...'.

The integration of the new technical device and the practices growing around it with the space, time and relationships of the family was another distinguishable component of my respondents' narratives. It was a story of the struggle for control over the processes of change, and conservation set off by the new medium. The communication with people and groups outside the home through the Internet represented yet another structural component of respondents' narratives.

It would be inaccurate to say that this narrative structure emerged spontaneously out of my respondents' story-telling. My questions contributed significantly to people's recollection of particular sequences of events and their focusing on particular aspects of Internet use. Yet, as I pointed out before, they were *not* diligently reproducing the model of their experience I had charted in advance and on which I had based my questions. The structure of their narrative was emerging as a collaborative achievement of the respondent and myself. He or she was replying to the questions included in my interview guide in a selective manner, picking those on which he or she preferred to elaborate, branching into sub questions that I could not have raised, and completely ignoring others. Thus, unlike Propp (1928/1968), who found that 'all fairy tales are of one type in regard to their structure' (quoted in Mishler, 1986, p. 85), I cannot claim that I have uncovered a universal underlying structure of the Internet-use experience. My bounded claim is that the respondents and I managed to construct a framework comprised of those themes and concepts brought by me from the province of the scholarly literature that resonated with users' meaningful daily experiences of the Internet.

After I had discerned these structural components in respondents' narratives, I could use them to bring organization into the fragments that my analysis had created and to make sense of the commonalities and differences these fragments exhibited. Thus, for example, what the disabled single woman and the retired mechanical engineer had in common was that they both had received their outdated computers from close friends for free and had counted on the faithful assistance of those friends throughout the process of learning how to use the technology and how to make sense of it. Where their experiences differed was in how they felt about befriending others on the Internet and what they believed was appropriate behaviour in such relationships.

Summary

The four overarching themes that I formulated as a result of this movement between content analysis, structural analysis and comparative synthesis are as follows:

1 'Becoming a domestic Internet user', that is, building the home Internet connection as a network of technical (hardware and software), social and cognitive elements and relationships;
2 'Situating the virtual', referring to the discovery by the user of these specific affordances of the technology that made it an effective tool for tackling his or her particular social-biographical situation and to the emergence of use genres;
3 'Making room for the Internet', meaning integrating the medium in the spaces, activities, interaction and value systems of the family home; and
4 'Virtual togetherness', dealing with the networks of relationships transcending the home that are woven and sustained with the help of the new medium.

I delve into these themes in the following chapters. Under each of them I look for sources and expressions of user choice and agency with regard to the Internet. In each of these areas, I argue, the new medium stirs and transforms the pre-existing arrangements of domestic everyday life. At the same time, by interpreting, deliberating and making action choices in each of these areas in the course of their everyday lives, users contribute to the social shaping of the medium.

Notes

[1]Seiter (1999) reminds us that people who work long hours to make the ends meet, that is the low-paid, 'impoverished' working-class people can hardly afford to spend time participating in studies like this. I was attentive to this problem and did what I could to include some representatives of this category in my respondent group.

[2]Anthropologist David Hakken (1999), for his part, has identified a similar problem in 'ethnographic' projects in the field of information system development. Hakken is critical to such 'appropriations of ethnography' where engagement with informants tends to be 'shorter term, possibly involving attendance at some meetings and doing some interviews' (p. 43).

[3]Unlike other studies of Internet use in the home (e.g. HomeNet, 1999) where computers and Internet connections were provided to subjects by the researchers, all my respondents had brought the medium into their homes themselves.

[4]In contrast to studies of the Internet 'in everyday life' that have relied on telephone interviews or online questionnaires as their primary data collection methods (see Wellman and Haythornthwaite, 2002, for a collection of papers of this kind).

[5]As a matter of fact, this is the same anthropologist on whose (Marcus and Fischer, 1986) definition of ethnography Nightingale (1989, cited above) based her critique of audience ethnography. In his 1995 article, Marcus refers to media studies as 'one important arena in which multi-sited ethnography has emerged' (p. 103).

[6]Hine's (2000) study of the Internet-based activities surrounding the case of Louise Woodward is an excellent example of a multi-sited ethnography. Hine's ethnography remains 'virtual' inasmuch as the multiple sites she studies are, in fact, web sites.

[7]At the time I was collecting my data, I was a new immigrant from Eastern Europe. The income of my own household was below the 'poverty' or low-income cut-off line determined by Statistics Canada. I was at a disadvantage with respect to most of my interviewees in terms of my proficiency with the English language.

[8]As Smith (1987) puts it: 'My description is privileged to stand as what actually happened, because theirs is not heard in the contexts in which I may speak' (p. 112).

[9]I would advise any researcher employing this procedure to take care to equip herself with a screen-capturing device, preferably synchronized with the tape recorder, so that the link between the verbal explanations of the respondent (guide) and the visual content of the tour can be preserved.

FOUR Becoming a Domestic Internet User

the presence of a given kind of behaviour is the result of a sequence of social experiences during which the person acquires a conception of the meaning of the behaviour, and perceptions and judgments of objects and situations, all of which make the activity possible and desirable. Thus, the motivation or the disposition to engage in the activity is built up in the course of learning to engage in it and does not antedate this learning process. For such a view it is not necessary to identify those 'traits' which 'cause' the behaviour. Instead, the problem becomes one of describing the set of changes in the person's conception of the activity and the experience it provides for him.

(Howard S. Becker, 1953, Becoming a marijuana user, p. 223)

Introduction

In the conclusion of his article 'Becoming a marijuana user', Becker (1953) writes: 'This analysis of the genesis of marijuana use shows that the individuals who come in contact with a given object may respond to it in a great variety of ways. If a stable form of new behaviour toward the object is to emerge, a transformation of meanings must occur in which the person develops a new conception of the nature of the object' (p. 242). In this Chapter, I set out to analyze the process of becoming a domestic Internet user combining Becker's symbolic interactionist approach with the idea of 'actor network' (Callon, 1987, Cowan, 1987, Law, 1987). In the stories my respondents told me about their encounters and early experiences with the Internet, it could be seen that the domestic Internet connection had gradually emerged as a 'heterogeneous network' (Callon, 1987, p. 93) of technical, social, cultural and cognitive elements woven together in the course of everyday life. In the following analysis

I will attempt to identify the various components or 'actors' and 'actants' participating in this network and explain how and why the connections among them arose.

The Home Computer

The computer had been the first element to make its way into the future user's home. It usually had arrived there via an activity such as work or study, performed in the outside world. Most of the time, the need to use a computer (its relevance) had been externally imposed by a certain organization, or the expense of buying one had been justified by the expectation of increased efficiency in an income-yielding activity. Thus it was the dominant rationality of productivity and efficiency defining computer technology that had brought the machine into the homes of most of the people in my respondent group.

> We had the computer already. My wife had bought it for her research, she was doing her Master's at [university]. (Theodore)

> I went into business for myself for a few years. I had already a computer – a 286. It wasn't good enough for AutoCAD at that point. So I bought a 486 – at that time it was the best and today it is already old and out of date. So, I had everything already there, I only needed to add a modem. I got the modem when I got onto CompuServe. (Reiner)

> [What were you doing with your computer before you got the Internet?] Writing letters, word processing. I did some work in security business for a while, I did the basics – selling security products like cameras. So I did book-keeping and record keeping. (Jane)

Taking the computer home had often meant taking work home from one's job-site or turning the home into the primary site of paid work. As a direct reflection of the sweeping computerization of the institutions of production and education, computer technology had acquired imposed relevance[1] in the everyday lives of people who were not necessarily 'knowledge workers' of high education and status. In my respondent group, this use genre was enacted by a homemaker who had done book-keeping work for a security-device distribution firm, a technician who had had an independent consulting business, a proposal specialist who wanted to write and edit for her employer from home.

For a second category of people, the imposition of the computer as relevant to their situation had a more or less ideological nature. 'When we got the computer first, it was basically for the kids and for us to be upgraded, to be technically upgraded', Sophie explained. 'To be technically upgraded' stood for an effort to keep up with technology even when no immediately instrumental application of it could be found in the home. Similarly, Martha, a meat-wrapper for Safeway, felt compelled to 'upgrade' herself with computer equipment and skills in light of her job-related injury that made her look for occupational alternatives. Her exposure to computerized equipment for weighing and labelling at work, and the general discourse of the 'computer age', had led her to look in that direction. The computer was presenting itself to her as a source of job opportunities, even if still vague: 'And I took a basic programming course a year or two before that. I thought in this computer age I better stay in touch' (Martha).

For a third group of users in my study, the computer was handed down by a friend or relative who was upgrading his or her own equipment at work or at home, or otherwise had access to a computer of depreciated value that could be given away.

> Being retired I basically try to minimize my expenditure on and around the computer. I started with an MX which was free. Someone was throwing it out. Then I bought a second hand 286, three years ago and then quite recently, this year, a friend of mine who is a computer programmer brought a motherboard for a 386 and put that in the computer. So now I have a 386. All I needed to go out and buy was a hard drive – I didn't have enough memory, so I bought a hard drive. (John)

This practice indicates an interesting mechanism of the social diffusion of computer technology. The machine, although a more or less out-dated model, becomes available to people in the social networks of computer and computerized professionals. Non-professionals and 'poor cousins' take up the computer waste and put it to uses of their own. Notably, in some of the cases falling in this last group, the explicit motivation for accepting the free computer had been its communication function.

> My brother had just upgraded his computer. My brother works, he is an actuary, so he uses computers all the time ... So, he was upgrading and he offered me this computer. He had offered it to me three or four times before and finally I said 'okay' because I had heard – I have had arthritis now since 1992 – that there was a site on there on which I could meet people with arthritis. So I said, here is my chance to use the Internet for something that would be useful to me ... . I'd seen them, computers, in the library and I was sort of intrigued, but I could never find how they could be of any use to me. I am not into learning something that is not useful. (Garry, a retired naval radio-operator)

For Ellen, a former editor with a disability preventing her from working, the home computer gained relevance when she became house bound due to her illness:

> My friend came and he said 'I'm going to set you up on the Internet, and I'm going to show you how to use it', and this specific function was different from when I used a computer at work. The main purpose was in order for me to be able to connect to a support group. (Ellen)

So, Ellen received an old Macintosh from her friend and got an Internet connection through the local Community Net, also for free. Predictably, Ellen's equipment, as well as that of the other people in this group, was far from being top of the line. Moving ahead of my analysis here, I would like to point out that these inhabitants of the margins of the computerized world seemed to have found rationales for engaging with computers (and the Internet) that were deviant from the dominant programs for action (Latour, 1992) embodied in the machines. Their main uses of the technology consisted of self-help, community building, talking back to traditionally one-way transmitters of information such as radio and television stations and branches of the government (see Bakardjieva and Smith, 2001). I will have more to say about these diverse appropriations of the Internet in the following chapter.

Hooking up

Let us now look into the different motivations that led the respondents to make the step from an isolated (stand-alone) computer, a machine for word processing, book-keeping and game-playing, to the Internet. Why did they want to bring home a new communication medium? How did the Internet, as a technology different from the stand-alone computer, gain relevance for the people interviewed? Comparing users' initiation stories three distinct types of motivations could be discerned: responding to outside pressure, buying into dominant discourses, and coming up with applications of one's own.

Despite the fact that the respondents in this study were not computer or Internet professionals, quite a few of them had experienced an outside institutional pressure to hook up to the Internet at home. This was most notable in the cases of those who had been involved in college or university education. There were also others who had felt the need to be able to transfer files between their office and their home, or to do work- or study-oriented research on the Internet from home. The Internet connection at home was seen as relevant in the context of the relations between work/education and family life. It was brought in as a mechanism for extending the work/education space or more precisely, in this case, for blending the spaces of work/education with that of the home:

> The Internet came next because I was in nursing [college programme], ... and they strongly recommended it as a research resource, for looking up all kinds of different things we'd need to do in nursing ... I thought I just could use the one [connection] at school to deal with the addresses that were assigned to us at school ... But he [her husband] said that the reality was that it's easier to use it from home, from the comfort of my own home, and he was right, because as soon as I was done with classes, I wanted to come home. (Sophie)

Similarly to what I found with computers, another kind of motivation for connecting to the Internet had to do with a more abstract impulse to fit in into the 'network society'. These were the users whose early motivation to hook up to the Internet had not been predominantly instrumental and institutionally imposed as in the cases quoted above. For them, the Internet had acquired a non-utilitarian, culturally imposed relevance.

> Why I wanted to have an account? Because the Internet is something of fashion, there is a lot of talk about the Internet and I could see some business possibilities. The excitement to have something new was the primary reason. (Patrick)

> I guess initially I was attracted by curiosity only. It was so much in the news, in the media hype and whatever. I guess you want to see what is really going on. I think one of my sons said once: 'If you don't have it, you feel like an outcast. You don't know what is really going on. If you don't have e-mail, who are you?' (Reiner)

A third kind of motivation to install an Internet connection at home – most often driven by the desire to do something concrete, for example e-mail – could be characterized as giving the medium intrinsic relevance:

> Then a friend started telling me about the Internet. He had a son in Calgary and another one in Montreal and he told me how every night he got e-mail letters from them and he would e-mail back. And I said: 'How do you do that? How much does it cost you?' And he said: 'It doesn't cost me anything. Would you like to try it?' So he came and hooked me up with CompuServe. (John)

Users such as Garry and Ellen, quoted above, also fell in this category. They were orienting to the Internet as a matter of free volition looking for non-conventional solutions to personal problems and needs.

What was common for most people across the three motivation categories was their relatively modest disposable income and hence, their caution in spending unnecessarily on the computer/Internet equipment and service. Yet, there were marked differences in how the reasonable level of expenses was perceived, depending on the motives people had for bringing information technology into their home.

Intrinsic motivation did not lead people in this (mostly) lower-middle-class social bracket to make substantive investment in up-to-date equipment. Older people, who could not expect any tangible profit or even potential increase of their earning power to result from the adoption of the Internet, had been reluctant to expend on powerful equipment. With younger people, a factor that I labelled 'the user-technology relation' seemed to have an expressed influence when it came down to equipment expenses. I will examine this factor in detail in one of the following sections.

The tangible outcome of these differently patterned motivations was a difference in the levels of power and speed of the equipment installed in the home. 'Low-tech' users put up with a limited access to the Internet in terms of both time and features, and navigated much more cumbersome interfaces than those with advanced equipment, software and service.

Most of the discussions of unequal access to the Internet have worked with a binary model – a person either has access or not. At this stage of the social diffusion of the technology, the question *what kind of access* is available to a user or a category of users needs to be raised more insistently. The answer to this question could orient the practical shaping of the Internet on the part of site and service designers. The inequality in technical equipment opens new gaps among people who *have* access to the Internet. A whole new social stratification seems to be emerging among Internet users themselves.

Both high-tech and low-tech users, as well as the myriad of intermediate states between them, find meaningful uses of the medium. However, commercial and political players chart the course of the technical and institutional development of the Internet with predominant consideration for the high-tech users. Low-tech designs and technical solutions, for example, textual browsers are not pursued. This marginalizes Internet users with older equipment and slow connections, and limits the range of applications to which they can put the new medium. Respectively, some social and cultural practices that could be sustained by low-tech devices remain underdeveloped or even become obsolete (for example, the decline of community nets).

I argue that if the Internet is to be developed as an equitable social resource, the actual circumstances and substantive interests of low-tech users have to be taken into account by software and service designers, as well as content providers. What sense would it make, for example, to develop flashy web-based job-advertisement sites if unemployed users cannot afford the type of connection that would allow them to view these pages? Content presented on the Internet typically caters to users occupying higher educational, professional, income and technical-equipment brackets. And this problem is further aggravated with the advance of e-commerce. This deficiency in application and content development can infringe on vital democratic processes, allegedly supported by the new medium, when it is reproduced by public organizations such as government, unions and civic associations.

I will return to the discussion of this problem and its implications for public policy later. At this point of my analysis, it would be useful to point out that the weaving of the complex network of actors and actants constituting the home Internet connection has barely begun with the arrival of the computer, the modem, the communication software and the Internet Service Provider's more or less responsive line. In the following two sections I will consider two other critical and quite complex components of this network: first, the acquisition of the knowledge and skills necessary to operate the system and secondly, the emergence of a stable user-technology relation.

Networking Knowledge and Skills: The Warm Expert

The acquisition of a minimum of networking knowledge and skills is a crucial condition for the stabilization of the home Internet connection. My respondents had traversed a complex path to pick up such knowledge and skills in both formal settings – an Internet course at the college, an instructional session at the library – and within their own homes with the help of more experienced friends and relatives. Notably, even when the introduction to the Internet had been initiated elsewhere, the 'domestication' (Silverstone, 1994) of the medium had been intensively assisted by a close friend. The computer/Internet literate friend or relative was a recurring character in all respondents' initiation stories.

This character first appeared as someone who precipitated the encounter between the user and the technology. This was the person who 'started telling me about the Internet' (John), or insisted that 'if you don't have it, you don't know what is really going on (Reiner; see quotes on p. 96), or that the respondent should have it in order to be able to maintain e-mail communication with that friend or relative. In Jane's case, it was her brother in Montreal, who also gave her the modem; with Reiner, it was his son.

An even more important role that the friend's character played in these stories, however, was one that I would like to call the role of the 'warm expert'. The warm expert is an Internet/computer technology expert in the professional sense or simply in a relative sense compared with the less knowledgeable other. The two characteristic features of the warm expert are that he or she possesses knowledge and skills gained in the System world of technology and can operate in this world but, at the same time, is immediately accessible in the user's lifeworld as a fellow-man/woman. The warm expert mediates between the technological universal and the concrete situation, needs and background of the novice user with whom he is in a close personal relationship.

In Martha's story, this role was performed by a friend from a remote suburb who came to her house when she bought her new 486 and stayed there for a while helping her with her computer: 'We played on the computer, we just played with it and he used a lot of metaphors'.[2] That friend was on CompuServe, so Martha too took a subscription with CompuServe. Subsequently, the correspondence with that same friend would be one of the main streams in the flow of her e-mail.

In Theodore's experience, the warm expert was a cousin (a professional 'tech support person') living in the US who, like a missionary, visited the homes of his relatives dispersed throughout North America and hooked them up to the Internet. Theodore's modem and the idea about his first mailing list subscription came as gifts from that cousin.

Garry took it upon himself to learn how to use his newly installed computer and Internet connection by relying on what he had heard at an introductory session in the library, and by trial and error. However, when his computer crashed shortly after he started his explorations, he had to call upon a computer-knowledge friend:

> So there was a misconnection in the mouse and the pointer wouldn't come up, so I thought it was something wrong and pressed every button on the key board in sequence trying to find out ... And during that procedure I crashed the machine. That was the first thing I did. Luckily, I have a friend who is just super technical! He lives and breathes technical things ... (Garry)

John was often walked through his computer problems on the phone by some of his expert friends. Sophie and her husband sometimes needed to call as far as California to receive personalized computer help from her husband's stepfather, a systems analyst.

In Ellen's case, her friend gave her the computer as well as the idea to connect to a support group for her illness: 'David was the one who heard about it and told me about its existence. Because I was so ill that I couldn't really, wasn't in a state to do any research of my own'. The same friend held her hand in both the literal and figurative sense in helping her learn what sequence to go through in order to get connected. Ellen's mental problems, stemming from her illness, made the learning process extremely painful, but both she and her friend persevered:

> So David would sit there and show me: here you do this and this, and he had to go over and over it again. I was like a two-year-old. I would write down painfully and slowly all the steps and had no idea what he was talking about, but only knew that I had to write this down and somehow there will be a moment – a day from now, or a week, or a month, when I will actually be able to follow it and to figure it out.[3] (Ellen)

Sandy hooked up to the Internet from home following the advice of one of her professors. She was planning to drop his course because it required Internet research. Sandy found it impossible to go to the campus computer lab given her part-time job, young child and family responsibilities:

> And he [her professor] provided a guy named Stanley who came over and helped me to get hooked up to the Internet. Very nice, very nice guy, and since then Stanley and I have become friends. So we met at the university and he told me what I needed to have and then he said 'I'll come over to your place' because I was confused. And he came, hooked me up and got me the software. (Sandy)

With Stanley's help, Sandy learnt how to use a chat program: 'I think I phoned Stanley and he told me – by that time I had Netscape and a connection thing – so Stanley told me to go to this place called www.talkcity.com'. Armed with this knowledge she went on to discover richer sources of technical help on the network itself:

> Quite often, once I had that chat line hooked up, a lot of my help came from people in that chat line like Roland who had a computer science degree. And he made it easy ... There's a lot of people online and if you go into the computer chat rooms, that would do the same thing, you just have to ask for the help and I think asking for the help and knowing where to go for the help is the hardest part online. (Sandy)

At the time we spoke, less than two years after her initial introduction to the Internet, Sandy was often called upon to teach other people who wanted to set up their own Internet connections at home. In her teaching, she drew on what she had learnt from Stanley, Roland and her own discoveries:

> Lots of people now get me to hook them up to the Internet because they know that I hang out there. One of the first things that I download is a chat line program and I say: this is where you go for help – and if they have a Macintosh I will set it up so that they just go in there – in the Macintosh room. And if you go in there and ask for help there are hundreds of people that will help you – they'll tell you where to go and what to do. Then you form relationships with other people who have computers. [ISP] has their own software, but I don't recommend people to use it … . That's how Stanley taught me – 'Don't use [ISP] software, Sandy, use your own software because you are in control of it'. (Sandy)

Martha, who was initially taught by her friend, also found herself on the other side of this ubiquitous process of informal mutual teaching about the technology and the medium:

> and it's the same that goes around, comes around. Whenever any friend, mostly women friends, whose husbands don't have the time to show them or don't know what this piece of equipment is in their home … . I'll go over for lunch, the trade off is they get me lunch and I show them how to get around on the computer. And it's not like having to take a full course in how to use this software or that software. In fact I have been paid by a couple of students because the word got around that I could teach people how to use their computers and I end up being paid for computer tutoring. So I've come quite a long way. (Martha)

Note the translation of higher order activity terms such as 'teaching', 'learning', even 'using' to the level of the immediately experienced, to the situated indexicality of everyday life: Martha 'shows' women friends simply 'what this piece of equipment is in their home' and how to 'get around' on the computer. The return for this showing, as in a typical 'gift economy' (Mauss, 1967), is lunch and, as one can imagine, the enjoyment of spending time with a friend. Having recently been in the shoes of her present students and caring about their feelings as a friend, Martha had an empathic understanding of the difficulties they faced:

> Everybody has to start. People I am teaching often say 'this sounds stupid' … . But I tell them no, nothing sounds stupid. I remember having the same question. (Martha)

Interestingly, the gender of the Internet teacher or champion who had helped my respondents with their first steps on both the computer and the Internet was in all cases male. However, the people in my study who had later become teachers and Internet experts themselves were both women. Indeed, they were divorced single mothers who at the moment of the interview, and for some time before it, had either worked part-time or had been on leave from work. In that sense, they had a family situation different from the Standard North American Family pattern (see Smith, 1999, p. 159). They were in virtually full control of their domestic time (unlike married mothers) and also had relatively more of it than women working full-time and raising children by themselves typically do. With this qualifying circumstance in mind, it should be noted that traditional gender inequalities with respect to technology did not necessarily transpire in the practices of the people in this study. In fact, as I will show in Chapter 6, in the homes where women were taking leadership in Internet adoption and use, specific domestic arrangements and use genres involving the medium emerged. Thus women were laying their mark on the shaping of the medium.

The learning experiences of new domestic users of the Internet recounted here thus exhibit a profoundly social character. The obverse of this social learning process in which non-professional domestic users typically engaged, was the process of socialization of personal knowledge of the technology and the medium. Friends and relatives, and to some degree online helpers, had taught my respondents not only how to navigate the interface but also what they themselves had discovered the Internet could do for them as a communication medium. They were passing along their understanding of the relevance of the new technology, crystallized from their own experience. As the cases of Sandy and Martha illustrate, the same had happened later, when some of my respondents had become capable of playing the role of the warm expert for the less knowledgeable others.

Examining the mechanisms of 'socialization of subjective knowledge' Schutz writes:

> The general and fundamental presupposition for the acceptance of subjective elements of knowledge into the social stock of knowledge is their 'objectivation' [sic]. This expression is meant to characterize, in general, the embodiment of subjective processes in the objects and events of the everyday life-world. (Schutz and Luckmann, 1973, p. 264)

The ongoing process of teaching others and learning from others that my interviews exposed suggests that subjective knowledge, or in constructivist terms, subjective meanings of the Internet as a technology and communication medium are indeed 'objectivated' in the objects and events of the everyday lifeworld shared by tutor and student. Thus, even though users, as de Certeau (1984) has observed, cannot lay their mark directly on the shape of the technology that they put into use, they still have the power to 'objectivate' their subjective knowledge of it. Other people in similar social-biographical situations, having similar problems to solve, pick up the discoveries made by their fellow-men and women and spread them around. In this way, the particular category of everyday users produces its own culture of understanding and application of the medium. This practice, I contend, represents an important source of user activity in the generative process of technology. I will examine in more detail the characteristic forms of such situated rationalizations of the medium in the following chapter.

User-Technology Relations

Let us go back to Becker's (1953) argument that 'in order for a stable form of new behaviour toward a particular object to emerge, a transformation of meanings must occur in which the person develops a new conception of the nature of the object and his or her own experience with it' (p. 242). I see the emergence of such a 'stable form of new behaviour' toward a technical object as 'stabilization' (Pinch and Bijker, 1987) of the definition of this object at the personal and local level. The new conception of the nature of the object and the user's experience with it characterizes the 'user-technology relation' that can take different forms depending on the user's social-biographical situation and the specific interactions and reasoning that have led her to recognize the technology as relevant.

In her book *The second self: computers and the human spirit*, Turkle (1984) pioneered an inquiry into the kinds of relationships that people from the first generation of personal computer owners (who bought and built small computers in the late 1970s) established with computer technology. She drew attention to the fact that even though many users were buying the machines with clear-cut instrumental purposes in mind (word processing, record keeping), 'once they are in the home, personal computers get taken up in ways that signal the development of something beyond the practical and utilitarian. People buy an "instrumental computer", but they come to live with an "intimate machine"' (p. 185). What made the machine intimate, according to Turkle, was the fact that its importance for users derived not so much from 'what it might do', but from 'how it made them feel' (p. 186). Users' experience with computers was intertwined with their sense of self.

The work of Margrethe Aune (1996) transposed a similar investigation into the world of Norwegian home computer owners of the early 1990s. Aune distinguished ideal types of users on the basis of their 'style of work' – a category describing the relationship of the user with his or her computer. The two styles of work discerned by Aune – 'instrumental' and 'expressive' (p. 102) – bear close resemblance with the categories introduced by Turkle (1984): the 'instrumental computer' and the 'intimate machine' (p. 185).

Notably, Aune (1996) did find some users forming an intimate relationship with their home computers, but this relationship was in no way characteristic of all or most of the people she studied, as was the case in Turkle's research. Users were demonstrating different profiles that Aune subsumed under several ideal-types. A substantial number of them did not feel intimate with their machines. They perceived the computer as a mere tool. On the other hand, there were those who demonstrated an 'expressive relationship' with the computer very much like the early adopters studied by Turkle (1984). These users were absorbed in the technology and very intense in their computer work (see p. 111).

The conclusions that Moyal (1992) reached in a project examining the use of a quite different communication technology, the telephone, by women in Australia, reproduced the 'instrumental' versus 'expressive' dichotomy in its own way. Moyal distinguished between 'instrumental' and 'intrinsic' calls made by women. The former were calls of a functional nature, while the latter comprised calls 'covering communication with relatives and friends, volunteer work, counselling and all intimate discussion and exchange' (p. 53). They were more spontaneous and related to people and activities defining women's sense of self. Although all women in her sample were found to make both types of calls, some tended to think about the telephone in more 'intrinsic' terms than others.

Moving into the terrain of the Internet, Markham (1998) discerns three types of user experience of the technology: the Internet as a tool, as a place, and as a way of being (see pp. 86–87). The 'tool' perception corresponds to Turkle's instrumental relationship. The 'place' and 'way of being' perceptions indicate an increasing investment of the self in the Internet where cyberspace becomes an arena for action and interaction as important as users' offline life. These two types of experience seem to constitute two distinct degrees of intensity of the intimate/expressive relationship with computers observed by Turkle and Aune.[4]

When I tried to apply the 'instrumental' versus 'intimate' dichotomy in my analysis of the relations that my respondents had formed with the

Internet, I ran into a number of contradictions. The major obstacle had to do with one particular kind of user. These people's relation with the Internet was very intense. They were deeply interested in the technology and strove towards a transparent understanding of how it worked, but at the same time, they did not seem to be emotionally involved with it, nor were they engaging with it for its own sake. By means of the Internet, they were pursuing particular interests and goals lying beyond the technology itself – in that sense the technology remained instrumental to them. At the same time, they invested considerable time and effort in keeping up with the latest technical developments and obviously found pleasure and some pride in that. This type of user involved the Internet in a whole range of different activities related to work, leisure, education/learning, socializing and others. No matter that most of them derived no immediate benefits from their computer and Internet use and their household incomes were modest, they regularly upgraded their equipment.

In contrast, another type of user remained in a strictly instrumental relationship with the Internet. The spectrum of their Internet applications was much narrower than the previous group. They were preoccupied exclusively with the particular goal lying beyond the technology with respect to which the technology was nothing more than a means. These people demanded 'transparency' of the technology in the sense of not having to pay special attention to the tool. Failure to find such transparency was a source of frustration to them, but they were unwilling to invest time and money in upgrading either their equipment, or their own skills for dealing with it. They admitted to being too impatient and stated that they would never look into a program's help. Those who had old computers and low-speed connections were annoyed by their limitations, but insisted that the equipment was just fine for their purposes. Put simply, they did not care about the technology as such. Here is one representative statement for this kind of relationship to technology. The respondent had complained about 'the amount of time that I have spent in frustration over the computer', so I asked him to explain what the source of his frustration was:

> It seems to be quite simple: I don't know the terminology. I don't know what they are referring to. I remember my first question in that regard. They were referring to 'default'. I had a different idea of what default was. And it's like, I had to learn that from hours and hours of making mistakes. I find that quite frustrating. I go to the help section and it doesn't help me because I don't know what they are referring to. And to be honest, I don't want to know the language. I just want the damn thing to work. (Garry)

For a third kind of user, the Internet and the computer in general were exciting as technologies before and beyond anything else. The practical goals of their Internet use seemed to be overshadowed in importance by how the technology 'made them feel', to evoke Turkle's (1984) formulation. Here is a short excerpt of the explanation one such respondent gave me while he was leading me on a breathtaking tour of his computer interior:

> In fact it is extremely simple to use my machine, but I have done some tricky things that other people just haven't. I can provide anybody with very simple little routines to do what I do. Most of my gimmicks people don't use, but I love them ... There is nothing on my screen that I don't want on my screen now. It is clean and simple. ... The beauty of this program is that [it] will only take about 100K ... . (Merlin)

Clarity, simplicity, beauty, tricks, gimmicks, love and hate defined the aesthetics of Merlin's computer and Internet use. His intensive preoccupation with re-programming, customizing, and outsmarting the original software made him feel in control of his computer space. ('There is nothing on my screen that I don't want on my screen now'.) It gave him a sense of autonomy and achievement. The 58-year-old Merlin had started his computer career as an enthusiast in the late 1970s. He was coming from the same culture that Turkle (1984) had described in her early account.

A similar relationship could be identified in the case of a young college student (Larry). Partly disassembled appliances lay all over Larry's room. He took pleasure in examining what was hidden underneath the cover just for the challenge of it.

In this way, three types of relationships between users and Internet technology were emerging from my observations. I will initially label them 'curiously instrumental', 'indifferently instrumental', and 'intimate' where the attributes curious, indifferent and intimate refer to how users felt about Internet technology itself.

In my attempt to interpret these descriptive categories, I will draw on (and adapt) Ihde's (1990) phenomenology of human-technology relations. Discussing the different ways in which technology is taken into the subjective lifeworld, Ihde posited four types of relations: embodiment relations, hermeneutic relations, alterity relations and background relations[5] (see Ihde, 1990 and Chapter 2). I wish to determine whether any correspondence exists between Ihde's taxonomy and the empirically observed relations I just described. If I manage to find such correspondence, I would be able to apply the analytical system of critical phenomenology that I elaborated in Chapter 2 to my empirical material. Thus, I would be able to go beyond the descriptive typologies proposed by earlier studies.

The Embodiment Relation: (I–technology)–world

The 'indifferently instrumental' users in my respondent group took computer and Internet technology as an extension of their perceptual and actional self, in an embodiment relation. In this relation, expressed by the formula: (I–technology)–world (Ihde, 1990, p. 73), the technology is between the seer and the seen, between the doer and the object of his or her action. The referent of the seeing and the doing is on the other side of the techno-logical tool or system. These users expected the technology to be unobtru-sive and not to divert attention and/or energy from the referent lying beyond it. That is what the exclamation: 'I don't want to know the language. I just want the damn thing to work' (Garry) stood for. For the people who established an embodiment relation with the computer and the Internet, the world was on the other side of the technology and lent itself to more or less successful comprehension and manipulation depending on how smoothly the technology was embodied. Interestingly, even the most poorly equipped and technically uninformed users seemed to have been able to work out a certain, even if awkward, routine for handling the technology, so that it ended up withdrawing from their attention, and yet served their purpose.

Ihde (1990), as discussed in Chapter 2, points out an essential ambi-guity existing in this relation: it has a necessary 'magnification/reduction structure' (p. 74). Embodiment relations simultaneously magnify and reduce what is experienced through them. But such an ambiguity, I argue, exists in all types of human-technology relations. It is a potential source of user alienation and subordination to technology. That is why critical understanding of the amplifications and reductions constituting this ambiguity in the case of each particular technology and each particular relation is a necessary condition for user emancipation.

The Hermeneutic Relation: I–(technology–world)

The group of the 'curiously instrumental users' in my study represented a relation with technology that could be described by Ihde's (1990) 'hermeneutic' formalism: I–(technology–world) (see p. 86). Building on Ihde's definition of this relation, I propose that, in this case, the attention of the user is focused on the technology, but not for its own sake rather, *for what it represents*. Here, I depart from Ihde by investing this statement with a dual meaning. First, features and events of the world outside – a landscape (represented by a map or picture), a friendship (represented by an electronic message) – are read off the technological medium. Second, in a more global sense, technology and the world become inseparable: the world is seen as technologically defined, and technology becomes a code for understanding the world. For the people in this group, the importance of their Internet use lay not only in what it allowed them to do, but also in *how it allowed them to relate to the world*. Here is the place to recall Martha's remark: 'And I took a basic programming course a year or two before that. I thought in this computer age, I better stay in touch'. Staying in touch with a highly computerized and networked world was the high stake that people in this category had in the Internet.

For Alex, for example, there was a rising tide of information out there that he felt compelled to orient to in order to remain in control of his life. For that reason, having the Internet connection was essential to him:

> I have an interest in computers in principle and the Internet connection is a big inseparable part of this interest. This is an industry that is developing at a super fast rate, no other industry has ever grown at such a rate. In the coming few years there will be a huge boom – like, for example, the number of people online has been doubling every eight months. Last year it doubled in three and a half months ... We are speaking about millions of people ... . (Alex)

In Sandy's world, information technology had two quite different, and paradoxically related, faces. Sandy, a telemarketer, worked in a highly computerized environment and was an object of technologically mediated monitoring and control throughout her working day:

> We sit thirteen-fourteen people into a, we call it, 'pod' and a supervisor sits there and she can pull up on her computer everything that we are doing. So she just sits at her desk and watches all our little, we call them, 'heads' on the computer and we are measured and we have daily stats and online stats – how many calls we made, how many minutes we spoke to that person, how many sales we made, what's our wrap time – that's the time from when I stopped talking to you and when I took the next call. It logs idle time; we had this joke that it logs how long you pee for and how many times. Because, really, it does! (Sandy)

When she was being trained for this job, Sandy recalled, she was having nightmares about the computer chasing her down the street. The huge pressure of the beginning had now been relieved to a great extent thanks to a good trade union at Sandy's workplace. Nevertheless, her relationship with technology at work remained the same – she was the object of it. In contrast, when she was at her computer and on the Internet at home, Sandy felt in charge:

And I have set up this thing called 'My Yahoo' which is through the search engine. I have it all programmed to load up to things that I am interested in – stocks that I own; and it tells me whether the stock is up or down and headline news stories that I am interested in – and it loads those automatically ... My chat program, my ICQ, stuff is neatly organized. The hard work is learning the technology, after that it's easy to organize. (Sandy)

'Organizing is essential', Martha also insisted. A substantial part of her world of interests and relationships with people was consciously structured into her bookmarks and e-mail folders. Having achieved a good command of Internet technology, Martha felt she could navigate the world outside and order her relations with it in accordance with her needs, values and priorities. In this process she was not only extending and enriching the content of her lifeworld; she was re-inventing herself. Thus, Martha had gradually become a resource person for many of her friends and relatives. She had done research on film related jobs in Britain for her aunt, on the Gulf War Syndrome for one of her brothers and on Attention Deficit Disorder for her local parent support group. She was learning that she actually enjoyed doing research and that: 'I think I would be really good at researching. That's why I want to find a job in research. I am good at finding things'.

She was also keeping up with technical developments in Internet technology and indirectly associating, through an electronic newsletter, with a community of web designers in Vancouver:

I keep track of it because I think if I get into this sort of industry, people have their companies on here, it's local, it's in Vancouver. It's a job potential, good way of collecting info on what's going on locally, people who are developing sites and making a lot of money out of it. (Martha)

The three respondents whose experiences I have used as an example of the hermeneutic user-technology relation, unlike Garry who simply wanted the 'damn thing' to work, were eager to learn the language of the technology in order to be able to relate to the world it represented and construed. However, knowing and speaking the language of Internet technology required constantly keeping an eye on the new technical developments. Not surprisingly, a big portion of these users' bookmarks and the newsletters and newsgroups they subscribed to were technically oriented. In terms of software and hardware, all these people were constantly 'upgrading'. An interesting 'information overload' paradox could be observed in this particular use genre: In order to be able to better know, organize, control and master the world of information to which the

Internet was giving them access, they needed to open the door to ever more information – about new programs, applications, upgrades and pieces of equipment.

The Alterity Relation: Technology as a Quasi-Other

By his third type of human-technology relation – the alterity relation – Ihde (1990) seeks to characterize 'the positive or presentential senses' in which humans relate to technology as a 'quasi-other' (p. 98). In this relation, Ihde observes, technologies emerge as focal entities that may receive the multiple attentions humans give the different forms of the other' (p. 107). This type of relation resembles what Turkle (1984) meant by her metaphor of the intimate machine – a machine or technology experienced in ways, and producing emotional reactions, typically associated with other human beings. The examples of this kind of relation in my respondent group, Merlin and Larry, were excited by the challenges technology posed. They appreciated its 'beauty'. They strove to outsmart a program, to prove their own intellectual superiority over a machine or to overcome its resistance.

These three human-technology relations do not exclude each other. They can coexist within the same personal experience of a user with regard to different technologies, or at different stages of the user's dealings with the same technology. Which type of relation would be preponderant in every concrete case of Internet use seemed to be a matter of biographically and situationally determined structure of interests and relevances. On the basis of the cases I have studied, I would suggest that people who found themselves in comparatively stable and generally unproblematic social-biographical situations were more inclined to look at computers and the Internet as means for achieving concrete, well-defined goals. For others, whose social-biographical situations were in flux or were fundamentally problematic, it was more likely that a hermeneutic relation with the Internet would arise. People who defined their situations in this way felt in need not so much of concrete solutions to daily problems, but rather of new ways of knowing and manipulating their environment. That is what the Internet technology taken into a hermeneutic relation allowed them to do.

Finally, the alterity relation involved playful experimentation with the computer and Internet technology, satisfying the user's curiosity and testing his or her own abilities. This relation had been formed in the distinct situation of the young college student (Larry), as well as that of the long-unemployed 58-year-old professional (Merlin) who similarly needed confirmation of his wits and skills, as well as a form of escape.

Amplifications and Reductions

Different forms of amplification and reduction ensued for users in these three different relations with the Internet. The users who had taken the Internet in an 'embodiment relation' seemed to suffer an immediate reduction in the range of approaches and possible operations that would get the task done. The technology provided an extension of their zones of actual and potential reach, but it also forced them to re-format these zones in sometimes undesirable ways. Theodore (an Ethiopian immigrant to Canada), for example, could gather information about his faraway native country's political life from the Internet. However, the fact that Internet protocols did not support the Amharic[6] writing, combined with his inability to afford a graphical interface to the World Wide Web, prevented him from receiving material in the language of his country of origin. Therefore, he had to put together his radio programme for the local Ethiopian community, which was his main use of the Internet, exclusively out of English language publications and to remain constrained to their perspectives and agendas.

Don could announce a meeting of his voluntary organization's Board of Directors by sending a carbon copy of the same message to all board members, which was a clear amplification of his communicative power and efficiency. At the same time, he had no way of getting reliable feedback about who had actually received and read the message and who had not. On one occasion, when Don decided to rely on e-mail for doing this kind of organizing, the designated host of the meeting did not receive the message and everything failed. Thus without the flexibility of synchronous human communication, the affairs of a community had become dependent on a technical system.

Vera liked drawing on online sources for her journalistic research, but she was aware of how much time she could sometimes waste in the process wading through irrelevant material.

The struggle for control of Internet technology necessitated reconfiguring the structure of amplifications and reductions built into the medium. For this type of users this involved conscious efforts at ascribing the technology the right place in their lives and, more particularly, learning what tasks could be entrusted to it and what not. Contrary to Reiner's son, who had said to his father 'If you don't have e-mail, who are you?',

Vera advised her ex-husband, who was eager to get an Internet connection: 'Consider how much you actually need it. Why would you get e-mail if you don't need it?' Part of the struggle was also determining what can and cannot, or should not, be given up in exchange for Internet time and virtual communication: Theodore contemplated: 'There are friends on e-mail, but we don't correspond that much. It's ironic, I don't know why ... Because of time constraints, I don't have the time. There is a life that I have to live here too – you have your social connections, your friends here. You just don't prioritize these e-mail connections as much as others'.

The role the Internet was playing in the lives of users in a hermeneutic relation with it was more pervasive. The discourse of 'the computer age', 'the information society', and ideas like 'millions of people going online every day' streaming from influential sources underlay these users' perception of the medium. The people in this relation dedicated conscious effort to studying and understanding the Internet with the purpose of being able to competently find their way around the 'computer age' (Martha), in which they believed they were living. Ironically, as the information overload paradox suggests, the more these users tried to be agents in this technologically driven world, the more they were becoming consumers of technological products. The nature of the 'hermeneutic relation' where technology was an interface, a code for interpreting the world and expressing oneself in it, involved a substantial degree of submission to the technological lead. Technology was appropriating its appropriators.

Were these users victims of the powerful discourses and systemic imperatives of the network society? Were the forces of alienation overpowering creative self-expression and individual control? The analysis of users' experiences does not provide a unilateral answer. Everyday Internet use was a field of struggle for a meaningful balance between personal autonomy and inevitable submission to rules and recipes. In some cases, what was beginning to emerge as a result of this struggle was a hard-earned reflexivity. People were beginning to reflect on the mechanisms of representation of the world implicit in Internet technology and content and the subtle ways in which these mechanisms both amplified and reduced personal control:

> Well, I can go to MacDonald's and I can be linked then to Burger King, Wendy's, etc., etc. ... But I can go there for the rest of my life and never have a nourishing meal, and not even miss it ... . (Don)

> You can go into the American Yahoo! site and you can search a route – how to drive from one city to another by the least amount of miles – it gives you a map. Which is very limiting because it is biased, based on their criteria. On one hand it frees me up because I don't have to worry which way I go

to Florida, but on the other hand, I haven't learnt so much. And I am probably the only nerd who thinks about those things – most of them will print the map and drive to Florida. (Sandy)

In fact, she was not alone. Martha too was quite self-conscious as far as her Internet use was concerned. She admitted that initially she was 'addicted', and insisted that now she was trying not to take the medium too seriously. 'I want it to become just a tool like anything else, like using the phone'. She saw the attainment, or restoration, of the embodiment relation, the 'technology-as-a-tool' position, as the salvation from the overwhelming experience produced by the hermeneutic relation.

Don, the psychological counsellor, explicitly called for careful gauging of the amplifications and reductions involved in a technologically mediated understanding of the world:

Now, question one is, do we really need all that information, what is it really doing for our existence? Then another aspect, psychologically, to me is this feeling where people go 'Yes, we are talking to people in India, we are talking to people ...'. I say: Well, are you really? Number one again, whoever's got the computer there is economically, socio-economically, even educationally just about in the same bracket – whether I am a Christian Baptist Korean or a super reformed Jew raised in Canada whatever, we are speaking white middle-class language. Not to say that it is wrong or right, but I don't know the smell and the sound and the sight of where you really live, I am in my little cubicle, with my nice little screen and obviously your screen is going to look damn close to my little screen. Are we again enclosing ourselves in a very nice data-filled bracket? My thing is, why do I need all this data? I'd rather crush a leaf, smell a leaf ... . (Don)

Thus, it can be argued that some users were starting to relate to the Internet in a *critically hermeneutic* manner. Out of their intense preoccupation with the technology as an interface to a technological world, an awareness of the reductions and distortions implicit in this interface was emerging. In fact, as can be sensed in Don's reflection above, the critique of technology was translating into a critique of the world that it helped reproduce in people's everyday lives. The critical juxtaposition of the possible and the real (see Lefebvre, 1991), of the exciting illusion of equality and intercultural reach and the reality of the narrow uniform middle-class 'data-filled bracket' was anchored in the 'nice little screen' which was screening out 'the smell and the sound, and the sight of where you really live'.

I conclude that achieving this *critical-hermeneutic relation* with technology in everyday life is a potential route of emancipation for users. It is a prerequisite for technology to become an instrument of critique of the real with the possible at the level of the everyday life of the ordinary men and women who get drawn into its network. The fluency that some users achieve with this technology, combined with their critical understanding of the amplifications and reductions built into it, allows them to imagine alternative, and yet viable, technical and cultural forms. Their competence puts them in a position to teach and assist newcomers to the Internet world as demonstrated by the phenomenon of the warm expert. This enables them to disseminate their critical understanding of the technology along with their skills in making meaningful use of it.

These observations do *not* lead me to a grand optimistic theory of the Internet as a vehicle of empowerment. All I see in the practices of these users is the germs of a knowledge of the Internet that is 'for us' (Smith, 1987, p. 153), knowledge that helps ordinary users to grasp the social and technological relations organizing the worlds of their everyday experience of the medium and conceive of adequate means of resistance and self-empowerment. The 'critical hermeneutic' relation does not follow automatically on the heels of technical proficiency. It emerges out of hard and broadly informed signifying work towards coming to terms with the new technology. It is more likely to obtain in the case of users with broader life experience, as well as where a user has failed to accomplish a significant personal project due to the medium's limitations. In a mature technological culture, the achievement of a critical hermeneutic relation with the Internet should become a conscious goal in the education of new users. Technical instruction centered on 'how-to' questions marked the early stage of educating the public about the new medium. At present, a much broader spectrum of critical issues and reflections have to be allowed into the agendas of both user education and public deliberation around the Internet. The pressing matter is not to universalize access and skills across social categories as governments and industry may have it, but to stimulate critical reflection on the amplifications and reductions the medium brings about in the context of personal and group lives.

Summary

The observations reported in this chapter invite the question: How does the micro-process of 'becoming a domestic Internet user', and the different human-technology relations that emerge, fit in the big picture of the 'network society' (Castells, 1996, 2001)?[7] I argue that macro-sociological analyses that derive the main principles of the present and future social organization from the structure of computer networks operate with an image of the user as what Garfinkel (1967) called 'the judgemental dope'.

In Garfinkel's definition, this is 'the man-in-the-sociologist's-society who produces the stable features of society by acting in compliance with pre-established and legitimate alternatives of action that the common culture provides' (p. 68). Because the organizing forces of contemporary culture identified in recent accounts are technological, the 'cultural dope' of the network society is also a technological dope – a man or woman-in-the-sociologist's-society who produces the stable features of the social structure by acting in compliance with pre-established and legitimate alternatives provided by the dominant technology.

However, when the social trajectory of Internet technology is traced at the level of the everyday lifeworld, an unsuspected realm of choice, and hence technological indeterminism (see Feenberg, 1993a, Zuboff, 1988 and Chapter 1), opens up. The unconditional acceptance of the medium, envisioned by some commentators, or its blanket rejection, recommended by others, turn out to be crude constructs that do not capture the actual dynamic of user-Internet relations. In practice, a person encountering a socio-technical system such as the Internet faces a richer gamut of choices. Depending on the local situation and its inherent interests and relevances, engagement with the medium can remain instrumental, or it can grow into a more substantive and absorbing relation. These different relations breed different use genres and, respectively, different sets of opportunities and threats for users as individuals, workers, consumers and citizens. I believe that awareness of these choices and their reflexive navigation can contribute to the production of different, humanly chosen, as opposed to technologically determined, 'stable features' of the network society.

Finally, I want to re-assert the legitimacy of the comparison between the process of 'becoming a marijuana user' as depicted by Becker (1953) and the process of 'becoming a domestic Internet user'. The contexts in which the two processes unfold appear to be poles apart. American legislators labelled marijuana use as deviant in the Marijuana Tax Act of 1937 and the Federal Bureau of Narcotics waged a crusade against the use of the drug that was believed to lead to physical and moral degradation (see Becker, 1963). On the contrary, the Internet has been portrayed as the gateway to economic and moral well-being and its use has been strongly encouraged by the economically and politically powerful.[8] Against the backdrop of the hostile accounts of marijuana use proliferating in the 1950s, the goal of Becker's analysis was to challenge the taken-for-granted notion of *deviance* and to expose the complex social process that was packed into it. Similarly, one of the objectives of my argument in this chapter has been to challenge the taken-for-granted notion of user *compliance* with the indomitable techno-logic of the Internet. Deviance and compliance are ultimately a matter of labelling.[9] Therefore, both moral panic and connection enthusiasm, sooner or later, have to give way to the patient work of 'describing the set of changes in the person's conception of the activity and the experience it provides for him' (Becker, 1953, p. 223).[10]

Notes

[1]Recall Schutz's (Schutz and Luckmann, 1973; Schutz, 1970) notion of system of relevances. Intrinsic relevances are 'the outcome of our chosen interests, established by our spontaneous decision to solve a problem by our thinking, to attain a goal by our action, to bring forth a projected state of affairs' (p. 113). Imposed relevances, on the contrary, are the outcomes of our being not only 'centres of spontaneity' but also 'passive recipients of events beyond our control' (p. 113) that occur without our interference. Imposed relevances are not connected with interests chosen by us. Having no power to modify them by our spontaneous activities, we have to take them just as they are (see p. 114 and Chapter 2).

[2]Unfortunately, I did not appreciate the importance of this theme at the time of the interview and did not ask Martha to explain what these metaphors were. I can only speculate that they translated the concepts of the technological system into the categories of the lifewordly stock of knowledge that tutor and student had in common.

[3]I am convinced that many healthy people would recognize in this description their own first steps on the computer and/or the Internet. I feel compelled to express special thanks to my own friend David Smith who patiently held my hand and to Richard Pinet who knew how to draw the cables of my first pathetic home computer.

[4]Another typology of Internet users has been proposed by Miller and Slater (2000). It is based on the socio-economic status of the users they find in four distinctive neighbourhoods in Trinidad and does not address the instrumental versus intimate continuum.

[5]This type of relation does not represent a direction of my exploration in what follows. I have included it here for the sake of completeness.

[6]Amharic is the official language of Ethiopia. It is a Semitic language that employs an alphasyllabary script. (see http://en.wikipedia.org/wiki/Amharic).

[7]See also Wellman, 2001. For a critical version of the sociological analysis of the network society, see Robins and Webster, 1999.

[8]Note, however, the similarity: both 'technologies' are believed to be addictive.

[9]One of my respondents admitted that he had used the Internet to rally for the legalization of marijuana, which, I thought, was an ironic turn in the Internet-marijuana and deviance-compliance analogies developed in this chapter. What from a macro-perspective looks like compliance with the dominant rules of the network society, may comprise deviant practices at the local level.

[10]I wish to acknowledge the very helpful comments on this chapter that I received from the late Rob Kling.

FIVE

Situating the Virtual: Little Behaviour
Genres of the Internet

Introduction

In this chapter I continue the exploration of the social process of becoming a domestic Internet user. Here, I examine in more detail that critical point in it where users discover important, personally meaningful applications of the Internet. I am looking for the emergence of what Becker called a 'stable form of new behaviour toward the object' (Becker, 1953, p. 242; see also Chapter 4) that is responsible for the continuation of use. In constructivist terms this can be seen as the stage of stabilization of the domestic Internet connection as a technology with a clearly defined meaning, even if only at the level of personal experience and for a limited period of time. This relatively stable conception of the Internet as an object of relevance is an expression of the situated rationalization of the medium.[1]

'Situated rationalization' is a concept in which I have blended and somewhat trivialized Feenberg's (1991, 1993a, 1993b) idea of subversive rationalization, Haraway's (1995) concept of situated knowledges and Smith's (1987) notion of standpoint. My study, as pointed out in Chapter 3, follows the method of Smith's 'sociology from the standpoint of women' in locating a subject who is anchored in a material and local world and engaged in his/her projects as a knowledgeable actor. My goal is to grasp the logic and rationality of the applications users find for the Internet from their standpoint in the actualities of their everyday lives (their social-biographical situation). I want to know how and why the Internet becomes drawn into the subjects' systems of relevance and activity. What I am hoping to uncover through this investigation is a repertoire of uses of the Internet that are meaningful to people; applications that help users gain control over characteristic situations in their everyday lives. In such instances, users elaborate locally rational conceptions of the technology and ways of its application that resonate with their plans and interests in their individual situations.

These situated rationalizations would be too microscopic in scale and negligible with respect to the social genesis of the medium if they were isolated, random and infinitely diverse. The account offered in this chapter suggests that this is not the case.

Putting together coherent narratives about their experience with the Internet, my respondents felt compelled to provide a rational explanation of why they valued their Internet connection. In order to do that, they had to explicate aspects of their situations with respect to which their actions on and through the Internet made sense. Typical expressions of this rhetorical move were 'because' clauses immediately following the statement of their discovery of a personally attractive function of the medium. A survey of these 'because' motives reveals a set of recurring situational characteristics that made the Internet needed, useful and significant to users:

- social isolation brought about by circumstances such as illness, dysfunctional marriage, single parenthood, retirement, unemployment;
- relocation or recurrent change of location;
- globally spread family and social networks;
- uncertainty or dissatisfaction with current job;
- sense of belonging to a dispersed community of interest, quite often – a community of suffering (such as rare diseases and adverse circumstances).

These situations with their sets of relevances, I suggest, offer glimpses into the human condition in a globalizing post-Fordist capitalist society. Facing characteristic problems in their social-biographical situations, users discover affordances in Internet technology that promise help in their struggle for regaining control over their lives. These are, then, the properties of the technology that users actualize on a systematic basis in the course of their everyday lives. By doing this they generate new practices anchored in that technology. These 'little behaviour genres of the Internet', as I would like to refer to them invoking Voloshinov's (1929/ 1986) theory of language, represent an important force in the dynamics of the generative process of technology.

Isolation

Maybe the most graphic crisis situation breeding loneliness and desperation was that of Ellen. About three years before our meeting, the 49-year-old editor and freelance writer had fallen ill with a rare, poorly understood and 'devastating' condition which had had a debilitating effect on her social and intellectual functioning and had made her housebound. On certain days Ellen, who is divorced, has no children and no close relatives in town, couldn't walk to the store to buy food, and often couldn't even go downstairs to check her mail for weeks. Most of her friends were puzzled and frightened by the change in her personality and practically abandoned her.

Against this backdrop, two years before our conversation, one of her few remaining friends came to visit her and said: 'I'm going to set you up on the Internet, and I'm going to show you how to use it'. Ellen had known about the Internet before she got ill and even used to belong to a professional editors' list to which she connected from work. But the specific function to which her friend was introducing her now was 'in order for me to be able to connect to a support group'. Since then, the Internet had become a 'lifeline' for Ellen:

> and what I found was that it became a lifeline for me, literally a lifeline, *because* [emphasis mine] I was in complete despair, really in a very desperate situation and terribly isolated, feeling very lonely because nobody around including my doctor actually understood what I was going through and how much I was suffering from the illness ... . (Ellen)

In another story, Sandy, a 35-year-old telemarketer, was first introduced to the Internet through a university course she was taking about a year and a half before the interview. She worked part-time and had a young daughter, so she found going to campus to use the computer lab too demanding and was planning to drop that course. Her professor advised her that she could actually connect to the Internet and do her research from home. He even put her in touch with a student knowledgeable about computers who came to her house and set up her connection. Very soon Sandy discovered the chat lines and started regularly visiting a room where she could find Macintosh help: 'the people in there would help you with all the technology stuff'. Sandy diligently worked through the different chat programs and channels until she found her way to a chat place called talkcity.com. There she actually discovered how the Internet was relevant to her life:

> I went into this room about parenting. *Because* [emphasis mine] I lived in such isolation, because my husband didn't allow me to have any friends or anything, I discovered this whole area. He thought I was writing essays for university and I have a ripping good time [laughs triumphantly] meeting people in there and having a great time talking to them. Just meeting

people because I wasn't ever allowed to do that. In my relationship with him he was very controlling and isolating. I lived with a lot of fears. And now I could just lie to him about what I was doing and meet people. (Sandy)

Isolation and discovery were the two key words dominating Sandy's account of her early Internet experience. While Ellen's isolation was caused by a physical illness, Sandy's confinement was produced by an abusive marriage. Less intentionally than Ellen, initially following the externally imposed requirements of her university course, Sandy acquired the tools and the skills to explore and re-define the educational medium promoted by her university. She found a medium that supplied her with the social support and self-esteem, so sorely missing in her original situation. This precipitated the end of Sandy's marriage – her online friends 'held her hand' throughout the painful experience of leaving her husband – and the beginning of her struggle to resume control over her own life: 'I think because I lived in such isolation and then all of a sudden I was reminded that I was a real person [speaks emotionally], with real emotions, and real feelings and I was likable by people. Because I was no longer isolated' (Sandy).

Isolation, albeit of a different form and origin, came up again as an element of Sandy's new situation following her divorce, which reinforced the relevance of the Internet. This time it had to do with her daily life as a single mother cautiously balancing her limited financial means:

Because [emphasis mine] once I get my daughter to bed at night, being a single mom now, I don't have a lot of social network availability because I don't have a lot of money – I am trying to pay for my bills here and this last year has cost me a lot of money, I have debts to pay. I can't pay a babysitter so that I could go out and do something. So, quite often I log onto the computer and read at web sites … . (Sandy)

In the case of John, a 73-year-old retired mechanical engineer, the Internet acquired relevance in the wake of the transition between employment and retirement. Despite the fact that this transition is considered a natural moment of one's social biography, it brings about isolation and loneliness nevertheless. Struggling to cope with the change, John returned to his youth's hobby – radio-controlled motor gliders. Later, the Internet, mainly in its e-mail function, was recommended to him by a friend as a means for staying in touch with his children – his daughter and her family lived in another province – and with his newly developed hobbyist network. Asked whether the Internet had changed his pattern of daily life, John explained that what had happened was more complicated:

Because [emphasis mine] my life changed because of being retired. This filled something which I missed when I retired and that was daily interaction with people, the people at work, travelling to work in the car pool. ... I find this [the Internet] helps to have this connection with people through the Internet – people on the mailing list and my friends, or unknown helpers, the general activity on the Internet helps to fill a void that I felt when I first retired. (John)

The capacity of the Internet to connect users with other people and to allow them to form new relationships from within their situation of being 'housebound' – physically, socially or financially – had been the affordance discerned by these three respondents. A similar element of limited physical and social mobility could be detected in the situation of other users who did not explicitly describe themselves as housebound. Jane, a suburban homemaker, was quite well integrated in her local community. However, she had to spend her days doing her domestic routine, practically alone, because most of the people she knew were at work and thus unavailable during the hours of the day when she had 'the time to think about contacting them' (Jane). E-mail with its non-intrusiveness and flexibility was a good tool for Jane to perform her part of the communication with people while her children and husband were out of the house and she had her own time. Her addressees could then respond at their own convenience, most likely during the hours of the evening when Jane had to attend to her family's needs and was unavailable to take phone calls.

Merlin, an unemployed 58-year-old mechanical engineer had suffered a major disruption of his established pattern of existence, or in Schutzian terms, his taken-for-granted lifeworld, when he was laid off from his job in Montreal after twenty years with the company. Merlin had been unemployed for six years at the time I visited him. His precarious financial situation had forced him to sell his house in Quebec and move to Vancouver where he and his wife could live in the house of his in-laws for several months a year, and rent a small apartment for the rest of the time. Although Merlin tried to stay active in the local Association of Professional Engineers, his daily access to a professional community was essentially cut off. After having worked as an engineer for more than twenty years, this had obviously been a heavy blow for Merlin. His job and the professional interaction it involved had been an important part of who he was as a person. The Internet had helped Merlin try to overcome this enforced isolation from his professional peers by joining a discussion list dealing with electrical vehicles. His original motivation was to educate himself, to expand his understanding of the area. However, the Electric Vehicle discussion list also gave him symbolic access to a 'semi-professional community, you don't need to have credentials to get in it', a pretty 'grown-up group of people' as he described it, sharing knowledge and experience. Merlin used to download and read the digest of the discussion list every day and felt an old-timer in it, although he admitted that he did not contribute very often. He had even visited the homes and shops of four list members when on a trip to California.

Merlin evaded explicit reflection about what the belonging to this community meant to him socially and emotionally. Instead, he spoke about expertise in handling technical problems, sharing stories of who built what vehicle, meeting some of the guys from the list at exhibitions. A sense of the importance of his Internet involvements in the context of his situation was conveyed in a remark made by his wife.[2] When I asked her whether she approved of his everyday, almost full-time preoccupation with his computer and the Internet, she said simply: 'It's saved his sanity since he's lost his job. So, that's fine with me'.

In his *Television: technology and cultural form* (1974), Williams draws attention to the condition of 'mobile privatization' characterizing everyday life in an earlier phase of industrial capitalist society and sees the technology of broadcasting as a resolution, at a certain level, of the contradictory pressures generated by this condition:

> This complex of developments included the motorcycle and motorcar, the box camera and its successors, home electrical appliances, and radio sets. Socially, this complex is characterized by the two apparently paradoxical yet deeply connected tendencies of modern urban industrial living: on the one hand mobility, on the other hand the more apparently self-sufficient family home. The earlier period of public technology, best exemplified by the railways and city lighting, was replaced by a kind of technology for which no satisfactory name has yet been found; that which served an at once mobile and home centered way of living: a form of *mobile privatization* [italics in original]. Broadcasting in its applied form was a social product of this distinctive tendency. (1974, p. 20)

The lives of the socially isolated people I talked to did not seem to match this description. First of all, these people were not sufficiently mobile – their automobiles could not take them to places socially denied to them. Second, they felt ambiguous about the self-sufficiency of the private homes in which their existence was circumscribed. Thus, they were not withdrawing into their homes to find comfort. They felt trapped in their homes and were ready and eager, each one to a different extent and different degree of rationalization, to trade the privateness of their existence for human contact, community and broader social involvement. Their Internet-based practices could be characterized as constituting an attempt at 'immobile socialization'. Users employed the medium for associating with other people and social entities without leaving, which represented a resolution, at a certain level, of the pressures present in their original situations. That was not necessarily the safe and inconsequential socializing at which critiques of computer-mediated communication have been levelled (Borgmann, 1992; Kumar, 1995; Postman, 1992; Slouka, 1995). Neither was it the absorbing fascination with virtual life discussed in the early 'cyberspace' literature (see Slater, 2002). In many cases, for example with Merlin and Sandy, there was a desire to extend relationships established online by face-to-face contacts. With John, the distinction between 'virtual' and 'real' links was less marked. He had been able to shuttle between involvement in actual events with his fellow-hobbyists and the electronic communication that sustained their organization.

In general, users encountering the Internet from within a situation of social isolation were quick to discover the socializing affordances embodied in the medium. These people defined and employed the Internet as a social technology, as a solution to the problem of loneliness, helplessness and the resulting loss of self-esteem. Typically commanding limited resources and deprived of mobility in the physical as well as the social sense, these users found in the Internet a handy and affordable means for transcending the limitations of their social-biographical situation. Sometimes, as in Sandy's case, the Internet had been instrumental in transforming this situation substantially. It should be noted however that most of the time the Internet-related practices had helped users to cope with problems, not to eradicate or radically solve them. Merlin remained unemployed despite the hundreds of job applications he had e-mailed. Sandy continued to be deprived of the vigorous social life she craved because of lack of resources.

At the same time, users' being 'out there', in cyberspace, the actions through which they geared into the virtual world – chatting, joking, sharing, helping and being helped, or in Sandy's playful formulation 'rescuing' and being rescued – constructed the medium of the Internet by giving it particular properties that others would later (or simultaneously) 'discover' or learn about and that would be deposited in the social stock of knowledge about this technology.

Relocation

Alex, a 36-year-old jewellry designer, and his family (wife and son) had left their East European country in the wake of the fall of the Berlin Wall. They had lived as refugees in London for four years before emigrating to

Canada in 1996. For Alex and his wife, cyberspace had provided vital information about the economic and social landscape of the new place they were settling into and, most importantly, about the job market. Alex had explored the Canadian jewellry-making business through online indexes at the time he and his family were making a decision to move. Later, he drew on that information to find himself a job in Vancouver. Then it was his wife's turn to apply the strategies he had developed in finding employment as a proposal specialist. It had worked for both of them. The new social territory seemed to have been more easily penetrable because of the availability of its charts in cyberspace.

The existing World Wide Web sites of newspapers from their native Bulgaria and of international news agencies allowed Alex and his wife to stay in touch with the 'imagined community' (Anderson, 1983) of their small nation, even in the total absence of any mention of it in the mainstream news media of their new home country. The same practice of putting together a geographically and culturally fragmented identity could be observed in the case of Radul, a 36-year-old auto body technician, originally from Romania. He and his elderly father, also an immigrant to Vancouver, would regularly sit together in Radul's basement to read newspapers and listen to radio stations from their native town.

This practice was common in the cases of other immigrants in my respondent group (eight from Europe, three from the United States, two from Africa). One notable example of this phenomenon came from a respondent who was using the information about his native Ethiopia found on the Internet to produce a co-op radio programme for the Ethiopian community in Vancouver. Theodore, a 45-year-old parking patroller with a bachelor's degree in political science had been active in the founding of the Ethiopian National Congress, an organization meant to represent a united front of Ethiopians in exile 'attempting to galvanize the opposition groups that are in Ethiopia'. In the following excerpt, Theodore describes how this political organization emerged out of the everyday life of Ethiopians in North America, sitting just like himself at the screens of their home computers:

> It was out of the EEDN – the Ethiopian Electronic Distribution Network. This professor in Ohio was pushing for the establishment of the Ethiopian United Front. Individuals on the list started talking about this thing and said we should do something about it and so it started as a virtual organization and it transformed itself … . There was a meeting in Los Angeles – the initial meeting for individuals to get together and discuss this thing and then there was another meeting in October 1997 where the actual organization was proclaimed and established in Atlanta. (Theodore)

For Theodore and the rest of the immigrants in my respondent group the Internet was a cultural and political technology providing them with the means for preserving an important side of their identities. They could stay informed and, when they chose to do so, be politically active Bulgarians, Romanians, Ethiopians, etc. while living in a different geographical location. In their everyday lifeworlds, their original states and cultures remained within 'attainable' and 'restorable reach' (see Schutz and Luckmann, 1973 and Chapter 2). Despite the novelty of the technology, one could recognize in this practice a repetition of the history of old communication technologies creatively employed by individuals and pockets of immigrants to sustain ethnic and cultural identities at a distance from their countries of origin. Early-20th-century immigrants to North America, as Cohen (1990) has shown, did that with the help of phonograph and radio. Punjabi young people living in England in the 1990s incorporated a combination of communication media such as television, videos and radio in the negotiation of their ethnic and immigrant identities (see Gillespie, 1995). The use of the Internet with regard to ethnic and national identity not only repeated, but also expanded the earlier practices based on other technologies in terms of reach and possibility for action.

It was interesting to contrast the experience of immigration in the age of the Internet with that of earlier generations of immigrants as exemplified by the 62-year-old Reiner, a retired mechanical engineering technician of German origin. Reiner's account presents a vivid illustration of the situated rationalization of the technology. Explaining how and why he began to use the Internet, Reiner recalled:

So curiosity was at the beginning, but then I realized – hey, there is something really good happening! And as you probably realize, I am not an original Canadian, just like you are. I am from Germany. And at the beginning when I first came here I was more of a Canadian than any Canadian probably. I said I am here now in Canada, forget about the past. And only later I realized, hey, there is something missing. I was 28 when I came over. My background, my history is in Germany, my schooling is German. My wife is Canadian so we didn't speak German at home. I almost lost my German. It was so bad. When my mother was on the phone, I couldn't respond to her in German. So, I suddenly woke up and said: there is something wrong ... So, I realized – this World Wide Web, it is not just English, it is German, it's Russian, Chinese. And suddenly I realize, hey, *I am connected again to Germany! Really, I am connected!* I can read German newspapers. I lived in Germany in Ausburg and I can read now (I just found it a couple of weeks ago) *Der Ausburger General (Algemeine)* with the local news of Friedburg which is the town where I more or less grew up. *So, I am at home again*! And I am reading another paper from Koblenz, where I went to engineering school and I lived there for four years, so I am still interested. So this is the biggest thing that the Internet did for me! (Reiner)

There is an irony in this story. The most postmodern of technologies is contributing to the persistence of typically modern sentiments and practices like these related to nationalism as a collective identity (see Anderson, 1983). Thus identity in the age of the Internet seems to be constructed through the computer screen as Turkle (1995) has pointed out, but this is occurring in ways quite different from those on which she has focused her account. My study found not electronic play lands such as MUDs, but rather cyber-projections of long-established social institutions formative to the personae of my respondents. The materials, the languages, generally, the resources on which people drew to construct identity both online and offline did not appear to be as free-floating and randomly accessible as postmodern theorists (Turkle, 1995, Stone, 1995) may have it. They remained socially and biographically rooted and as unequally distributed as ever before.

Upon further reflection, a question arises about whether the very existence of cyberspace projections of 'real' institutions is making the constructed character of these institutions themselves more easily recognizable and negotiable. Latour has argued that in fact 'virtuality ... is a materialization of society and not a disembodiment of society' (1998, paragraph 5). The digital images of social institutions, Latour maintains, have provided us with a more material way of looking at what happens in society. They have made our social links visible in a much more simple and archaic way than before. Virtuality allows us to see the 'building blocks of social order being re-invented anew' (1998, paragraph 8). Perhaps this is the same insight that inspired Zuboff to write about information technology in the production process: 'the same technology simultaneously generates information about underlying productive and administrative processes through which an organization accomplishes its work. It provides *a deeper level of transparency* to activities that had been either partially or completely opaque' ([my italics] 1988, p. 9). This observation led Zuboff to believe that information technology could 'informate' (p. 10) the human actors and open a new level of reflexivity to them.

Whether a new relationship between citizens and institutions was emerging based on this increased transparency of social process is a question that certainly applies to the experience of immigrants and Canadians alike. An impulse to talk back to the online representations of political and media institutions was clearly discernible in my respondents' stories. Theodore talked back critically to a mailing list distributed by the Ethiopian government (and lost his access to it as a result). Garry, a

67-year-old retired naval radio-operator, had turned the practice of talking back to mass media and governmental sites into his main activity on the Internet:

> I was never writing letters like that before. Because e-mail has made it so easy to send a letter. I have often had thoughts about what had been said on the radio before. But now it is so easy for me to send a message that I just send it. I sometimes smoke dope and I don't think dope should be illegal. I have sent letters on e-mail through the Internet on that subject. I would never send that before, but now it's *so easy*! I have written to my MP, I got their addresses through the Internet, the minister of health, the minister of justice. (Garry)

Sophie, a 35-year-old nutrition consultant, talked passionately about a health policy issue that she followed from a co-op radio show onto a web site suggested during the talk, and was finally left wondering how she could express her own feelings through the Internet:

> and I was reading, and reading, and I thought 'this is awful!'. Because who wants to read about this, who wants to know about this, because what can we do? ... Other than leave what you are doing now and go and [searching for a word] protest or whatever ... It takes a heck of a lot ... It is interesting, may be through the Internet, you can protest, people can protest, and that would be easier, because it's a link to everywhere, right? And that's what they are trying to do with these web sites. (Sophie)

The 'it's so easy' sensation should not lead us, as analysts, to underestimate the significance of the impulse to talk back. We should consider whether 'easy' is actually a code word for something else. People do not talk back simply because 'it's easy', but because they have always had things to say to the world of policy and mass media. These institutions have been experienced as a separate sphere of practice to which ordinary people have had no access in terms of their everyday action. They have not been able to afford to 'leave what you are doing now and go' as Sophie put it. The handiness of the Internet access to these institutions – from amid everyday life – now generates the feeling that they are within 'attainable reach', that people, as citizens, can actually perform action onto them, that they are part of the subjective everyday lifeworld and not a detached 'province of reality'. Thus 'easy' may actually mean 'it is now possible for me to act politically from where I stand'. As much as this can be a naïve illusion, it is a very important pointer to 'the possible' in Lefebvre's (1991) terms, the possible application of the network toward the empowerment of citizens who otherwise cannot leave their daily affairs to take part in politics. The fact that this possibility remains a matter of rhetoric and largely unaddressed in practical terms represents a powerful critique of the 'real' Internet development.

Some of my respondents, just like many academic analysts, were less than hopeful with respect to the touted citizen access to institutions of power via the Internet. Institutions, they thought, would pay no heed to e-mail comments from ordinary men and women talking back to them on daily basis. Institutions are modelling their Internet-based communication with the public on the time-tested practice of public relations. They *present* themselves through their web sites and tend to limit the use of the interactive features of the new medium to delivering individualized information in response to searches performed by clients. At the same time, citizens seem to want their voices heard and taken into account now through the new functionalities of the Internet. This suggests that there is indeed a democratic potential in the Internet – its capacity to galvanize response and to conduct it back to previously one-way transmitters of powerful discourse. However, in order for that potential to start materializing, innovative social and political interfaces between citizens and political institutions should be imagined and implemented to match the technical interface already in place.

Globally Spread Family and Social Networks

When I first moved to the States I was completely lost. I was in the middle of nowhere, in the middle of the cornfields. I knew nobody. I had nobody around. I desperately needed human contact. You go there [to the university], your professor tells you to start studying this and that, to read this and that, but everything else is just dead. (Myra)

The speaker of these words was a 28-year-old Albanian woman who had moved to the United States to pursue an academic degree. The void Myra was describing was not the same as the situations of isolation discussed earlier. Myra was a member of the nomadic tribe of relatively young and educated people of different national backgrounds who venture across state and cultural borders in their pursuit of a variety of personal goals. Yet at the level of everyday life, Myra and others like her still have a need 'for human contact' in their here and now. Cultivating such contact usually takes time, sometimes longer than the nomads actually spend in the same place. Note the life style Myra sketches below and its 'natural' match with the ubiquity of the Internet:

I was lucky in some sense because most of my friends from the time I studied and worked are now scattered around the world – doing PhDs and post-doctorates here and there. As grad students or post-docs they all have *the access,* so we keep in touch that way. Well, I have made a few friends on the Internet too. [Where are your old friends?] Sheffield, England, several in France, several in Italy, several in Germany, in Russia, in Bulgaria, Japan, of course, the States. They are not only Albanians. I tend not to make a difference. I have been here and there in Europe usually for three to six-month exchange, working at a university you get those ... . I made friends here and there, basically all over the world. (Myra)

Like Myra, throughout their wandering, Alex and family had been leaving behind a scattered social network that could only be experienced as restorable and maintainable through e-mail and online chat – parents in Bulgaria, cousins in Spain, friends in London, the USA and throughout Canada.

The wish to stay in touch with one's globally dispersed extended family is a major impetus behind the adoption of the Internet in the home. Thanks to the channel opened by e-mail, loved ones seem to be within restorable reach. As research on the telephone (Moyal, 1992; Rakow, 1992) has suggested, women are the main beneficiaries of this new possibility because it is their job to maintain the family networks. Men in Internet households, however, especially when they were the main users, as was the case with in my study Reiner, John, Don and Merlin, seemed to be getting more involved in this practice too. The question of what the communication within these electronically sustained family and broader social networks means to participants is worth an extended discussion. I will limit myself to putting forward an observation regarding the experience of electronic writing. Both men and women in my respondent group expressed in different ways a feeling of a dual liberation of their communication with close friends and relatives – from the cultural authority of the epistolary genre and the intrusiveness of the phone ring.

[How do you communicate with your sister in Toronto?] Well, since we have the Internet I prefer the Internet, it's easier, quicker, I can just sit down and write. I have noticed that my writing is often very messy which it wouldn't be in a letter. It's interesting, because as you are typing along, thinking and typing, and then you tend not to proofread too much here before you send it off. And it works like you just sort of, okay, next thing, right? But I don't mind writing letters, but once I got the Internet, I prefer to use it. It is more like talking on the telephone, whereas writing down with pen and paper is more formal somehow, really from learning this in school, whatever, you are very strict how to write ... . I don't know, maybe this is where it comes from, but I see it as more important being correct in one's grammar. But on the Internet it is more easy-going ... I won't think twice before writing her something and just sending it off. (Sophie)

My brother gave me the machine, and it has vastly improved my communication with my brother. He lives in south Vancouver. I never would think about phoning him if I hear a joke at the swimming pool. And he would do the same for me. And we would have never done that before, never. We exchange little things, really not very important but it makes it much more exciting when I meet him in person. I have something to discuss with him and so go on from there ... Or, you are walking home after seeing [friend's name] at the pool and I think, oh, I've got to tell him about this and I go on e-mail. (Garry)

And I talk more to my brothers now. If I have a question – like this one line question – I probably wouldn't write to them. I might phone them but the chance to get them at home is very unlikely because they are never at home, and then the time difference – they are three hours ahead ... . That way I can just e-mail them and they can answer it whenever they want and it doesn't cost them anything. It is easy. (Jane)

Jane went further to construct a shared world with her distant friends and relatives by looking at their local newspapers on the web: 'it is kind of fun to see their headlines'. Sandy did the same for her friend's local weather. Along with the transcendence of distance, the second notable functionality, resonating with users' needs, was the element of time management. People in contemporary society are not separated only by space, but also by conflicting schedules. E-mail provides more room for negotiation between 'subjective time' and 'social time' (see Schutz and Luckmann, 1973, p. 47 and Chapter 2). It produces moments of imagined intersubjective time out of temporally separated but mutually oriented (textual) actions.

There was a whole range of conflicting evaluations expressed by my respondents as far as the norms of appropriateness and the overall value of this electronic social networking was concerned. Different ideologies and sensitivities become invested into these debates that sound similar to earlier negotiations and struggles around the definitions of other new technologies of communication, for example the telephone. Is online chatting enriching or degrading; is sending multiple-recipient messages with jokes and other 'cute junk' as one respondent called it, a reassuring form of phatic communication, or is it a de-personalized and superficial pseudo-contact? Considering, debating and settling such issues in their online relationships with others, users contribute to the public understanding of the Internet.

Uncertainty or Dissatisfaction with Current Job

Job uncertainty and dissatisfaction were other recurring aspects of respondents' social-biographical situations that motivated their Internet use. Having a job that is 'boring and it takes absolutely zero intellectual capabilities' (Sandy), being 'boxed in' (Theodore) in a job situation where the kind of the work was not gratifying but the pay was good, feeling 'in limbo' (Martha) due to a work-related injury and the unpredictability of insurance coverage and employment future, having been unemployed for an extended period of time (Merlin) – these were characteristic conditions that led people to look to the Internet for intellectual challenge, self-realization, shortcuts to employment information and potential business opportunities.

Sandy, who was an object of pervasive performance monitoring by a computer all through her working day, was responding by learning and mastering the technology of the Internet so that it would serve her to arrange and feel in control of her personal world outside her telemarketing pod. Theodore was drawing on Internet sources to create his co-op radio show. His programme was 'as close as it comes' to his field of study – political science – a field in which he never had the chance to work professionally because of his unresolved immigration status at the time he graduated.

Martha, who had injured her shoulder working as a meat-wrapper at Safeway had developed a passion and skills for Internet 'research' and was starting to envision for herself a future as a researcher and Internet site developer. Sophie had voluntarily made it part of her job as a consultant at a nutrition supplement store to search the Web for specific information on herbs in order to better help her customers. She and her husband were thinking of opening their own herbal store with an Internet connection where they could 'educate' people along with selling them products. Even Don, who was otherwise making a conscious effort to remain cool and critical in the face of the common fascination with the Internet, was keeping his connection alive for the purpose of job searching. Thus job searching and 'research' were emerging as two central applications meaningful to my respondents that justified their continuing Internet use.

The notion of 'research' is particularly interesting as it points to a potentially important change in the way everyday life activities are performed. Routine ways of doing things and the application of unquestioned common sense knowledge have been considered among the main determinants of the everyday lifeworld (Schutz and Luckmann, 1973). In contrast, equipped with their Internet connections, the people I interviewed seemed to approach their everyday life activities with a heightened awareness of the diverse choices and possibilities available. They were taking a questioning and reflective stance towards their environment and seeking to elaborate rational strategies for dealing with it. They were using the Internet to be intellectually creative, especially when such a chance was denied them at their jobs. They were opening up new areas of meaningful activity and production, in Lefebvre (1971) extended definition, in their everyday lives: Theodore's radio show, Martha's Attention Deficit Disorder support group site (see p. 133), Sophie's customer education or Merlin's Electric Vehicle mailing list, leaning on the Internet.

The interest in 'doing research' was most clearly expressed in the field of health and pharmacy. People were drawing on both medical school sites and newsgroups discussions in their effort to understand and manage their health problems. Research was performed on places to travel to, on apple trees to be planted in one's garden, on forage to feed to one's cows, on historical events drawn into current media discourse, on musical releases, on locating long-lost members of one's family, on equipment and other items to be bought. All these heterogeneous interests and actions can be subsumed under one trend – the effort to make informed and thus 'rational' choices about matters of daily action, including consumption:

> Another aspect I like – when I want to buy something – whatever it is, be it shoes or books, I can actually get more information about products from the Internet than I can receive from sellers, or a clerk in a store. I think I probably get more factual information because it has been presented to you in a written fashion. It is different when someone puts it on paper and when someone gives it to you verbally. You never know whether this person actually knows anything. So, that I find very helpful – knowledge about anything I would like to purchase ... information is very good for me. I can compare different offers on the Internet and I find I am going to the store much better prepared and I know much more even than the clerk. (Reiner)

> For example, last week I needed a fax, I looked here [on the Internet] what faxes there are on the market .... Instead of asking technical information from the store and the salesmen, who know nothing about that, I went directly to the web site, looked up all things that I needed, downloaded them and chose exactly this fax, which helped me a lot because it saved me a lot of time searching the stores. It also saved me some money because I didn't decide to buy a more expensive fax given that this one would serve me just as well to do the same job. (Alex)

Compare these efforts at 'situated rationalization' to the rationality behind the massive movement toward turning the Internet into a gigantic electronic mall, advertising machine and a hunting ground for customer data. The contrast between the 'real' and the 'possible' can hardly be more glaring.

Sense of Belonging to a Dispersed Community of Interest

Three distinct manifestations of this condition could be found in the situations of Ellen, Garry and Martha. Meeting other people with the same syndrome online, Ellen could 'put her situation in perspective' and start learning what to expect and how to deal with the most difficult moments from others who had already been there. That is, she entered a process of enculturation in her disease. At a later stage of her involvement, Ellen was among the initiators of a sub-list, a group of people who went on searching for alternative treatments including herbal, traditional and spiritual elements. In fact, one such treatment the group had been able to find consisted in their mutual emotional support. Futhermore, Ellen's online relationships and the self-understanding she acquired through them gave her the strength to start working on the reconstruction of her local friendships. Now she could reach out to people and tell them that despite the illness, 'I am the same friend you once had'.[3]

For Martha, the rationalization and subsequent stabilization of her domestic Internet use happened in relation to a problem her son had as a child – his Attention Deficit Disorder. Initially, Martha joined a chat room on this topic at CompuServe. Later, when her Internet 'research' skills improved, she went on collecting information on the topic and putting it together for the purposes of the local parent support group she had helped organize. Martha's online and offline activities helpfully complemented each other. She ended up becoming the web master of her local parent support group. She created a web site about attention deficit disorder featuring informative material found on the Web and publicizing local activities. Since the site was put up on the Vancouver Community Net server, Martha had regularly been receiving mail from parents in the area looking for information about the disorder and interested in joining the local support group.

This weaving of the local and the global, the 'virtual' and the 'real' through involvement in groups of common interest both online and face-to-face could also be observed in the case of Garry, who drew on discussions in the arthritis newsgroup to advise people with the illness as a volunteer for the local Arthritis Association telephone line. Jane was searching Internet sources for ideas to implement in her arts and crafts group at the local church. On one occasion she searched the Internet to help a friend with information about support groups for male victims of sexual abuse. Theodore's radio programme was influential in the life of the local Ethiopian community.

Summary: Little Behaviour Genres of the Internet

In conclusion, I would like to go back to the perspective on the generative process of language proposed by Voloshinov (1929/1986) in his *Marxism and the philosophy of language*. The special value of Volshinov's theory, as I argued in Chapter 1, lies in his dialectical conception of language as a system that determines what speakers can and cannot say, but that is also susceptible to transformations originating from the social process of speaking. Brought to bear on technology, or more precisely on what I have called the generative process of technology, this perspective allows us to see the Internet simultaneously as a system that determines what users can and cannot do by virtue of given design, but that is also susceptible to change in the process of use. For Voloshinov, the everyday speech acts that spur the evolution of the linguistic system grow from little behaviour genres arising in typical situations. These situations, for their part, are shaped by the larger process of material social reproduction.

Building freely on Voloshinov's (1929/1986) linguistic insights, it can be argued that users are indeed an active force in the generative process of technology but not in any random or voluntaristic way. Typical social-biographical situations in which subjects find themselves give rise to specific little behaviour genres including genres of technology use. Under certain conditions, such genres can induce changes in the technology itself.

In this study, I have been able to identify a number of 'use genres' invented by everyday users of the Internet: participation in online support groups; holding together a fragmented national and cultural identity; sustaining globally spread social and family networks; political organizing from amid everyday life; talking back to institutions of power; reflexive (rational) conduct of everyday activities; connecting local and global interest groups, and others. Most of these ways of using the Internet have been widely known and discussed in the Internet literature of the last ten years. My aim in this chapter has been to present them as *use genres* linked to typical social-biographical situations characteristic of contemporary society and culture. I have proposed a perspective on these genres that construes them as a product of users' situated rationalizations of the new technology. I have also attempted to explain how – in these particular use genres – the technology of the Internet has been bent to empower 'boxed in' ordinary people to transcend certain limitations of their situations and to open up spaces for meaningful individual and collective action and creativity. I contend that by these creative engagements with the Internet, ordinary users have performed important signifying work that has expanded the public understanding of this medium.

A logical question to be asked in the face of such an observation is whether the empowering potentialities discovered by ordinary users find an adequate consideration in the political and economic processes shaping the Internet. For this to happen, the little behaviour genres enacted by everyday users have to converge and stabilize as Internet content and communication genres supported by the technical and institutional struc-ture of the medium. These structures have to ensure spaces and accessi-ble resources for doing the things that ordinary users find meaningful and empowering as, for example, the case of the local parent support group using the server of the Vancouver Community Net as well as the mailing lists for associating with people with similar health problems or beliefs.[4] As Lefebvre (1991) has observed in his *Critique of everyday life*, the rift between the 'possible' and the 'real' can remain wide open, espe-cially if the empowering potentialities discovered by users resist trans-formation into profitable business models for the industries operating the Internet. After all, from capital's point of view 'the important thing is that human beings be profitable, not that their lives be changed' (Lefebvre, 1991, p. 230).

Recognizing the structural realities of the world in which we live, however, should not prevent us from identifying 'the possible' as it emerges out of the everyday efforts of ordinary users to find meaningful applications of the Internet. This locally produced knowledge of the medium can represent a resource for the development of the type of critique that Lefebvre called for – 'the critique of the real by the possible' (1991, p. 9). A democratic counter-project for the shaping of the Internet as a communication medium can only be conceived on the basis of a careful study and emphatic understanding of the situated rationality embodied in what the ordinary users of today are trying to do with it. In the absence of such a project, users will be forced to surrender to the totalizing stabilization of the consumption possibilities (e-commerce, Web TV) foisted on them by the dominant economic and political rationality.

Later in my analysis I will attempt to derive suggestions for civic action and public policy from the set of mundane, user-initiated use genres I have identified in this chapter. Before I do that, I will examine another form in which the pragmatic relevance of the medium to users' lives is established. By choosing an appropriate location for the networked computer in their homes, users determine the domestic rules, roles and rights with respect to it. Placement discourages and reinforces particular patterns and genres of use within the 'moral economy' of the household (Silverstone et al., 1992, p. 17).

Notes

[1]Typically, worked out with the help and collaboration of other people such as the 'warm experts' introduced in Chapter 4.

[2]I have chosen not to give pseudonyms to the respondents' spouses whom I have interviewed for two reasons. First, I would like to avoid the overloading of the text with names and second, I want to keep clear the relationship between the main respondent and the spouse. I refer to male spouses as 'husband' and female spouses as 'wife', in most cases following respondents' own example. There were no homosexual couples in the group of people I interviewed.

[3]I feel compelled to dampen the optimistic overtones of this comment in light of what Ellen shared with me two years after the interview. Despite the hopes for revival of her local friendships inspired by her participation in the online group, most of her social relationships in Vancouver had floundered and faded away.

[4]Matthew, one of my respondents who acted as moderator of an amputee mailing list, started his list at a time when he could use the equipment of a local organization. He had an interesting saga to tell about what happened after that organization withdrew its resources. Matthew's list was saved by its own participants who raised money for him to buy a computer. This didn't quite solve the recurrent problems Matthew ran into struggling to cover the expenses of the list's busy electronic communications.

SIX Making Room for the Internet

Introduction

The title of this chapter plays on Lynn Spigel's (1992) book *Make room for TV: television and the family ideal in postwar America*. In her study, Spigel set herself the task to explain how, over the course of a single decade, television became part of daily routines and how people experienced the arrival of television in their homes. In order to be able to recover this lost history, Spigel turned to popular women's magazines from the postwar period and found them saturated with representations of the new technology of television and the new practice of viewing in the home setting. Popular magazines expressed a 'set of cultural anxieties' surrounding television and engaged the public in a dialogue concerning television's place in the home' (1992, p. 2). Thus they contributed to the shaping of the way in which the new medium operated within the culture: 'Television spurred a host of debates in popular media and what was said about the medium in turn affected television's ultimate cultural form' (Spigel, 1992, p. 4).

Engaging in this project, Spigel wished to complement the 'industrial' history of television that concentrated mainly on invention, production and regulation with a social and cultural history of the medium. In this 'other' history, Spigel maintains, the role of women is central. Contrary to their marginal position in 'industrial' history, women were main players in the integration of television into domestic life. Looking at popular magazines allowed this kind of television history to be written as magazines 'gave women the opportunities to negotiate rules and practices for watching television at home. They addressed female readers not simply as passive consumers of promotional rhetoric, but also as producers within the household' (Spigel, 1992, p. 5).

Following Spigel's (1992) example, in this chapter I make an effort to uncover the contribution of consumers to the shaping of the Internet as a communication medium by looking at the immediate domestic context in which it becomes incorporated. 'Making room' in this sense refers to integrating the new medium into the space, time, activities and relationships of the home. Unlike the case of television in Spigel's study, the appropriation of the Internet is not past history. It is possible for a researcher to observe this process as it unfolds in the present, in the space and time of real individuals, rather than restoring it from magazine texts.

In what follows, I discuss the patterns of placement of the networked computer in the homes I studied and locate them with respect to the normative coordinate system organizing domestic space. Like Spigel (1992), I discover a process of intensive cultural production within the household, a production that is an integral part of the medium's evolution.

The Micro-regulation of the Internet

The arrival of the Internet in the home stirs up anxieties and respective negotiations of roles and rules of using it. It precipitates a process that I would like to refer to as the micro-regulation of the medium. This regulation involves making decisions about issues of placement, access, preferred, discouraged and forbidden activities on and through the Internet, and the allocation of resources, including time, space, money and attention.

Underlying the micro-regulation of the new medium is a set of values characteristic of the particular family: the 'moral economy of the household' (Silverstone et al., 1992, p. 17). Silverstone et al. insist on conceptualizing the home in terms of a 'different kind of rationality – different, that is, from the rationality dominating the world of public affairs and the formal economy' (p. 27). This alternative rationality, they suggest, guides the appropriation of commodities in domestic culture – their domestication. Commodities (media and technologies included) are re-defined in accordance with the household's own values and interests (see p. 16).

Silverstone et al. (1992) have proposed an elaborate model of the domestication of commodities including several dimensions. They use the term 'objectification' to refer to the physical dispositions of objects in the spatial environment of the home: 'objectification reveals itself in display and, in turn, reveals the classificatory principles that inform a household's sense of itself and its place in the world' (p. 22). The arrangement of physical artefacts making up a particular environment, Silverstone et al. argue, objectifies the values, aesthetic and cognitive universe of those identifying and feeling comfortable with them. It also reveals the 'pattern of spatial differentiation (private, shared, contested; adult, child; male, female, etc.) that provides the basis for the geography of the home' (p. 23).

The integration of a new artefact into the existing fabric of the physical disposition of objects and into the patterns of spatial differentiation in a household requires creative engagement on the part of its inhabitants. As it became clear in the case of television, new technologies do not descend on the household along with a precise description of their appropriate place and surrounding. Women, men and children living alone or together have to make more or less conscious decisions about where the novelty belongs. Thus, even if users of new technologies do not literally write and publicize their own definitions of artefacts' meanings, they objectify these meanings by inscribing artefacts into an already meaningful structure of objects. In this sense, Silverstone et al.'s concept of objectification stands for a form of 'objectivation of subjective knowledge' as discussed by Schutz (see Schutz and Luckmann, 1973, pp. 264–286 and Chapter 2).

The concept of 'incorporation', another central component of Silverstone et al.'s (1992) domestication model, focuses on temporalities (see p. 24). While Silverstone's team applies the term broadly to cover 'ways in which objects, especially technologies, are used' (p. 24), I interpret it as a reference to the temporal arrangements and patterns that arise around a new domestic artefact. The organization of time-sharing of the artefact among different family members and the way in which its use fits into the overall structure of the day represent another measure of social and cultural significance. As Spigel has shown in her cultural history of television, the timing of housewives' engagement with the new technology of television has been at the root of both the development of particular television genres (cultural forms) and the redefining of the role of women within the home. This provides, I believe, a strong example of the intricate interconnectedness and two-way dependence between subjective time and social time (Schutz and Luckmann, 1973) as they are structued around a technological medium.

'Houses are shaped not just by materials and tools, but by ideas, values and norms. They should not be regarded simply as utilitarian structures, but as "designs for living"', states Corlin (1982, p. 173, quoted in Drucker et al., 1997, p. 46). Adopting the logic of this observation, I argue that the placement of technology within the physical and temporal setting of domestic life represents a *design for acting* with technology and as such, it is an important aspect of the use genres that I have set out to investigate. In what follows I will examine the search for the proper place of the Internet that my respondents and their families had gone through. The general driving force behind this search had been, as Silverstone (1994) has noted about television, the 'struggle for control and identity, both by the household itself in its involvement with the world beyond its front door and by the individuals within it' (p. 103). Placing the computer connected to the Internet had been a statement of the acceptable and preferred ways of using the medium within each particular home, and simultaneously, it had reinforced the Internet-related roles and competencies of family members.

While in some homes among those that I visited, the computer connected to the Internet had found its more or less stable place, in others it still was, or had been until recently, a wandering object. Across the different homes there was no emerging convergence of views regarding the right place of the networked computer. Depending on the overall structure of the home (number of rooms, computers, and inhabitants), the types of activities associated with the computer, the identity of the main user (if any) and the degree of use by other family members, several patterns of spatial arrangement could be discerned.

The Wired Basement

The spatial pattern that I have called 'the wired basement' could be found in its most representative form in the case of Reiner, a retired mechanical-engineering technician. The basement room in his single-family house, out of which he had run his own business, had become his computer and Internet room. Although Reiner's computer was not top of the line – it had been bought for his business years ago – he had high-speed Internet connection. The space had kept its business-like character, the bookshelves still stuffed with technical guides, books and CD-ROM packages. Several clocks on the walls showed the time in different time zones. A television set connected to a satellite dish on which Reiner used to watch German news programmes from *Deutsche Welle* was also in the room.[1]

For Reiner, who had retired from his job at the relatively early age of 56 and had only run his own business for a few years after that, this room seemed to accommodate the need for a space for intellectual, quasi-professional activity. It helped him reproduce the pattern of going to work, withdrawing from the domestic space shared with others (in this case his wife and the three little girls she used to baby-sit on regular basis) and delving into pursuits of his own. He was going downstairs every day to attend to his interests in news, technical and political topics and German language programming. That is how Reiner's wife sketched the Internet-use arrangements in their home in terms of personal versus shared time and space. Note also the vertical gender-zoning of space in the home:

> And also I find that it keeps him occupied and out of my hair. Because it was a bit changed after he retired and he was around quite a bit and now this takes whatever time I need to be alone and he is out of my way. And he needs that. He has an inquiring mind and it is very good for him. It is good for me too because he is busy with that …. Now he comes up at 8 o'clock and he sits with me and watches TV with me. (Reiner's wife)

Reiner's wife had only abstract curiosity toward the Internet and something of a puzzlement as to what her husband was doing on the computer for all those hours. However, if the amount of time he was spending on the Internet had been an issue at some stage of his usage, at the moment we spoke things seemed to have settled down. His wife could not completely understand his attraction to the computer screen, but had learnt to see the bright side of it – it gave her the opportunity to enjoy her own 'quiet time'. She did not exclude the possibility of becoming a user herself, but right now her hands were full with the job of nearly full-time baby-sitting of three young children and her duties related to the house, the farm,[2] and the garden. Her lack of time during the day and tiredness at night had kept her away from the Internet connection despite her feeling of being 'a little bit left out'. Writing messages that Reiner would then e-mail to one of their sons and to a friend on her behalf was as far as she had gone in using the net.

> It is not quite the same as it would have been if I was doing it myself. My work stopped in 1966, so I had no dealings with computers. I am just awestruck, I am just amazed and I would have been even more amazed if I knew what was out there …. (Reiner's wife)

This state of affairs was, according to Reiner's wife, her 'own fault' because she only needed to ask Reiner to show her what to do, but then the time factor intervened again. Furthermore, 'there are a lot of things for me to do before I sit down in front of the computer'.

The same pattern of division of space, time and computer/Internet competence between husband and wife could be observed in the case of another couple – John, a retired mechanical engineer, and his wife living in a single-family house in an affluent residential area. John had his computer and Internet hook-up in a room on the ground floor where he also kept his technical literature, hobbyist magazines and motor glider models. While Reiner's wife's lack of active interest in the Internet was nuanced with a certain sense of guilt, John's wife was completely comfortable with the fact that she did not have anything to do with this technological marvel. She had the clear sense of inhabiting a sphere of knowledge and activity different from her husband's. The themes of time and passive sitting in front of a screen as deterring factors recured in her explanation:

> WIFE: No, I am not interested. I do other things. It takes too much time.
> JOHN: [Wife's name] is the gardener.
> WIFE: Can be quite time consuming.
> JOHN: It's her hobby.
> WIFE: John likes to sit more than I do. I like to be moving.
> MARIA: You can learn a lot about gardening on the Internet, or maybe you prefer a book?
> WIFE: Oh, I pick it up as I go. My father used to like to garden. First of all I learnt it from him, and later neighbours exchanged plants and things like that ...

Similarly to Reiner's wife, John's wife had quit her job as a secretary in the 1960s to become a full-time mother and homemaker. As John explained, she had never been an 'adventurous lady'. She had always shied away from machines if she could. She never drove. In this home one could observe the same up-down gender zoning of space as in Reiner's case:

> I go up there in the evening to watch TV only if it's something very interesting. Then I come down here until it's time to go to bed .... One thing that puzzles me in this relationship is that she expects me to go up there and spend some of the evening with her, I ask her: 'Why don't you come down here to spend some time with me?' She doesn't want to do that. (John)

Both these wives seemed to experience a kind of identity conflict when it came to using the Internet. Their sense of who they were and of their role in the home was incompatible with the idea of passively sitting in a chair in front of a machine, especially during the day. Their specialty was the immediate physical dealing with domestic objects, people, animals and plants. For these women, the time when they felt they could afford some passive entertainment was in the evenings, but by then they were physically and mentally tired. In the television set, they found an undemanding and yet engaging source of pleasure. The pressure they put on their husbands to come and join them in television viewing was reminiscent of the cultural pattern of the television set being perceived as the hub of family togetherness established in the postwar years (see Spigel, 1992). Thus, although after retirement husbands experienced a void in their daily life that they sought to fill with intellectually stimulating and social activity resembling paid work, wives could never retire from their domestic duties. They continued to perceive their homes as work places where indulgence in a detached form of activity was simply out of place.[3] Moreover, they did not seem to suffer as severe a breakdown in their social connectedness as their husbands did after retiring.

The wired basement was an exclusively male domain. Even if not always literally a basement in terms of architecture, it was characteristically a space where one person could seclude himself for a lengthy period of time and attend to interests and pursuits of his own. With Reiner and John, the practice of 'going downstairs' was a symbolic and relational substitute of going to work and their use of the Internet in a way emulated the 'serious' activities they used to do at work. In the case of the 35-year-old Norris, a single man with a part-time teaching job who shared the home with his mother, the wired basement served both as his office, and information-gathering and entertainment centre.[4] A transformed family den, it was spacious and accommodated, besides his desk, a sofa and an old television set that Norris used to watch videos. Two more television sets were located on the upper floor and were used for family viewing.

Yet a third version of the wired basement was Radul's ground floor family room turned into a computer/Internet and TV/Nintendo room for himself and his son. Radul, 40, was an auto body technician originally from Romania who lived with his wife and 14-year-old son. Radul had bought his computer a year and three months before we met.

> Mostly, I bought it for my son, you know, to work or to play games, and after I bought it, we said, oh, okay, let's try the Internet and see what's going on. I had had absolutely nothing to do with computers before that. (Radul)

Since then, Radul had become quite interested in computer games himself and the Internet had turned out to be a great source of new game programs. The computer was initially installed in his bedroom, but often the long downloads of games and other programs from shareware sites disturbed his wife who wanted to use the room for its main function – to sleep. Then, the family decided that the 'TV room' on the ground floor of their three-level townhouse would be a better place for the computer and its related activities. That is how that room had become a sort of (predominantly) male entertainment centre. After supper, Radul would 'disappear', in his wife's words, to surf game sites, to download and play games. Radul explained:

> Because, I tell you honest, I didn't have this kind of toys in Romania. That's one reason. I bought this because I said: 'Okay, I wanna do my pleasure.' [We laugh.] I like it. I try to keep up with the generation of my son. (Radul)

In response to my question about whether he felt isolated from his family when he withdrew downstairs to deal with the computer, Radul replied that his son would often join him there to watch television or play Nintendo. They didn't do much together on the Internet itself, but sometimes, after a new game had been downloaded, Radul would show his son where to click to install it and they would try playing it together. Thus Radul's relative leadership in computer and Internet competence and his sharing in his son's interest in games served as a platform for a father-son bond, anchored in technology, from which the mother was practically excluded.

On weekends, the Internet helped to transform the wired basement into a piece of Romania and thus provided a space for another inter-generational bonding – that between Radul and his father, who also lived in the Greater Vancouver area:

> Because when my dad comes here for the weekends, he just sits in and I put on the radio, on RealAudio, from Romania and then he sits here for hours and listens – music and news, and all that. Sometimes I like that too – some of the news, to listen how …. And because we get the radio from my city, from Timisuara, a few times I even heard my ex-boss's name on the radio, and I feel like, oh – I got those – uh, the goose bumps. Because I feel you know, I go back in memory, you know, because we worked together …. (Radul)

Romanian newspapers were bookmarked in Radul's browser and he would normally go over the latest issues and download articles to take to his dad when he went to visit him during the week:

> He lived with us for about four years after my mom passed away five years ago and then he moved to Burnaby, we found him like a bachelor – and now almost every second day I go to see him, to bring him some food and then he phones me: 'Just don't forget to make some newspapers for me'. He likes politics, that's the truth, he likes to be updated. I don't read the whole article. Just at the time when I print them out what I think interests me, I read it. Not the whole thing because I don't even know, there are so many politicians now and all the time they are changing and I don't know what that guy did, or, I don't know – [But your dad follows?] Oh, yea, he understands that thing. He cannot read the English newspapers, he understands no English, nothing. Me and my sister put the money together to bring them here. But to be honest, I don't [think it was a good idea]. Now he started to

be a little bit more mellow but before, he couldn't find it, you know. He watches the TV, he doesn't understand nothing, he listens to the radio, then even the music here on the radio is not the same like, you know from … So I print him a paper, I make him happy. (Radul)

Radul's wife (37 and working full-time at a bakery) would sometimes leave her preferred leisure space – the main floor living room with the large television set – to go 'downstairs' and participate in listening to the Romanian radio stations. Other than that, she had no interest whatsoever in the computer and the Internet. Here, the wired basement was a clearly delineated male leisure space without much pretence for 'serious' work-like activity apart from Radul junior doing some homework on the computer. Radul, the father, admitted that his computer/Internet engagement had nothing to do with his actual job and was just a strategy 'to kill some time' and have some fun. As was noted, however, the Internet in fact played a significant part in his relation with his son and his father. It was not just an instrument for personal entertainment, but created – in the phenomenon of the wired basement – a space for enacting and meeting of male cultures characteristic of the three generations represented in Radul's family.

The Family Computer Room

The family office/study was a different form of spatial arrangement of Internet-related practices. It was a space shared by both husband and wife, and sometimes by more mature children. It had usually emerged as a designated space for in-home paid work, education, voluntary work and finally, entertainment. It could be observed in larger home units where putting aside such a designated space was possible. The family study was a more equal territory, even though sometimes contested. There existed privileged users, but others could lay claims to the space, the computer, and the Internet connection as well. In these cases, family members worked out rules of access. The women in such families, in my respondent group, were typically educated above the secondary level and employed in jobs for which computer competence was one, if not the central, prerequisite.

The most clear-cut case of an equitably shared family computer room was presented in Don's home. Don was a psychological counsellor working from home. He had his office and reception room in the basement of his single-family house. The computer with Internet connection was located in another room on the main floor. Don's wife, a book-keeper employed outside the home, did some of her work and e-mail correspondence on that computer. His grown-up sons, 18 and 22, also used the computer – partly for work, partly for games and in pursuit of their own interests in computer technology, sports and other leisure topics.

Don would usually have undisturbed access to the Internet connection while the rest of the family members were at work or school. In his words, his main activity on the Internet was 'searching for employment' which involved regular visits to job advertisement and government sites. Along with that, he maintained numerous contacts with family and distant friends, co-workers from his voluntary community board, and with some patients. Both he and his sons spent some time playing computer games, but priority would be given to the family member with a more 'serious' need for the computer and the Internet at any given moment.

Theodore and his wife also shared a common computer room which had been set up initially so that Theodore's wife could write and do research for her Master's degree in psychology. After she had completed her programme and had started work for a governmental organization, Theodore had become the main occupant of the room. It was the place where he was gathering information on Ethiopian politics through the Internet and putting together a programme for a community radio station. This activity was Theodore's hobby, but was also a realization of his interests and skills as a bachelor of political science. Theodore had never had the chance to work professionally in that field because of his unresolved immigration status at the time of his graduation. Instead, he had taken a job as a parking patroller which allowed him to effectively support his family. The computer room, then, was a constructed professional space for Theodore and the Internet was his access to a world of political information and action.

Although his wife's graduate studies had been the original reason for purchasing the computer and her student account had provided the initial access to the Internet, her use of the medium had remained very limited.[5] Their 8-month old baby was also an indirect user of the computer room space by virtue of a few items of baby clothing hung to dry there.

The family computer room or office in Rita's home was shared between herself and her husband who was a computer professional. At the time of the interview, Rita's husband had started his own business and the family study was his main working place. Rita, a chartered accountant working for a big local company, had a separate computer for her own needs that she could use at any time in the same space. The children in this affluent home, a 13-year-old girl and a 9-year-old boy, possessed their own personal computers each in her or his separate room and used them for homework and Internet surfing, e-mailing and games. This was the only family in my respondent group whose annual income exceeded 100,000 Canadian dollars. They had a local area network in the house, high speed (ADSL) Internet connection and individual e-mail addresses.

Spatial Improvisations: Work versus Pleasure

The idea of a computer room inside the home took different physical and conceptual expressions in single-adult homes. Sandy, a single mother of a 5-year-old daughter employed in telemarketing, had set aside a bright room on the second floor of her house for her sewing machine, her books and her computer. 'I also sew here and read', Sandy explained. The computer room in her case was mainly a leisure space and yet it had an intellectual feel to it. It was the room where Sandy was not a paid worker or a housekeeper but a social person and a self-motivated researcher and learner. Here, she could pursue her own interests and passions, and in that sense, the room was her demarcated zone of personal freedom. Not long before our interview, however, Sandy had expelled reading as an activity from that room. The reason for that is only touched upon in the following quote and warrants further examination which will be provided in the next chapter. What I would like to emphasize here is an instant of micro-regulation of Internet use through space designation and object placement:

> I used to have the green armchair that is downstairs up here and I used to read up here at night. Now, because I decided that I don't want to see this man any more – the one I met online – for now, I took my chair downstairs and I separated them because otherwise the temptation for me to go on there and talk to him is too great. With the computer here it is like a bottle in front of an alcoholic ... So I had to move my chair downstairs. I don't want to chat online that much any more, at least for now. I think I want to establish social relationships in the real world instead of in the virtual world right now. (Sandy)

Vera, a freelance writer working from home and a recently separated mother of two children – 4- and 6-years-old, organized her space along functional and emotional lines. In contrast to Sandy, Vera perceived her little office as 'a really dreary room'. That was the place where she used to write non-fiction such as magazine articles and the guide book on which she was working at the moment. She also did her book-keeping and some e-mail there using the fast and powerful Pentium computer hooked up to the Internet. In contrast, when she worked on projects involving free creativity such as writing fiction (a novel) she tended to use a notebook computer in her bedroom: 'Because there is a lot more light and I can see the plants'. In order to connect to the Internet from her bedroom through her notebook computer, Vera had to plug and unplug the telephone line as opposed to the permanent hook-up that she had in the office. In terms of Internet use, again, free interests and pursuits related to creative work, curiosity and correspondence with close friends would rather be performed in the bedroom than in the office. The office, on the other hand, was open to her children who would play games on the 'fabulous' computer there.

Vera's case, where a home office existed in the strict sense as a place for doing paid work, demonstrates how the lines between (mandatory) work and leisure, imposed and intrinsic interests and activities are conceptually drawn inside the home. Like Sandy, she was demarcating a space for free play and creativity that was extracted from the 'dreary' site of paid work – the office.

Ellen, the 49-year-old former editor disabled by a chronic illness, had set up her computer room (she referred to it as 'my office') in a walk-in closet adjacent to her bedroom. Ellen would squeeze in there when she wanted to communicate with her online support group, correspond with distant friends and relatives, or collect information about her illness from the Internet. Ellen felt it important to be able to keep her immediate space tidy and manageable ('because I personally cannot live in chaos') while recognizing that the outside world she was bringing inside her home through the Internet resisted any neat arrangement. It was messy and overwhelming, particularly to a person with limited physical energy and a number of mental problems. That is why Ellen wanted to be able to close the door of her office/closet and separate the peaceful, aesthetically organized interior of her bedroom from the piles of paper on her desk and the disarray of files on her small Macintosh.

Garry, a 67-year-old retired naval radio-operator, also living alone, had set up his computer room 'like a little radio station'. The model of connecting one's ship to the often vital information carried by the radio waves had been adjusted to include the computer and the Internet: 'As you see, I've got my radios there and my short waves are there, my computer is here, and under there is my keyboard and in here is my printer'. Garry was pointing to a neatly arranged set of pieces of equipment on and under his desk in a small room adjacent to his dining room. Garry would come here when he wanted to communicate with the outside world. On the other hand, as he explained: 'I have a different room that is quiet and sunny and looks over the lawn and when I want to be alone and relax, I go there, but here, here is where the action is'.

The Gate in the Living Room

The 'gate in the living room' was a form of spatial organization observed in families with a shared computer and no extra space to be assigned the function of a computer/Internet room. Apart from this spatial deficiency however, there were characteristic features of the use genres preferred by these families and respectively their concrete use practices that made the living room look like the most appropriate place for the computer with Internet connection to be installed. These features included first, the openness, or interfamily publicness, of Internet use that was encouraged in these homes. Second, Internet use was enmeshed in a set of other activities taking place in the same room and at the same time. Finally, in these homes the computer and the Internet were often used collectively or in the presence of other family members.

In Alex's family, both he and his wife were competent computer and Internet users. Alex, a 36-year-old jewellry designer had developed an interest in computing as a hobby and was the real computer/Internet fan in the home. His wife, a telecommunications engineer by background and proposal specialist for a networking software company by occupation at the time of the interview, had more professional technical knowledge in this area, but was not so well versed in the ways and tricks of the Internet. Nevertheless, she used the computer and the Internet on a regular basis for both work and leisure.

In the two-bedroom apartment where the family lived, the living room represented the only space, other than the bedrooms, where their computer with its manuals, disks and books could be installed. The computer desk was located across from the dining table and the television set. The television set, for its part, was placed on a wheeled table, which made it possible for television to be watched from both the sofa and the chair in front of the computer. This arrangement facilitated a seamless transition between routine daily activities and Internet use. Here is what Alex's daily Internet use would normally look like:

In the morning, I take a fifteen to twenty minute break, I drink my coffee, [smoke] my first cigarette, I check my e-mail which comes mainly from Bulgaria and Britain. Because 8 a.m. here is 4 p.m. in Britain, and 6 p.m. in

Bulgaria. If someone has sent something during the day there, it must have already arrived. That's everything I do, nothing else, I turn the computer off. In the evening, when I come back [from work], while we move around the house preparing dinner, doing this or that, my wife checks the e-mail first. Then, when my son goes to bed, about 8–9 p.m., I check the news .... (Alex)

Alex also said that while he waited for a large file to download, he would often turn his chair to the television set and watch TV. Television viewing and Internet surfing and communicative use were in open competition for Alex's domestic time. In his account, the Internet had taken over time traditionally spent watching television. Alex thought that the integration of the new medium into the life of the family had not taken away from the communication among family members:

I notice that the time in which most people would watch television, I spend on the Internet. In that sense, the communication at home isn't changed very much because whether you sit by somebody's side in front of the TV eating chips, or in front of the computer looking at the Internet and from time to time say: 'Hey, come and see what an interesting thing I found', I don't find much of a difference. The only difference is that the TV pours it directly over you. If I weren't on the Internet, I would probably be watching TV because it is also a way to relax after work. Most people watch TV at that time. (Alex)

Alex's wife did not accept his view of the Internet being without consequences for the communication in the family. According to her, television viewing presupposed more sharing between family members while the Internet was 'individually absorbing'. She objected not only to extensive Internet use, but also to domestic time spent with the computer 'one-to-one' in general. She preferred joint activities on the computer such as multi-player games – she often played computer games with their son – and designing. A good example of appropriate computer use for her was the collective creation of a Valentine card. Alex and their son had designed the card on the computer, she had cut it out and everyone was happy with their 'interaction'.

Echoing the same basic concern for family togetherness, Alex felt compelled to explain that: 'There are many things that we do together as a family on the Internet – talking to people, showing things we have found to each other ...'

Indeed, an examination of Alex's narrative reveals a lot of collective agency in his Internet use expressed through 'we' and 'our' pronouns. He and his wife, for example, jointly developed and implemented a job-search strategy for her, drawing on Internet resources. They had numerous family friends and relatives around the world with whom they talked and chatted over the Internet in multi-participant sessions that they found a lot of fun. They listened to radio programmes together. Although the issue of whether the Internet separated them, drew them closer together as a family, or had no effect on their bond was far from being resolved in this home, the very dialogue around it, as well as the positioning of the computer with the Internet connection in the middle of a shared and multi-functional domestic space, suggested a possible style of use anchored in the value of spousal equity and collective activities.

The family computer in Sophie's home had also been intentionally put in a place where it could be used by everyone:

> We wanted a place where everyone could have access to it and we figured, if we had a den, that would be a good place, but we don't, so the living room was where everybody could have access to it. Because we just have the one [computer], if we had more than one, it may have made sense to have it in a study, or a bedroom, but just the one, we put it, you know, central. (Sophie)

Interestingly, the computer (hooked to the Internet) was occupying a television rack located centrally in Sophie's living room. It had literally replaced the television set as a focal domestic object. The family had a small television set located elsewhere in the house that was used for watching videos but they did not subscribe to cable television. However, in the practice of this family the computer had not come to represent the successor hearth around which the family members would gather to enjoy time together as many advertisements picture it. Sophie, her husband and two sons, 11- and 13-years-old, took turns using the Internet, each for their own interests and purposes, according to a casual schedule determined by their work and school time, and not the least important, by the fee-schedule of their Internet provider. This was a typical example of time-zoning (see Munro and Madigan, 1999) of a shared, or 'public' area of the home.

Sophie, the main user of the Internet, studied herbology from home by correspondence and the Internet was essential for her programme-related research. She would also gather information to answer inquiries by customers of the nutrition supplement store where she worked part-time. Sophie would usually get on the computer to do her research in the morning when nobody was home and the access was free (their Internet service provider charged for the time online between 3 and 11 p.m.): 'When I am working on research, I prefer some quiet, but I usually get that in the morning'. Her sons would occasionally go online in the afternoon, and her husband after 11 p.m.

One important thing Sophie wanted to ensure was that she or her husband were home when their sons went on the Internet. The location of the computer worked well in that respect. It was indeed central enough to allow the parents to keep an eye on what their boys were doing in cyberspace even when they were busy with something else around the house. Monitoring the children's use of the paid time and the printer was one consideration:

> They'd like to download a lot of pictures and things and get them printed out, but we try do discourage them because it is too expensive. I mean, if they need a picture for a project or something like that, that's fine. But if they just want to hang it on the wall or whatever, they've got to kind'a watch that. (Sophie)

The second, and more alarming reason for keeping an eye on the boys' Internet use was pornography. Notably, Sophie's anxiety did not stem simply from the knowledge of pornography being available 'out there' in cyberspace. She was mainly disturbed by the fact that pornography was actively and uninvitedly reaching into her home and intruding on her and, potentially, her almost teenage sons' attention. One small-scale technology-out-of-control experience prompted Sophie and her husband to start looking for preventive measures against the influx of pornography: 'Because you can put in something very innocent and have quite surprising things come up on the Internet'.

What had happened to Sophie was that she entered 'Toyota Previa' in a search engine because she and her husband were thinking about buying one. All of a sudden, she was confronted with a number of shocking 'previews' of hard core pornographic sites. The search engine, she thought, 'must have misunderstood'. Or, because she was in a car-related site, Sophie speculated: 'maybe those [cars and pornography] go together, maybe people think they go together, I don't know'. In any case, it was not only too easy to get into these hard porn previews, it was confusingly difficult to get out: 'cuz when you push "back" you'd normally get out of the site quite easily, but this one just kept going with this horrid stuff'. If the kids had been looking at the computer at that moment, Sophie concluded, she would have been very upset. That was why she and her husband bought two different patrol programs and installed them on the computer. Only to be disappointed quite soon. The patrols, they found, were useless: 'too overbearing, too knit-picky'. Next thing Sophie knew, she could not get into a herbology site. The CyberPatrol was coming up saying that the site was being protected. In the end, Sophie and her husband decided that they simply had to be present when the boys were online.

Considerations of common access and monitoring children had also kept the computer in the living room in Carol's case: 'For the first year and a half I had it right here in my living room, so I could see it, so I could see what was happening'. Their Pentium PC computer with Internet connection was used by Carol, a marketing manager who had recently quit her job, and her two sons, 11- and 14-years-old. Her husband, who used his own Macintosh mostly for the purposes of his job as a movie producer, had not figured out how to find his way to the Internet yet:

> And he is a very intelligent man, and very technically oriented, but he could not master – and to this day he can't sit down on our computer and dial up the Internet. We didn't have Windows at that time. He just didn't seem to be able to grasp it – he just cannot understand how everything can be in different places. He got left behind and he hasn't caught up yet. He just got too frustrated. (Carol)

So, it fell upon Carol to follow their sons' exploits in cyberspace. Having the computer in the living room and going on the Internet herself helped her intercept a disturbing phenomenon:

> Now, after about half a year, I don't know exactly how it happened, but my son somehow got connected to some pornography sites and we started to get a lot of pornographic mail, and we still do to this day. I get sometimes up to seven pieces of pornographic mail every single day on my AOL account. It's a line that says: 'X-rated sites, open us up' and really horrible stuff ... and I have that computer here in the living room and at one point my 11-year-old downloaded pictures, *disgusting* [speaks with indignation] pictures, so I disconnected the Internet for about a week. They didn't know how I'd done it, I disconnected the phone lines from the box and I told them that if I ever caught them on ... (Carol)

When she contacted their Internet service provider, America Online, Carol found that her sons were probably not to blame for what was going on. They had not necessarily been actively searching for pornography. Pornography had sneaked in by way of seemingly 'innocent', as Sophie had put it, activities. AOL explained to Carol that 'these pornographic people' would go into the chat rooms, and most certainly into the teen chat rooms that her sons frequented at the time, and they would collect up all the addresses of the users they found in there and start sending them stuff. Then, if one of her kids ever went into a pornographic site, his address would be picked up and 'be sold over, and over, and over again' to similar content providers.

153

This put Carol on the alert and looking for measures to closely supervise her sons' use of the Internet. The placement of the computer in the living room contributed to that for some time.

> But finally after that length of time my husband wanted the mess gone. The kids had their games everywhere and they were always downloading stuff and the computer was always sitting here in the living room and my husband wanted to sit here and listen to music and, he is a very quiet man, and that really bothered him. (Carol)

Then, the gate in the living room arrangement in Carol's home was transformed into a family computer room set up. The computer and Internet activities were relocated from the central, shared, visible, lively space of the living room into a designated separate space with open access for whoever in the family wanted to use the computer:

CAROL: And so I moved the computer down to its own room and so that's where it is now.
MARIA: Is it like an office now? Do you work there?
CAROL: No, it's just our computer room. Because my youngest son has four friends that visit and they all sit there all day Saturday and play Sim City. And that way they can be alone with their games and my older boy can be in the other room.
MARIA: Do you feel okay with the fact that you cannot monitor them?
CAROL: I go down and look at them very often. Now, that I am home,[6] if the door is shut, I always open the door and look at them ...
MARIA: So, you prefer the door to stay open?
CAROL: Yah.
MARIA: Do you yourself go down to do your stuff?
CAROL: Yah. Sometimes we have problems with that.
MARIA: Why?
CAROL: Because my son wants to be on it and I want – but we have a lot of computers in the house ...

The competition with her sons and the felt obligation to weed out pornography from their mailbox had shaped Carol's temporal pattern of using the Internet. Thus, another example of time-zoning had been put into place in this family. Carol would go to the 'computer room' more often at night 'because the kids are in bed and they are not on the computer'. Usually, in the morning she would do her 'computer work' – writing reports, announcements, and other documents related to the voluntary organizations she belonged to – and she might also 'sit on the Internet to see whether I've got any messages and to clear off any pornographic mail that's coming through the night'.

Sharing computer/Internet related space and time with her 16-year-old son was also an issue that Martha, a single mother, had to consider. Deciding where in her home to place the computer, she went through the options of her bedroom, where, subsequently, her son would have to come to play 'doom and kill and blast and that sort of thing'. Or, his bedroom which she could rarely find her way through ... In a two-bedroom townhouse, Martha had to be flexible and creative, and so she came up with the hallway:

> So, because we have this hallway which is basically used as an access to the living room and we have access through the kitchen. So I turned the hallway into an office. And it works. It's a neutral place. I can look outside if I want and the [outside] door is open during summer time. I can be aware of what is going on. If I put it upstairs, I'd feel a little claustrophobic upstairs and there is where I sleep ... I like to feel like I am outside all the time, people pop in and I don't feel secluded ... This is a crammed space, but it works ... And there is that feeling that everything is still close at hand.

A neutral place, where you do not feel secluded, where you can be aware of what is going on and have the rest of the home facilities close at hand matches the definition of the gate in the living room arrangement discussed above.[7] Martha dealt with the pornographic threat in a more relaxed manner than the previous two mothers, although she too had to do her share of monitoring of her son's Internet use:

> He has done the typical teenage-boy thing – gone to pornographic sites. He leaves a trail of crumbs behind. I can always tell where he has been. [Laughs] I can check in the cache and see what graphics there are. So I say: oh, okay. But I don't make a big thing out of it because it is there. There is freedom of speech and there is going to be subversive information out there, but I think it is like television – you don't have to turn it on, you don't have to go there. I knew that he would go through this stage and he did and it is not a big deal any more. (Martha)

On her part, Martha was sensitive to the possibilities of having her home invaded by unwanted content and had elaborated strategies for protecting the boundaries of her (and her son's) private space. One trick she used was juggling two e-mail addresses, one of which was anonymous in that it didn't reveal any personal information about her. She also avoided using newsgroups because of the well-known practice of advertisers collecting addresses from there and then distributing electronic junk mail. On one occasion, a Yahoo chat partner had led her son to believe that he was communicating with a 14-year-old girl, when actually, after real addresses, telephone numbers and names were exchanged, it turned out that the chat partner was a boy sexually interested in Martha's son. The discovery had come as a shock to Martha's son. She, however, had not disconnected her telephone line, as Carol had once done. Instead, she had taken the opportunity to educate her son about how 'it is totally whatever you want to perceive and whatever they want to tell you. You are totally' at the mercy of this thing, so you have to be very cautious'.

Internet Parenting

Although the theme that I am discussing here is spatial arrangement, I cannot dissociate it easily from the intervening theme of Internet parenting. If we recall Radul's case, we had a father who shared his son's interest in computer games and respective Internet sites. That was a predictable example of male bonding based on typical male things – technology, games and domestic leisure. No trace was to be found in Radul's account of any concern about the possible pornographic invasion into the world of his 14-year-old son. In contrast, the three stories I just told all involved computer- and Internet-literate mothers vividly aware of the shadowy side of cyberspace and deeply concerned about the threats it bred for the moral and social well-being of their sons. For these mothers, the Internet had added one more area of their children's development to guard. Or, to confirm Cowan's (1983) earlier observation, new domestic technology was bringing in 'more work for mother'.

In this context, it would be useful to recall Smith's (1999) argument that the 'dominant school-mother T-discourse'[8] lays the primary responsibility for the individual child's school achievement, and even further, his/her success as an adult, on the family. The ideological code of the 'Standard North American Family' (see Smith, 1999, pp. 157–161) helps to translate in practical settings 'family' into 'mother'. Thus, mothers are charged with the responsibility for the overall success or failure of their children in terms of academic and moral achievement and expected to do the work required for fulfilling that responsibility. Understood in that way, the work of mothering that had to be done in these Internet-connected families had become more complex and demanding. It required technological competence and knowledge of the medium on the part of the mother. The technological imperative was experienced by the women in these families in relation to their motherly duties. They felt it as a pressure to upgrade themselves as mothers with technological skills and knowledge.

Notably, the different reactions the three mothers demonstrated with regard to cyber pornography were not motivated by different moral philosophies or parenting styles alone. At the core of these reactions was the mother's technological confidence and Internet experience. Sophie and Carol were insecure novice users. They were coming to know the new medium alongside and maybe even a step behind their sons. For them, cyberspace was still an unpredictable terrain, the technology was hard to harness and these two circumstances put together represented a major source of anxiety. Martha's reaction, on the other hand, was based on the superior knowledge and understanding of both the technology and the medium that she possesed, compared to her son. She was moving ahead of him, she knew what could be expected and she felt capable of educating him, while the other two women were looking for mechanisms for protection.

Furthermore, Martha was making a conscious effort to uncover to her son the creative and knowledge-yielding powers of the medium. She was in the process of developing a web site for his art: 'He's an artist – he draws a lot and I want to get his pictures out there. It's a sort of self-esteem thing. He can feel really good about his work'.

She had downloaded an English-Spanish translator program to help him with his Spanish classes and kept his bookmarks organized in a separate folder in Netscape. A look into this folder gave her a synopsis of at least some of her son's interests and pursuits at any given moment. She thought she should take the opportunity to better understand those interests and possibly shape them as far as she could: 'Art Crime – he is very much into world graffiti and what people are doing out there and what kind of impact and statement they are making'.[9]

Thus, in Martha's case, a less easily predictable mother-son bond seemed to be growing out of Internet use. The technology and the medium were becoming implicated in a previously less typical relationship. Mother and son were jointly exploring cyberspace and learning more about each other along the way.

Jane, a 35-year old homemaker, and her 12-year-old son represented another example of this phenomenon. Jane had two boys and a girl. Her husband, a metal builder, had no interest in the Internet mostly because he worked long hours, but also because, as he put it himself, he was more 'mechanically inclined'. Mechanical versus literary, or symbolic inclination was a line of identity formation in this family. The older boy, 14, according to Jane's characterization, was like his father:

interested in mechanical things, how to repair [machines]. He fixes cars, he can do an oil change. The big box outside [Jane points to a box in the

157

yard] – he built that. He likes to work with his hands, to see how things work, and machines. He would use a computer to make a card for someone's birthday, or make a sign, or do a homework. He is not that interested in the Internet at this point. (Jane)

On the other hand, the younger son, 12, was perceived to be like his mom who liked to read a lot. He was also a voracious reader: 'In grade five he read grade seven books. If they told him at school to read two novels, he would read ten'. He was attracted to the Internet 'for the reading part'. Jane and her younger boy would often dial up the Internet together after he came back from school. They tried different search strategies: 'He'll show me different things he's done to find something, and I'll show him things that I have done and we sort of exchange information'. She encouraged him and helped him correspond with e-mail pals from other parts of the country. This was a sort of collaborative project between the two of them as her son would write to those pen-pals about his Lego, Tamagochi and boy-scout activities, while Jane would add geographical descriptions of their location, their city and other information that she thought might be educational. Thus, in this family, the Internet was being appropriated by the mother as a tool for building a new kind of special bond between herself and her growing son.[10] For the time being, it was competing successfully with the 'male' mechanical involvement with machines, cars and carpentry.

A complex dialectic of oppression and empowerment with regard to these women can be detected in their everyday stories. On one hand, the technological system was invading their homes through the ideologies of progress, personal success and motherly responsibilities. It was forcing them to do additional work in order to meet the challenges involved in ensuring adequate technological and moral education of their children in the unsettled context of the new medium. A boy's toy was turning into a mother's toil.

On the other hand, the new medium was delivering a new tool into the hands of the mother to teach resistance, dignity and integrity of being (recall hooks, 1990; see also Chapter 2). Internet mothers, similar to the black women hooks wrote about, resisted by making homes where their children could strive to be 'subjects, not objects' (p. 42) in the face of a powerful technological system driven by the impetus to transform these children into perfect consumers.[11] The pornography example being an extreme case of consumption gone wild. In order to be able to play that role, mothers had to understand the technology critically and to imagine alternative possibilities for its use that would affirm the subjectivity of their children as learners and creators. The women I talked with found themselves at different stages in this process. The discussion of children's (boys) interest in cheat-codes for computer games illustrates the journey of critical discovery that mothers had to make in order to interpret the new phenomenon:

> My son started getting interested in, for example, he was playing a CD ROM game, he'd go to a site where there were codes so that he could do better at a game. (Martha)

> but he also goes into the game sites, and he downloads cheat-cheats ... Do you know what that is? When you play a game on a Sony playstation ..., but he can go on the Internet and find whole pages of codes, and he loves that. My son trades them with his friends. (Carol)

Martha and Carol were just registering an instance of their sons' Internet use. Martha sounded quite indifferent to it, while Carol seemed to appreciate to some extent the subversive nature of this activity serving as a stimulus for her son to engage with the new medium. After all, it put the Internet in service of his own pre-teen interests and socialization efforts (he traded codes with friends).[12]

> [Laughs.] You know what he does? He finds the Game Boy, the [unclear] video game thing. He goes on the Internet and he finds how to cheat so that he can get further ahead in his games, little tricks. The games usually have eight or ten levels and the farther you get, the more interesting it becomes. So they want to skip levels cuz they want to get as far as they can. (Jane)

This description of an annoying habit that my own son was developing at the time struck me with its emphatic quality. Jane had found an explanation of why her son needed the cheat codes from his own perspective – to get faster to more interesting levels of his computer and video games. She seemed to understand and justify the kind of pleasure her son was deriving from this.

Sophie, for her part, had gone a longer way toward relating this playful subversive activity with the big picture of the computer game industry:

> And they use it for, unfortunately there is a lot of cheating, what they call, oh, I am not sure what they call it, but anyway it's cheating. There's answers for games they play, so they go on there and I don't know how they find these addresses, but have them at school, friends have them at school ... .[13] They go on there and find answers for games they can't figure out. So you'd say, why? That's the whole point of the game, challenge is over. *And then they want a new game* [emphasis mine]. I don't know ... So, it's a very different pace these days, I am not sure ... . (Sophie)

159

Summary: Inscribing the Internet

As noted at the beginning of this chapter, domestic interiors are designs for living. As such, they represent the material expression of families' interpretations of domestic technologies. In the case of the Internet, the placement of the computer with the Internet connection within the home speaks of the meaning of the technology for this particular family and embodies the micro-regulation of its use. By placing the device in a particular way, the families I studied were defining its properties. One of the main dimensions of interpretation and regulation expressed in these patterns of placement was constituted by the choice between individuality versus togetherness of use. This was the range between 'It's peaceful to me to be in the bedroom and close the door. Whoever is using it [the Internet] can be on one's own in there' (Jane) versus the preference for joint activities and the refusal to accept a use practice that is 'individually absorbing' (Alex's wife). The values underlying these choices were on the one hand the respect for the privacy of individual family members, and on the other hand, the felt need to reaffirm the family collectivity by engaging in joint activities.

The available technical configurations could clearly support the need for privacy better than the desire for collective engagement. The togetherness ideal was much harder to sustain in the face of a technology based on the *personal* computer with its single-person operated input and output devices. In this respect, technological design was limiting the possibilities for collectivist interpretations and applications. The gate in the living room placement pattern represented an attempt to compensate for this technologically imposed disintegration of the family into separate individual spaces of attention and engagement. In homes where women played the leading role in Internet appropriation, togetherness, or at least mutual awareness, through central and public placement of the computer with Internet connection was being sought. In contrast, the wired basement pattern allowed different family members to be alone during certain periods of the day as a mater of routine. The case of the family computer room was similar – whoever needed to use it at any particular time could be there on his or her own or, as in the case with some of the children, with friends.

Another dimension of interpretation and micro-regulation of the Internet had to do with the equality/inequality of access. What was affirmed along this continuum was the question of symbolic ownership: who the privileged user of the medium in the home was, or who had the most legitimate access to the connection and the space and time allocated to it. As I have shown, what I have called the wired basement was an example of exclusive access, most typically granted to the man in the family. Other members of the family, most typically the wife, were not necessarily denied the opportunity to use the Internet. In the cases I examined, these wives chose to exclude themselves from the space and time of the new medium due to interiorized cultural attitudes regarding the role of the woman in the home and the relationship between women and technology. What Turkle (1988) has labelled 'computational reticence' (p. 41) seemed to play out in these cases in a specific way.

A further dimension of spatial arrangement concerned the type of relevance of the Internet activity: imposed (work) or intrinsic (pleasure, freedom, curiosity). In some cases, as for example Sandy and Vera, there was a clearly drawn demarcation line between the workspace and the pleasure/freedom space. Vera had assigned different computers to each of these spaces while Sandy had definitively placed her Internet-connected computer in her pleasure/freedom zone, as if in an effort to claim that technology back for herself in contrast to being its slave at work. In other homes, work and pleasure, imposed and intrinsic relevance of the computer and the Internet were intertwined and hard to distinguish. Characteristically, as in the cases of Alex, Sophie and Theodore, the Internet at home was being employed to introduce a pleasurable, exploratory, creative, even playful dimension into education and work.

In the choices made along these dimensions we see an expression and negotiation between the diverse values underlying the culture of the particular household. Thus, in the pattern of the wired basement we find a culture organized around rigid gender division of roles in the family. The men in these households have exclusive access to the computer, the Internet connection, and the space where they are located for the purposes of work or pleasure, whatever the case might be. Female identity is constructed in relation to different central objects, activities and spaces – the kitchen, the garden, the television room. In these homes, domestic space is the proverbial leisure realm for men and working place for women described in numerous studies by feminist and media researchers (see Drucker et al., 1997 for an overview of feminist discussions; Gray, 1992; Morley, 1986; Weisman, 1992). The practices of technology use supported by the spatial arrangements are constitutive of this gendered geography of the home.

In the family computer room arrangement, a more flexible definition of roles of family members can be discerned. Both husband and wife can make a legitimate claim on the computer and the Internet connection for imposed or intrinsic purposes. The individuality of their access is also confirmed by the separation of the computer from other objects and activities within a designated room where the person using it can be on his or her own and concentrate on his or her interaction with the outside world. The family computer room can be defined and experienced either as an office, that is, with an emphasis on the work being done there, or as a leisure room. More often than not however, it is both. An elaborate time-zoning scheme is usually put in place to ensure that the needs of individuals in the family are fairly met. Conflicts can occur in the process of the negotiation of an acceptable time-zoning pattern. Power differentials in the family or values associated with different kinds of activity affect the division of space and time between different members.

In both the wired basement and the family computer room, the demarcation line between the domestic or private space of the family and the public space with which the Internet helps members interact is clearly drawn. To invoke the metaphor of my naval radio-operator respondent, these two placement patterns resembled the radio room which is the point of connection between a ship at sea and the rest of the world. Individual family members withdrew from collective and strictly private domestic life into these spaces so that they could communicate with the public world. I would refrain from characterizing this practice as 'double privatization' (Morley, 1992, p. 120) as critics of the 'home based society' such as Kumar (1995, p. 59) have done. What I see in this practice is a dialectical paradox: the individual withdraws to the private realm of the home thus negating the public world at one level, and yet at another level, she withdraws from the private publicness of collective family life in order to return to the public world outside the home in a different way, from her own base. The repercussions this practice entails for public and private life will be discussed at more length in the next chapter.

In the gate in the living room arrangement, the spatial boundaries between private domestic space and the public world are blurred. Home-based activities are enmeshed with activities drawing on and addressing the public world. Less individual privacy of use and more publicness within the family are characteristic of this pattern. In this arrangement I see an attempt for 'double socialization' – typically private practices within the home are articulated to the public world and individual Internet use is exposed to the glances of the family public. With all that said, what happens to the long-standing dichotomies between the public and the private, between individual and community? The following chapter will take up this theme with a view to the various forms of actual and virtual togetherness in which the Internet is implicated.

As a new technology and new medium of communication, the Internet has stirred the existing spatial arrangements and significations inside the home as well as having induced a process of renegotiation and re-definition of the boundaries between the (private) home and the public world. The penetration of the new technology into the home does not simply represent an instance of further encroachment of System onto the Lifeworld. Individuals located in their homes are not simply drawn into a new technological and ideological structure of domination. They are involved in decision-making regarding the space, time and meaning that the new technology deserves from the perspective of their existing values and meaningful everyday activities. They are engaged in active work aimed at erecting the selective and protective mechanisms that would allow them to remain in control of their personal and family space while at the same time relate more flexibly and freely to their social environment. In the cases cited in this chapter, one can see a clear illustration of the strategies people invent in order to put such mechanisms in place. Zoning of space and time, sets of rules for access and appropriate use, articulation and re-configuration of values, re-definition of roles and tasks emerge as the means through which people resist technological dictate and strive at mastering the novel possibilities for action and living the Internet creates. Thus, with regard to the foreign technological object, placing and timing become means of appraising and taming. Some solutions follow the trajectory of old ideologies, including gender divisions and oppressions. Others become materializations of new, more equitable, imaginative and collaborative relations between partners and family members in general,[14] and importantly, between the household and its social exterior.

Notes

[1]This intense connectedness was in sharp contrast with the impenetrability of the physical boundaries of his estate. Located on five acres of farm land, his house was protected by a fence and guarded by two quite fierce dogs that scared me away at a distance from the door bell for a few embarrassing minutes after my arrival.

[2]Both spouses reported that after he retired Reiner had taken over from his wife the care for their animals. He expressed admiration for her having been able to carry on that work along with raising five children during all the years of his employment.

[3]Morley (1986) has observed a similar anxiety related to women's television viewing. Television was problematic for women because it necessitated inactivity in a space construed as both work and leisure.

[4]This description was verbally given to me by Norris. We met and talked in a college cafeteria. Norris was eager to respond to my questions but excused himself

for not being able to invite me to his home at the moment. I decided not to insist on paying a home visit in his case as I suspected that religious, customary or other considerations might be deterring this respondent from accepting me, a woman, in his bachelor's premises. This might have been a prejudice on my part given my ignorance about Norris's original culture – he was a Tanzanian of Indian descent who had moved to Canada twenty years ago.

[5] Although I met and had a pleasant short conversation with Theodore's wife, she had not agreed to participate in my study and Theodore did not feel comfortable to discuss her use of the Internet in any concrete detail. Everything he felt he could say without violating his wife's privacy was: [Does your wife use the Internet at all?] 'Seldom. Very rarely … She knows how to use it but doesn't use it very much.' (Theodore)

[6] Carol had quit her job a few months before our interview so that she could be there to meet the growing needs of her sons: 'But I felt, ten years from now, who's gonna care that I did a wonderful job marketing [company's name], and I am still gotta have to live with these two boys as adults, and what kind of adults are they going to be?'

[7] In Martha's case the computer desk was actually blocking one of the accesses to the living room and she called her computer space 'my office'.

[8] In Smith's (1999) terminology this concept refers to discourses representing 'skeins of social relations mediated and organized textually' that connect and coordinate the activities of actual individuals whose local historical sites of reading/hearing/viewing may be geographically and temporarily dispersed and institutionally various (p. 158).

[9] Martha did not show concern for her son's privacy being violated through these actions. She felt her monitoring of his 'trail' in cyberspace was justified and indeed an expression of interest and caring. I did not have the opportunity to interview the teenager himself and get any sense of whether he was aware of this benevolent surveillance and what he thought about it.

[10] Pornography was not a big issue in this home because they were using a text browser and still could not access any graphic files on the Internet. Nevertheless, Jane had learnt from her experience with newsgroups that: 'you have to watch them [newsgroup postings] though. Some have really horrible pornographic stuff in the text, even on kids' stuff. People put really weird stuff'.

[11] See the publications of The Center for Media Education (CME) for a comprehensive discussion of the commercial exploitation of children through the Internet.

[12] My own son wrote a column in the school newspaper entitled 'The Cheat Zone'. There, he used to paste cheat codes downloaded from the Internet. He countered my argument that this was not a creative way to run a newspaper column by telling me how popular this material was.

[13] No wonder! There was 'The Cheat Zone' column in the school newspaper (see previous footnote).

[14] An interesting and unexpected example of that is the fact that Internet competence becomes a part of the job characteristic of the mom and a tool in her hands for creating a new partnership with her son. Unfortunately, my data do not allow me to say anything about parent-daughter relationships involving the Internet as only four of my respondents had daughters, mostly quite young.

SEVEN Virtual Togetherness

Introduction

Two distinct models have emerged in the last decade as the main contestants for defining the social character of the Internet. I will label them 'the consumption model' and the 'community model'. The germs of the consumption model can be found in the early visions and subsequent efforts to put research centres, libraries and other information-generating and storing institutions online so that initially professionals, and later the wired public, could tap into an unlimited stock of data. This model further took shape in conjunction with the growing adoption rate of the new medium. As more and more comfortable middle-class users hooked up to the Internet, it dawned on businesses that a promising new virtual market was opening up. The conceptual step from information retrieval to retrieval of goods and services was easy to make. Technical solutions ensuring higher speed and capacity of transmission lines and graphical point-and-click interfaces are further furnishing the Internet as a global electronic mall. The characters populating this space are free, active consumers, viewing, picking, clicking and getting what various industries have to offer, not only never talking to each other (as in the traditional bricks-and-mortar commercial sites), but also never seeing or sensing each other's presence. Privacy, anonymity, reliability, speed and visual appeal are desired properties of this virtual space, mobilizing armies of designers in search of adequate technical solutions.

The community model originated in the side-track inventions of ARPANET[1] and later Internet builders who were simultaneously users of these networks in need of communicating and collaborating with distant colleagues. The remarkable popularity of bulletin-boards, e-mail and in the later years Usenet, Internet Relay Chat, mailing lists and similar applications came as a surprise to those who originally planned the networks with resource sharing and file-exchange as priority functions in mind (see Abbate, 1994). The discovery of human communication on computer networks provided grounds for the enthusiasm of early visionaries who conceived of the Internet as a community technology with the potential to provide spaces for people to come together as equals, as colleagues and generators of ideas, to deliberate and act collectively, that is, to form communities.

Predictably, the promises that a new technology would enhance community and extend it globally have elicited withering criticism. Skeptics (Borgmann, 1992; Dreyfus, 1998; Kumar, 1995; Postman, 1992; Slouka, 1995) have contended that nothing is more destructive of real community than its virtual counterfeit. The 'virtual community' debate continues unabated to this day for good reason. Community is the scene on which a large share of human development occurs. As such it is a fundamental human value mobilizing diverse ideologies and sensitivities. The possibility of realizing this value in a new domain and by new means is naturally stirring up optimistic excitement in many circles. At the same time, the eagerness to put hopes for community in a technical system flies in the face of an influential intellectual tradition of technological criticism. This eagerness seems even more naïve in the light of the latest development of the Internet driven by powerful players indicating the triumph of the commercial model.

The objective of this chapter is to explore some dimensions of the virtual community concept that relate to questions of user agency and empowering possibilities in the appropriation of the Internet by domestic users. I contend that users' participation in what has been called 'virtual communities' (Rheingold, 1993) over the Internet constitutes a cultural trend of 'immobile socialization', or in other words, socialization of private experience through the invention of new forms of intersubjectivity and social organization online. When I introduced the term 'immobile socialization' in Chapter 5, I intentionally reversed Williams's (1974) concept of mobile privatization. Unlike broadcast technology and the automobile that, according to Williams, precipitated a withdrawal of middle-class families from public spaces of association and sociability into private suburban homes, the Internet is being mobilized in a process of collective deliberation and action in which people engage from amid the private realm. Whether an analyst would decide to call the electronic forums in which this is happening communities or not depends on the notion of community with which she is operating. What has to be noted, however, is that by engaging in different forms of collective practice online, users transcend the sphere of the narrowly private interest and experience. They use their homes as bases for reaching out into the public sphere. Why do people do that? What does it mean to them? How does it reflect on the public understanding of the Internet? The concept of 'virtual community' has been of only limited help in the understanding of this practice and I will try to explain why in what follows.

Few studies of virtual communities (an exception is Turkle, 1995) have attempted to relate online community engagement with users' everyday life situations, relevances and goals. Most of the existing research (see Jones, 1995, 1997) has concentrated on the group cultures originating from the interactions of online participants, thus treating online group phenomena in isolation from the actual daily life experiences of the subjects involved.

In a recent paper, Wellman and Gulia (1999) have pointed out a common weakness of all these approaches to online community, including the empirically grounded anthropological studies. All these analyses are premised on a false dichotomy between virtual communities and real life communities. This split is unjustifiable. Both Wellman's (1979, 1988) community studies carried out through the methods of network analysis and Anderson's (1983) historical studies have demonstrated in their specific ways that the majority of the so-called 'real life' communities are, in fact, virtual in the sense that they are mediated and imagined. 'In fact most contemporary communities in the developed world do not resemble rural or urban villages where all know all and have frequent face-to-face contact. Rather, most kith and kin live farther away than a walk (or short drive) so that telephone contact sustains ties as much as face-to-face get-togethers' Wellman and Gulia (1999, p. 348) argue. 'All communities larger than primordial villages of face-to-face contact (and perhaps even these) are imagined', Anderson (1983, p. 18) insists, in a curious concord between the two quite distinct schools of thought.

Furthermore, Wellman and Gulia (1999) charge, all these accounts of virtual community have treated the Internet as an isolated phenomenon without taking into account how interactions on the Net fit with other aspects of people's lives: 'The Net is only one of many ways in which the same people may interact. It is not a separate reality', Wellman and Gulia observe (p. 334).

The missing aspects of people's lives are the actualities (Smith, 1987) in which virtual community members are situated. I believe this to be the crucial background against which questions regarding the social and individual significance of online communities can be raised and answered. Thus virtual communities cannot be declared inferior to 'real-life communities' simply because they lack face-to-face materiality. They cannot be celebrated as liberating or empowering by nature either, as people bring to them stocks of knowledge and systems of relevance generated throughout their unalterable personal histories and social experience. They cannot be studied and characterized exclusively by what is produced online as the cultures enacted online have their roots in forms of life existing in the 'real' world.

My attempt in this chapter is to initiate an exploration into the experiences and motivations that lead Internet users to get involved, or the opposite, to stay away from forms of virtual togetherness. I believe it is important to understand what needs and values and under what circumstances virtual forums serve. This will open a realistic perspective on the significance of this use genre to the shaping of the Internet. Examining closely my respondents' stories, I will offer a typology of different forms of online involvement with others, demonstrating that virtual community is not always the most accurate notion for describing people's actual social activities online. In fact, virtual togetherness has many variations, not all of which live up to the value-laden name of community. This fact however should not undermine the idea of collective life in cyberspace. On the contrary, I will call for appreciation of the different forms of engagement with other people online (virtual togetherness) that exist and the different situated needs they serve. In these multifarious practices I recognize new vehicles that allow users to traverse the social world and penetrate previously unattainable regions of anonymity,[2] as well as to expand their restorable social reach. In light of this formulation of the meaning of virtual togetherness, I will question the dichotomy between the private and the public that is at the root of both virtual utopia and dystopia.

Finally, and this is the central thesis that I propose here, the concept of (virtual) community with all the normative load[3] it carries, has led analysis into a unproductive ideological exchange disputing the possibility for genuine community to be sustained through computer networks.[4] This has deflected attention from the fact that a continuum of forms of being and acting together is growing from the technology of the Internet. Community, whatever definition one may choose to give it, would then be one possible form of virtual togetherness among many. Thus, I see virtual togetherness, not genuine community, as the core of the community model of the Internet outlined in the beginning of this chapter.

The opposite of virtual togetherness is not 'real' or 'genuine' community, as the current theoretical debate suggests, but the isolated consumption of digitized goods and services within the realm of alienated[5] private life. The issue, then, is not which (and whether any) form of togetherness online deserves the 'warmly persuasive' (Williams, 1985, p. 76) label of community. The challenge to analysts is to understand and appreciate the significance of these use genres, representing various forms of transcending the private and navigating the social world, for individual participants, for society at large and for the shaping of the Internet.

Infosumption: The Rationalistic Ideal of Internet Use

Accounts of participation in virtual groups cropped up in the stories of some of the people I interviewed, without specific questioning. Invited to explain how they used the Internet, they started with their online groups. With others, no mention of any social life online was ever made. My pointed question about whether they took part in virtual groups or forums received sometimes very sceptical and even derogatory responses:

> I am reading a few groups, not much. But again, nothing intrigues me to participate. So I don't know how widespread that communal thing is. I have no idea. I haven't participated. Chats, I find, are a horrible waste of time! I tried it once or twice and said, forget it! [What is so disappointing about it?] Oh, the subjects, the way they talked about it ... (Reiner)

> I am aware, like you say, of newsgroups or usegroups, whatever they are called, I tried, two or three years ago, some and I just didn't care. The crap that came back and the depth of the level of knowledge didn't really strike me, it wasn't worth going through these hundreds of notes – somebody asking this or that to find ... But I couldn't find any substantive issues and I did not care, I did not want to use it to advertise my own knowledge, so I just left them alone. (Don)

Garry, the naval radio-operator, summed up this particular position regarding Internet group discussions in a useful model. According to him, a good radio-operator sends as little as possible, but receives the maximum:

> Because the radio-operator is there just to get all the information he can about the weather, the time signal, about what's happening in different countries and orders from different places. And if he can get that efficiently without going on the air too much, then it is to the benefit of everybody. If everybody is on the air asking questions, then you cannot hear really anything but miles and miles of questions being asked. That's why the etiquette of the professional radio-operator was to say as little as possible. Like telegrams used to be ... To me, it is a matter of getting information across. (Garry)

Coming from this perspective, Garry, like the other respondents quoted previously, scorned the 'noisy people out there on the Internet', 'the empty heads' who were out there first: 'There are always people out there who just have their mouth hanging out and they are just talking, and talking, and talking, and just creating a lot of babble' (Garry).

These empty heads produced 'garbage upon garbage' on the Internet, a low level content with which Garry did not want to engage. He believed that his contributions, had he made any, would not have been appreciated. To post in newsgroups, for him, would have been like 'casting pearls before swine – that means it is pretty pointless to be intellectual when you are dealing with people who just want to talk about garbage'.

A closer look at the 'radio-operator' perspective reveals the underlying communicative values to be 'substantive issues', 'information', 'efficiency'. The respondents in this category upheld a rationalistic ideal of information production and exchange and judged the content of the discussions they found on the Internet by it. The high expectations they had to the quality of communication prevented them from contributing any content themselves because of an 'expert knowledge or nothing' attitude. From the perspective of this rationalistic ideal, these respondents repudiated sociability understood as the pursuit of human contact, acquaintance, friendship, solidarity and intimacy, as legitimate motives for using the Internet. The users in this category were going to the Internet for timely, accurate, reliable information and, quite naturally, were finding it in the online offerings of traditional information institutions such as news agencies, radio stations, newspapers, and government sites.

Instrumental Interaction: Rational and yet Social

My son has an Attention Deficit Disorder ... and it was really interesting to get online and to talk to people from all over the world about this issue. It was called the ADD forum – a really good way for providing information. (Martha)

In Martha's narrative, one noticed the persistent authority of the rationalistic ideal with information as its central value. Recognition of other users on the Internet, not necessarily experts or expert organizations, as sources of information and ideas was also apparent. Information remained the leading motive stated for going on the Internet, however 'talking to people online' was not perceived as its antithesis:

At one turn of the conversation when Martha admitted that she missed the ADD forum that was available only through CompuServe, she took care to emphasize: 'It wasn't chatting to meet people and get to know people. It was chatting about ideas and exchanging information', thus paying tribute to the rationalistic ideal.

Similarly, John perceived his participation in the SkyTraveler's Digest,[6] a mailing list for motor glider hobbyists, as a valuable resource in problematic situations when decisions regarding new equipment had to be made or technical problems to be solved. He had approached newsgroups in the same way: in cases when he needed a question answered, a problem solved, a new experience illuminated: his wife's diabetes, a new type of apple tree he wanted to plant, his new communication software, etc. He enjoyed the helpfulness and solidarity demonstrated by people who took the time to answer his queries in their specifically human and social aspects, but admitted that once the problem was solved, the interpersonal communication would fade away:

> We don't normally communicate socially – how are you, what's the weather ... It's usually when a technical question comes up. After that question is solved, we may talk a little bit about how old we are, what we did. But once the problem is solved this fades away. But yet, those people are still in the background. And when I am looking at postings and see their name, a bell rings. (John)

Thus people with expertise and experience in different matters of interest were coming into 'attainable reach' through the medium. John himself would only respond to questions others had asked on the mailing list when he had 'something positive', meaning well-established, proven, to say and believed that this reserved culture of 'positive', substantive exchange made his mailing list work well.

Merlin, too, was quite scrupulous as far as the quality of the contributions in his virtual group was concerned. He insisted he was on this mailing list in order 'to learn', 'to expand my understanding of the electrical components used in the electric car'. He saw the list as a 'semi-professional community' and only felt the right to contribute when he had hard evidence to show for it: 'somebody says something wrong or asks a question, especially connected to hybrids, because I have thought about it, I haven't done any real calculations, [only] very simple calculations which answered some questions that were asked'. Despite the preponderance of strictly technical content on the list, the personalities of participants had come through and Merlin had developed some curiosity as to what kind of people they were. When he had happened to be in the locations of some of the men on the list, he had driven by their houses or shops and had met some of them. Putting a face to an e-mail address or alias, a living image and context to stories told on the list, seemed to have been a transforming experience in terms of how Merlin felt about his list:

Now, I have met these people, so it actually means a lot more to me, now that I have met [emphasizes] ... I thought Jerry was a wealthy guy, in fact, you have to categorize him as poor, he is a postman and he hasn't worked for over a year, he is obviously not rich. And I have seen him, and I have seen his wife Shauna, I actually saw his two daughters in passing. I have seen the truck, the car, that had this plasma fireball incinerated inside of the car, I saw the battery – there were three batteries welded together in a T-junction, I mean really, to do that damage, it really had to have a lot of energy ... (Merlin).

Thus, unexpectedly, the rationalistic model of Internet use (Merlin insisted on his loyalty to it) was showing cracks where it would have seemed most unlikely – on a technical discussion list.

Exploring Ideas in Virtual Public Spheres

For Patrick and Myra, a young couple, 'chatting about ideas' was one of the main attractions of newsgroups. In this use genre, the high standing of information, ideas and knowledge was preserved, however it was inextricably linked to interest in socializing with people as knowers, interpreters, discussion partners and opponents. The contact between the two of them (Patrick and Myra) was actually established when Myra found in the Albanian newsgroup a posting from a guy who wanted to 'ask some questions about Albania to an Albanian, to a guy or girl who knew about the country'. Reflecting over a gratifying exchange they had had in an Internet newsgroup, they described it like this:

We started talking about serious politics ... Albanian, Eastern European. We were talking – long, long, long messages – political analysis, how this or that could be. No jokes, no stupidities like oh, I find you attractive, nothing like that.

In her description of another newsgroup exchange with a previously unknown contributor, Myra stressed both the quality of the ideas that were articulated in the posting and the relationship established between its author and herself as a reader:

There is a guy in the Russian group – and I saw a couple of postings of his and, of course, I sent him a message, a personal one and I said well, I am delighted, I like them and he replied – oh, I am delighted that you appreciate them. So you kind of establish a closer contact. We don't write to each other or anything but when I see a posting by him, I will go and read it. (Myra)

Myra used to write a lot in Albanian newsgroups and mailing lists (trying to express her opinion regarding various, mostly political, issues) but the highly controversial nature of the political topics she was addressing drew to her intolerable flaming[7] and disciplinary measures. Patrick, for his part, admitted that he was visiting newsgroups to some extent also for the controversy: 'But I like provocative topics and if someone starts flaming me, fine, I get what I deserve ... I have been flamed and certainly will be flamed. I don't avoid that'.

Both Patrick and Myra thought of newsgroups not simply as an information resource, but also as a space for intellectual sociability and political debate, a 'public forum' in Patrick's own words, where diverse opinions could meet and clash as a matter of course. The point of being there was to get exposed to others' perspectives and to argue for your own, to build alliances with like-minded people and to enjoy intellectually stimulating encounters.

An online political discussion that had gone the extra mile to subsequent organization and collective action was represented by the mailing list Theodore belonged to. The participants in that discussion had taken their interaction beyond collective sense-making of events and issues. An agreement over needs and directions of political organizing had emerged out of their exchange and debate. The grassroots Ethiopian National Congress had brought together Ethiopian refugees scattered all over the world who had reached agreement over their common cause and course of action in their virtual togetherness:

> Individuals on the list started talking about this thing and said we should do something about it and so it started as a virtual organization and it transformed itself, there was a meeting in July of last year in LA – the initial meeting for individuals to get together and discuss this thing and then there was another meeting in October where the actual organization was proclaimed and established in Atlanta. (Theodore)

Chatting: Sociability Unbound

The cases discussed so far derived in a significant way from the rationalistic model of Internet communication, albeit implanting in it interpersonal interaction and sociability in different degrees and variations. However, when I listened to Sandy I realized that a qualitative break with the rationalistic model was taking place. Sandy spoke for a markedly different model of Internet communication, one that had sociability as its central value. Ironically, as I explained in Chapter 4, Sandy was first introduced to the Internet through a university course she was taking. That means finding information had been the foremost rationale for using the medium presented to her by authoritative sources. However, it did not take long before Sandy discovered the chat lines and got fascinated by what they had to offer. In her open and emotional statement Sandy showed no signs of guilt or remorse for abandoning the rationalistic model of Internet use. In fact, she did not seem to notice the major subversion to which she was subjecting the medium as perceived from the 'radio-operator' perspective. She was happy to be one of those noisy people who were out there 'talking, and talking, and talking' (see Garry's quote earlier in this chapter). Her main reason for being on the Net was 'meeting people in there and having a great time talking to them' (see Martha's statement in the opposite sense above).

> I was drawn to the rooms that were like the parent zone, health zone and things like that, just general interest ... I would talk to people in there and then I met this guy who lives in Ontario and his wife and they had a room called the Fun Factory. It was about 10 of us. We just hung out there, we went in there and just chatted about life. All kind of fun things – we goofed around, told jokes, stories, whatever. The same ten people. Oh, I still talk to them all. In fact we've flown and we have met each other and some of us ... Lots of times other people came in, but this was the core. (Sandy)

Paradoxically, what started as 'goofing around' ended up having dramatic consequences for Sandy's 'real' life. In Sandy's own reflections, as a direct result of her hanging out in chat lines, her marriage fell apart completely. That was because online she met 'really good people' who helped her to regain her self-confidence: 'then, all of a sudden, I was reminded that I was a real person [emotional tone] with real emotions, and real feelings and I was likeable by people'. One of her new online friends was the first person to whom she revealed that her husband was beating her:

> And he just said – get out! You have to get out, Sandy, you cannot stay there! And he and I became really close good friends and he convinced me that life could go on and even that I would lose a lot of materialism, I would gain so much more, if I could fight this fight and get out. And I did. I left. (Sandy)

Another person Sandy met on the chat line also became a close friend and shared a lot in Sandy's marital problems. He was also instrumental in helping her with the technological challenges of the Internet. He was a computer professional and taught Sandy skills that she needed to move and act freely online. Thus, one can notice how, starting from a close personal relationship established online, Sandy had occasionally gone the full circle back to hard information and proficiency in one particular area:

> And he made it easy. I would say 'I don't think I can do that', and he would say – 'I remember you saying that about such and such, but if you just think about how it works'. And he would explain to me how it worked. And then I would go and do it myself. (Sandy)

The chat room Sandy was describing could hardly meet the high standards of community raised by the critics of the idea of virtual community. The interactions in that room had been vibrant, and yet superficial, intense, and fleeting at the same time:

> In the room it was mostly goofing around, telling cracking jokes. And also there was always stuff going on in the background in private conversations and then you'd have the public room. And often you would have three or four private conversations going at the same time as the room. (Sandy)

What was actually happening in this environment was that people were meeting previously anonymous strangers and treating them as someone 'like myself', someone who could laugh at the same jokes, talk about the same topics of interest and then walk away and go on with his or her own life. That is, what the room was providing for its visitors was an environment for 'fluid sociability among strangers and near-strangers' understood in a sense similar to that suggested by Philippe Ariès in his discussion of the sociability of pre-modern cities. Ariès writes: 'This is a space of heterogeneous co-existence, not of inclusive solidarity or of conscious collective action; a space of symbolic display, of the complex blending of practical motives with interaction ritual and personal ties ...' (cited in Weintraub, 1997, p. 25).

The chat room Sandy frequented, also displayed social proximity found across physical distance. Sandy's account indicated that the people she was meeting in her chat room were socially and culturally close to her: they liked rock and roll, Star Trek and kayaking. They had computers of the same make, and similar kinds of marital problems. The spirit of sociability sustained in the chat room was a product of the shared desire of these people to overcome the privateness of their existence, to go out and socialize some of their most personal experiences, anxieties and troubles. Mere contemporaries and social types, to invoke Schutz's terminology describing the social structures of the lifeworld, were turning into fellow men and women to each other through the creative appropriation of a communication technology. The merry superficiality of the chat room was only the first level of contact where, through the expression of one's personality in public, interpersonal affinities were sought and negotiated. The deeper effects of this activity were realizing themselves at the level of the private conversations breaking off from the party and even further, into participants' actions in the offline world. These were effects concerning again the private spheres of the individuals involved. However, the return to the private to deal with its challenges was performed at a different level, bringing in a re-affirmed self[8] and new interpretative frameworks for addressing vital problems of everyday life acquired in the online forms of intersubjectivity.

At the time I spoke with Sandy, the Fun Factory chat room had died out – its participants had left. Sandy emphasized that she did not want to chat online so much any more, 'at least for now':

> I think I want to establish social relationships in the real world instead of in the virtual world right now. That's important for me where I am right now. I still want to keep in contact with the friends that I have met online and I do that by e-mail now instead of chat rooms. (Sandy)

In Sandy's case, the involvement in a form of virtual togetherness had clearly been a situational phenomenon. The problems and relevance systems of a particular situation in her life had led Sandy to seek sociability, recognition, social support, and intimacy in the more or less anonymous virtual association of people she could meet through the Internet chat programs. The specific characteristics of her situation have already been discussed in Chapter 5. The most prominent of them were social isolation and dysfunctional abusive marriage. In her virtual togetherness with the other members of the chat room, Sandy had found the means to deal with the problems she was facing there and then. In a changed situation, she was consciously choosing a different route and different means for building togetherness with people. Yet, as it can be noticed in her statement, she valued the relationships she had created online and worked to translate them into a different format. Her 'virtual' friendships were in the process of becoming 'real', and as such, sustained through other communication technologies – e-mail and telephone. A transformation that once again exposes the fragility of the constructed boundary between real and virtual togetherness.

Community as in Commitment

With Ellen, the concept of community dominated the conversation from the first question. Ellen had hooked up to the Internet from home after she became housebound and diagnosed with a rare, crippling chronic illness. Her explicit motivation for becoming an Internet user was to be able to connect to a support group. She simply felt 'very desperate for information and help'. 'Getting information' and 'getting support' were two inseparable reasons for her to go online. Thus, Ellen joined an invisible, dispersed group of people who were logging on everyday to get the 'gift of making this connection' with each other:

> to discover that thousands of people are going through exactly the same incredible experience and nobody in their family understands, their husbands and wives don't understand, the doctor doesn't believe them and they have this terrible difficulty of functioning. And yet, there is this tremendously strong community of people who have never met and probably will never meet but who are so loyal to each other and have such a strong support because it is a lifeline for all of us. (Ellen)

The list was experienced as a safe environment by these people, a place where they felt comfortable saying:

> I've had a really bad day, I had to go see a specialist and I had such a difficulty and couldn't breathe and it was such a challenge to get there and then the doctor was awful to me. And then I got home and my husband was complaining because the house wasn't clean ... (Ellen)

And immediately after a complaint like that would pop up in members' mail boxes, there would be a 'flurry' of supportive responses. Loyalty, high tolerance for 'dumping', safety, family-like atmosphere, compassion – these were all attributes Ellen used to describe the quality of interaction in her 'wonderful group'.

The real-life effects consisted of 'a lot of confidence', 'getting my life in proportion again', 'getting a sense of myself' (compare with an almost identical formulation by Sandy) 'feeling much less a failure'. Learning a lot about the disease was among the benefits of list membership, however Ellen took care to distinguish the particular kind of learning that was taking place there:

> I learnt so much from these people who had had the disease for years. I had tried to get hold of some medical information. But getting online is different because there, for the first time, you get information from people who have trodden this path already! (Ellen)

For good or ill as the case may be, the victims of the disease Ellen had were short-circuiting the medical establishment and the expert knowledge produced by it and were learning from each other. More accurately, they were collectively appropriating and using expert knowledge in ways they had found relevant and productive in their own unique situations as sufferers and victims. On the list they were creating this culture of appropriation and a stock of knowledge stemming from their individual and yet intertwined lifeworlds.

A similar sense of gain from online support group discussions came through clearly in Matthew's comment. According to him, people with similar medical problems learnt from each other about the existence of a variety of treatment options, which, consequently, empowered them when dealing with the medical profession. Matthew challenged the very notion of a patient. In his understanding, people with health problems were clients, customers and in the best case, collaborators with doctors, nurses and prosthetists. To be able to act in this capacity however, they needed to be informed and acculturated in their disability. This is, Matthew believed, what online support groups, such as the mailing list for amputees he himself had initiated, were instrumental in doing. 'I learnt more about being an amputee in the one year on the mailing list than throughout the twenty years I had lived with my disability', Matthew insisted passionately.

What distinguished Ellen's experience from other, more detached, forms of learning like those described by previous respondents was the fact that the people she was interacting with online had come to constitute a collective entity with its own distinctive culture. Her virtual group had a relatively stable membership communicating on a daily basis and feeling responsible for each other's well-being. Both commonality of interest and diversity could be found in that group. Most of its participants were people seeking alternative approaches for dealing with the chronic devastating disease they had. In Ellen's estimate, most of them were highly educated and articulate. Women were in the majority. At the same time, members of the group came from different religious backgrounds and life experiences in terms of profession, family, nationality and other factors. Yet, characteristically, they were entering their shared space ready and eager to listen to interpretations coming from viewpoints different from their own:

> Like this woman in Israel, a Hebrew scholar, a convert to Judaism, she has the most fascinating perspective on things. There are amazing things coming from her … But nobody has ever tried to push one point of view above another. There has been very much a sense of sharing. (Ellen)

Ellen's account describes a 'warmly persuasive' version of a robust online community distinguished by interpersonal commitment and a sense of common identity that could meet the highest standards. Ellen's Internet was thus markedly different from the rationalist model of Internet communication defended by the 'infosumers'. Yet, as we have seen from the cases cited earlier, not all home users of the Internet recognized or were eager to grasp this opportunity offered by the technology. It took a particular configuration of situational factors: a rare disease, physical and social isolation, a vital need to come to terms with a radically new experience, and mastery of language and expression (recall that Ellen was a philologist, editor and writer) for this rather extreme form of online community involvement to materialize. And it should be noted that even in this case online community was not displacing face-to-face community where the latter did or could have existed. It was rather filling the gap left by the impossibility of face-to-face community or the inability of existing face-to-face communities to satisfy important needs of the subject. Furthermore, online community was, helping the individual member, at least in the evidence presented by Ellen's case, in her struggle to regain confidence and motivation for rebuilding face-to-face relationships.

I would now like to go back and revise the theoretical debate about virtual community in the context of the various experiences of my respondents. Let me start the interpretation of the emergent continuum between what I called 'the rationalistic model of Internet communication' and the 'community as in commitment' experience with the observation that in all of the cases discussed above, the respondents had access to principally the same technology with some variations in computing power, speed and access time which, I found, were not related to the prevalent type of use.

The users who denied the communal aspects of the Internet (most of them men) came from a strictly utilitarian value orientation. They were using the Internet to find positive, reliable, scientific, professionally presented information and were more often finding it in the virtual projections of institutions such as online magazines and newspapers (Reiner), radio and television stations' sites, government sites (Garry), news agencies (Norris) and scientific publications online (Sophie). To most of these users, newsgroups and mailing lists had little to offer and respectively, communal forms were questionable in principle. The everyday practice of such users, I suggest, is organized by the consumption model of the Internet. The everyday practice of the infosumer, for its part, continuously reproduces the consumption model of the Internet as a social institution.

On the other hand, representatives of disenfranchised groups – in my study these were clearly Ellen and Matthew, both disabled, but also in some sense Sandy (a victim of spousal abuse) and Merlin (unemployed long

179

term) – were using the technology as a tool to carve spaces of sociability, solidarity, mutual support and situated, appropriative learning in communion with others. As I tried to show, these two forms of Internet use were not separated by empty space but by a whole range of intermediate modalities. Martha and John appreciated the empowerment stemming from the opportunity to draw on the knowledge, experience and practical help of otherwise anonymous people in the areas of their specific interests and concerns. Myra, Patrick and Theodore were new immigrants struggling to make sense of the dramatic political events that had befallen their native countries, as well as to sustain a meaningful balance between disparate, and even conflicting, sides of their cultural identities.[9] They were leaning on both the informational and the communal affordances of the Internet, thus forging a medium for political debate and civic involvement.

On the basis of these observations, I feel in a position to define more accurately the difference between the consumption model and the community model of the Internet. The qualitative distinction between the two models lies in the absence or presence of users' involvement with one another. The degree of immediacy and depth of this involvement may vary in the different versions of the community model. It may or may not meet a normative standard of 'genuine community', but in all the expressions of this model, users *produce* something of value to others – content, space, relationship and/or culture. I believe that the legitimacy and the practical possibility of this kind of user involvement is what needs to be defended against the assault of the consumption model and its related practices.

Between the Public and the Intimate: Gradients of Immediacy

In the previous chapter, I turned around Williams's (1974) notion of 'mobile privatization' and pointed out that the behaviour of many of my respondents in relation to the Internet constituted a practice of 'immobile socialization' – associating with other people and social entities without leaving their private space. The forms of 'virtual togetherness' I presented above are further expressions of this practice. They undermine a central dichotomy that has been employed to frame the discussion of the social meaning of the Internet – that between the public and the private. My respondents' narratives revealed a process of subtle negotiation of the boundaries between the private world – the one that the individual user felt he or she had under control – and the public spaces created on and through the Internet. In fact, by the end of my argument here I will suggest that it would be useful to recognize the falseness of the dichotomy between the private and the public (at least in the context of Internet togetherness). Schutz's analogue model of the experienced social world as a continuum of 'levels of anonymity' (Schutz and Luckmann, 1973, p. 80) offers a more suitable basis for understanding 'virtual togetherness'.

Most of the people I interviewed, especially the women, spoke about an initial shock and fear for their privacy when using the Internet. As new users, they found it hard to imagine exactly how visible and socially consequential their various actions and interactions were. Sandy recollected her early anxiety with amusement: 'I remember when the modem hooked up the first time, I was scared. I thought, oh, no! I thought everyone was gonna know everything about me for some reason'. Jane was still at the stage where making a comment in a newsgroup or participating in a chat line felt 'creepy': 'So, I just made a comment. But I didn't like the idea because I realized later that anybody could read my comment and send me e-mail ... I didn't make any other comments'.

With experience, users were developing strategies for careful control of the degree of self-exposure they allowed for on the Internet in particular action contexts. Martha's approach involved complex manipulation of two e-mail addresses, one 'anonymous' and the other indicating her real name:

> The address I have at the VCN[10] forwards mail ... to my home address. When the people I am contacting are a non-profit web site I can contact them either way – from my home address or the VCN one. I like to have that anonymity. Then any mail that goes to the VCN, the people that have sent it don't know where it goes to until I contact them. (Martha)

Similarly, when Myra wanted to respond to a request for information posted in a newsgroup by an unknown person hidden behind a nickname, she reasoned:

> Robert Redford [poster's nickname]! ... Let's see what his true name is. (I am a scientist after all!) At the same time I wanted to be safe and because I had several accounts scattered around the world, I wrote to him from an account that I had in Italy. And on the next day when I checked that account, I found a message from that guy that I also thought was a Pole ...

The mystery guy and Myra started a 'serious' political discussion (referred to earlier in this chapter) which went in concentric circles from public issues to private thoughts and feelings:

And then after months, because he was always asking questions: how are things over there … After months, I started joking and said, well, the next message I expect something like ten questions from you. And here come ten questions: How tall are you? What kind of wine do you like? Do you like sailing? … things like that. So it got more into [I suggest personal, she doesn't accept it, preferring] ordinary human terms rather than talking about big issues. (Myra)

Myra was drawing the trajectory of a fascinating gradual movement between the public and the private, or as Schutz would put it, between different gradients of immediacy spanning the distance between the most anonymous – 'an Albanian, a girl or guy who knew about the country', 'that guy that I also thought was a Pole' – and the most intimate, as we will see shortly. Communication media varied accordingly. They were used with subtle discretion, like musical instruments by a virtuoso, to carefully negotiate transcendence of social and cultural boundaries, one infinitesimal step at a time:

And then it was almost a year after we started talking … I don't know, maybe I was bored again or I had other problems in my life when I decided again, well, what's this guy, let's hear his voice. Let's make him a real thing rather than just an e-mail header. So I asked him: 'May I give you a call?', and he said 'yes'. I was a little shy, because I knew nothing about his *private* [emphasis mine] life. You don't want to intrude into somebody's life and we were just friends, not even friends, not even close friends. But he said yes and I call him, and I talk to this guy who happens to have an accent, we talked about some rubbish, I guess. I don't even remember, nobody would have guessed then that things would get … (Myra)

As the story progressed, the phone conversations between the two of them became a regular event, alternating with hours-long Internet chats, e-mails and again hours-long phone conversations. Then, pictures were exchanged, then a marriage proposal from him came by e-mail in the form of a joke: 'And it was easier to make that joke on the Internet than on the phone' (Patrick). Then, 'things started getting more and more romantic' (Myra). And finally, a visit was arranged:

MYRA:	At the beginning of March of 1997 I came to Vancouver. We met at the airport and that was it.
MARIA:	How did you find each other after having all the correspondence? Did reality change your image of the other person?
PATRICK AND MYRA:	No.
MYRA:	I remember that I was very tense, of course.

PATRICK:	Me too [unclear].
MYRA:	I remember I got out of the gates. The first thing that I saw was him. He was coming towards me. We just hugged and we kept walking. I was talking all the time because otherwise I would explode. It was my usual way of talking – making fun of everything including myself. He was used to that, I guess. He wasn't surprised that I was behaving ...
MARIA:	How long did it take from the first time you exchanged messages to that moment?
MYRA:	A year-and-a-half.

As I explained earlier, in Sandy's story the interaction in the semi-public space of the chat room consisted of 'mostly goofing around, telling, cracking jokes'. In the private background, however, joking was turning into deeply intimate revelations:

Roland's and mine relationship was mostly joking around, but we at some point, got quite deep into his relationship with his wife and my relationship with my husband ... He was married and going through really tough times with his wife, so he and I got really good friends and we e-mailed each other back and forth every day and just having that relationship with him made me feel alive! And made me realize how much really I had going for me because after my husband diminished my self-worth and self respect so low ... (Sandy)

Sandy also walked all the way from 'cracking jokes' in public to a romantic relationship with one of her new friends from the chat group. The dynamic of the story of that relationship was similar to Myra and Patrick's – long chats, coming to know each other's life stories in detail, exchange of pictures, and finally, a face-to-face meeting. The ending of it all, however, was not quite so happy as in the previous case. Sandy's partner, C.K. had taken advantage of the manipulative powers of the Internet to lead numerous women into believing that each of them was the only one he was attracted to and exchanged intimate correspondence with. A discovery Sandy made by accident on his computer during a visit, opened her eyes to the fact that C.K.'s compassion and caring had been shared with many other women across North America at exactly the same time when her own romance with him was in full swing. In a theoretically quite interesting move Sandy chose to publicize her deeply private pain. Enraged, she sent a message to these women explaining what C.K. was actually doing thus creating a powerful, even if short-lived, united front against the trickster: 'None of them [the women she e-mailed] hated me, they were really angry with him. He took some pretty big flak over that'.

In the context of a disease-related mailing list, having hundreds of readers and dozens of contributors all around the world, Ellen also traversed a spiral of public to private and back to public communications. Initially, she was 'intimidated by the very hugeness' of the list and did not feel confident enough to contribute. However, in the midst of the big group discussion, after a while, Ellen would notice people that she 'would resonate with': 'I would find myself looking through the list of messages for their names – just to see whether they have written that day'. Finally, one day, she contacted a couple of people through the so-called 'back channels', sending private e-mail. This move coincided with the creation of a new sub-list by one of the women Ellen had contacted. So, about seventeen people, who had found through the big list that they shared similar interests and approaches to healing, formed a 'semi-private' group branching off from the open public forum and initially exchanging carbon copied e-mails with each other.

As the interest in that group turned out to be quite high, at one stage it had to be transformed into a new 'official', as Ellen put it, mailing list based on a server at St. John's University in Boston. This meant that from a closed 'private discussion', the list was going back into the public realm where everyone could read and join it. Some members feared that this would compromise the quality of the exchange, as well as the openness and the depth of the interpersonal sharing. The group deliberated on the problem and finally decided that it was 'the idea of keeping it private versus having new blood, and new information, and new ideas. Also importantly, being able to offer what we had to more people'. They chose publicness and, initially, Ellen was ambivalent about it:

> I felt very uncomfortable with the idea of becoming public. I wasn't sure I could continue posting because I am a very, very private person. I don't like the feeling of being on stage. It is a very personal medium – I find that people write very personal messages. They really reveal themselves very deeply. (Ellen)

Eventually, feeling that the characteristics 'very nice atmosphere and a sense of camaraderie and common ground' of the list were preserved, Ellen overcame her reservations and continued to be an active contributor. Thus, after finding re-affirmation of her interests and values in other individuals and later, in a close in-group, Ellen took her deeply private thoughts and sensations out of her walk-in closet (where her old Mac was located, if you recall Chapter 6) and came out on the stage of the public realm empowered as an actor. After some time on the new list, someone suggested that the members exchange personal biographies. This made

Ellen reflect on the dialectic of public and private, self-presentation and knowledge of the other person in the online environment:

> I found it so fascinating to read – first of all, what everyone chooses to say about themselves; and also think about what I want to convey about myself – here I am in this unique online environment where I can't be seen, I can't be heard and, yet, I want to convey something about myself ... I kept them all. So, that gave more of a sense of the individual lives and of being a group. (Ellen)

What this public–private–intimate continuum helps us realize is that, analogous to the consumption versus community continuum, there is no critical point where a person's or a group's behaviour can be definitively characterized as private as opposed to public and vice versa. People plan and experience their social action as combining privacy and publicness in different proportions. The task typically assigned to the Internet is to bring the determination of this proportion under the user's control. To whom do I want to listen; to whom do I want to talk; who do I allow to listen to me? For and with whom do I want to act; who do I allow to act upon me; how big and open a collectivity do I want to act with? The different answers individual users give (more or less consciously) to these questions led them to choose individual, 'private' e-mail or a dozen of 'carbon copies', a posting to a closed or to an open mailing list, 'lurking' in a newsgroup or contributing to one; joining a mailing list, or, as a matter of fact, creating and moderating one (Matthew in my respondent group).

If we look at Myra's and Ellen's example in detail we will recognize the multidimensionality of the notions of private and public that emanate from them. There are at least three senses in which publicness and privacy are perceived and respectively manipulated online – in terms of the forum, or space of gathering; in terms of the content of the communication; and in terms of the action taken – does it affect others or is it performed in perfect privacy 'within the lair of the skull' as Anderson (1983) has put it, in describing the act of reading the newspaper. What emerges is a multidimensional scale on which privacy and publicness of social action can be gauged. At all stations of the processes of encountering others and interacting with them online, people are located in their private homes. From this position, they turn themselves, initially as simple consumers/readers, to forums that are public. Later, they reach out to another private individual, sending him/her content that can itself be classified as dealing with issues of public concern or as the opposite – with private issues.

Thus all three components in which I have subdivided the process analytically – forum, content and action – can be either public or private and people carefully select the degree of openness of each component they permit at any particular moment. Virtual togetherness and immobile socialization defy the qualification of Internet use as contributing to the 'increased privatization and individualization' of existence and the 'evacuation and diminishing of the public sphere of contemporary western societies' (Kumar, 1995, p. 163). Neither do the 'networked nation' (Hiltz and Turoff, 1978) or the 'global village' (McLuhan, 1964, p. 93) metaphors accurately describe the actual practice of users. What I see happening is a careful crafting of boundaries and relationships between individuals and individuals and groups. These boundaries delineate new spaces of social knowledge and action spanning the public and the private spheres.

Summary

Two conceptual dichotomies powerfully shape the theoretical debate concerning social life on the Internet: virtual versus real and public versus private. The first polarity opposes 'virtual' to 'real' community. The second, compels us to choose between the images of the Internet as a medium fostering the extreme privatization of society and the Internet as an automatic community-building technology enhancing public participation. Instead of taking a side with respect to this received disposition of forces, I have questioned the usefulness of the very dichotomous mode of thinking that underlies existing debates. Users approach the medium, as my data have shown, from a variety of situational motivations, needs and ideologies. In doing that, they generate a rich repertory of use genres, each of which needs careful consideration and evaluation on its own merits, or, as Lefebvre would advise, in its own 'historical concreteness'. The preoccupation with ideologically constructed standards blinds commentators to the possibility of new, unexpected, unimaginable and yet humanistic and empowering variations of technological practice.

It is my belief that the careful examination of actual Internet use in its numerous forms should be oriented toward the discerning and articulating of the empowering aspects of the medium as they present themselves to people in particular situations. A struggle to direct resources towards the further development and re-enforcement of these aspects of the Internet as a technology and a social institution can start from that basis.

A quote I found by serendipity in Schutz's (1964) *Collected Papers* helped me to summarize what my somewhat confusing journey through my respondent's social actions on the Internet had helped me discover. In the conclusion of his analysis of Mozart's musical contribution, Schutz writes:

> I submit that Mozart's main topic is not, as Cohen believed, love. It is the metaphysical mystery of the existence of a human universe of pure sociality, the exploration of the manifold forms in which man meets his fellow-man and acquires knowledge of him. The encounter of man with man within the human world is Mozart's main concern. This explains the perfect humanity of his art. (1964, p. 199)

My study of the communicative and communal use of the Internet has uncovered a fascinating variety of forms in which individuals meet their fellow-men and women and acquire knowledge of them. The encounter of the person with the Other, in singular and plural, within the human world; the filling of erstwhile regions of anonymity with detailed knowledge of one's fellow human is one of the most exciting promises of the Internet. Discovering and promoting these manifold forms of human encounter in a new technological environment is, I believe, the central task of a humanistic study and shaping of the Internet.

Notes

[1] ARPANET was the predecessor of the Internet. The network was created by the US Defense Advanced Research Projects Agency (ARPA) in the late 1960s and became a testing ground for innovative concepts such as packet-switching, distributed topology and routing and the interconnecting of heterogeneous computer systems (see Abbate, 1994: iv).

[2] Recall Schutz's model of the social world presented in Chapter 2.

[3] Raymond Williams (1985), tracing the etymology of the word community, notes that it is 'the warmly persuasive word to describe an existing set of relationships; or the warmly persuasive word to describe an alternative set of relationships' that 'seems never to be used unfavorably and never to be given any positive opposing or distinguishing term' (p. 76). The heavy normative load of the concept of community explains why the early enthusiast have wanted to appropriate it for the legitimation of their project, for stressing its significance and nobility, while the critics have zealously defended an idealized notion signifying a higher state of human relationships that resists technological mediation. Williams' account of the historical development of the usage of the word reveals the interpretative flexibility of the term itself and hence its socially constructed character. There is no 'genuine' fact of nature or social history that the word community denotes. There is no consensually accepted definition of its meaning. Different social actors have appropriated the word at different points in history with different concrete contexts, goals and oppositions in mind.

[4]Ironically, in this debate virtual community non-believers (most of them moral philosophers and critical theorists) have passionately undermined the strongest alternative of the narrowly consumptive model of Internet development.

[5]Recall the forms of alienation that Lefebvre (1991) detected in private life and leisure.

[6]The name of the mailing list has been changed to avoid subject's identification.

[7]Flaming is an exchange of rude, sometimes abusive, messages online.

[8]Quite contrary to the floating multiple selves postmodern theorists anticipated.

[9]I should admit that this category of respondents was the one to which I could relate most closely because of my own personal social-biographical situation.

[10]Vancouver Community Net.

Conclusion

Everything is still at stake.

(Bruno Latour, 1988, *The pasteurization of France*, p. 160)

Starting this inquiry, I took seriously the proposition that users represent an active force in shaping technology together with various groups of experts and political players (Feenberg, 1991, 1999; Lie and Sorensen, 1996; Silverstone and Haddon, 1996). I adopted a view of technology that saw its actual reality in the concrete acts of its use and, more precisely, in the social event of technologically mediated interaction between the user or practitioner, and his or her physical and social environment.

My concrete object of interest was the Internet – a global computer network (technology) gradually evolving into a mass communication medium (a social institution). I focused on one of the most recent and significant developments in the evolution of the Internet – its penetration into the everyday life of a vast user population and specifically into one of its core sites: the home. The lack of conventional stock of knowledge regarding the 'appropriate' use of the Internet, I reasoned, would necessitate heavy involvement of users in signifying work. That is, these people would need to make sense and find applications of the medium with respect to specific tasks and problems they faced in their immediate environment. I expected to find early users actively discovering the relevance of the Internet to their social-biographical situations and initiating Internet-based practices that designers and promoters had not been able to imagine. To me, this meant that these users would be further inventing the Internet. Taking the Internet home, early users would not only act *with* it, but also *onto* it.

With my empirical study, then, I set out to understand the process in which users formed their relationship with the Internet that I believed to be mutually transformative. I was curious to discover the concrete courses of action and reasoning through which the new technology was drawn into domestic users' systems of relevances and how it was incorporated into their existing activities and relations forming the everyday life of the home. What did user agency look like in actual practice? What were the products of users' signifying work, how palpable, stable and portable were they?

Suggestions for Theory: Choices and Mediations in the User-Technology Relation

At the very beginning of the narratives that represented my avenues into users' authentic experiences, I discovered the figure of the warm expert. He or she was an expert in the sense of possessing working knowledge of the technology that was as yet unfamiliar to the novice user. However, she or he was not interacting with the user from a position in a formal set of relationships as it would have been the case, for example, with the expert from an Internet service provider's help desk or the instructor of a course. The warm expert inhabited the user's everyday life in the most direct sense, as a fellow-man or woman, who experienced the user's immediate situation. He or she acted as an interpreter between the technical system and the user's lifeworld, speaking the language of both. Notably, the warm expert was not an unbiased interpreter. She was passing to the new user her own understanding of the technology along with the universal meanings of technical features. She was teaching the user tricks for preserving autonomy and shortcuts to content of relevance. Thus, while the Internet in itself was infinitely open and diverse, new users did not rush to surf it at random as some surveys of user behaviour would suggest.[1] Neither did they diligently follow the instructions in their manuals or the bookmarks of their software providers. More often than not they entered the medium through a specific port suggested by the warm expert – an Ethiopian discussion group, an arthritis mailing list, a chat site, etc. In taking clues from their immediate social environment, users' learning of the Internet was no different from established patterns of use of traditional media, especially print. It was reminiscent of the two-step flow of mass communication discovered by Lazarsfeld et al., 1948 (see also Katz and Lazarsfeld, 1964). The new user was not facing the technology and the content and activities accessible through it as an isolated individual. Technology, content and activities were refracted by interpersonal influence and contextual relevance. Thus the interaction with the warm expert represented the first level of translation where the work of making the medium personally meaningful was started.

I found another expression of users' choice and activity in the variety of relations users formed with the Internet. I employed Ihde's (1990) phenomenology of human-technology relations to interpret the different ways in which the Internet mediated between users and their physical and social world. The blanket acceptance as well as the blanket rejection of the medium, I concluded, are crude constructs that do not capture the actual dynamic of the user-Internet relation. In practice, a person encountering a socio-technical system such as the Internet faces a richer gamut of choices. Engagement with the medium can remain instrumental, or it can grow into a more substantive and absorbing relation. These different relations produce different sets of opportunities and threats for users. I believe that awareness of this fact and, consequently, reflective navigation of the available choices contributes to personal empowerment with regard to the medium.

In the case of the embodiment relation, the Internet is simply a tool for accomplishing clearly defined goals in the surrounding physical or social world. It is mobilized by the acting person as an extension of his or her natural abilities. It can be experienced as an organic part of oneself, or on the contrary, as a poorly made prosthesis. In both cases, the world is on the other side of the technology and the limitations in seeing or manipulating it imposed by the mediational agent – the Internet – are accessible to reflection and action. In the hermeneutic relation, the attention of the user is focused on the technology as a representation of the world. The world and the medium merge. The technical and institutional codes embodied in the medium become codes for understanding the world. The advantage this relation brings to the user is an increased mastery of the technical and institutional code. The threat consists in the fact that the reduction of the world to its technical representation can easily be forgotten. In the alterity relation the world is bracketed out. The technology and/or the content it delivers become a source of emotions usually derived from the contact with another human being. Both technical creativity and technologically furnished escape from the problems of the surrounding world are viable outcomes of this relation.

In all these forms of human-technology relation a complex dialectic of amplification and reduction of human powers is involved. In order to be an autonomous agent in a technologically mediated world, the subject has to be able to question and realistically estimate his own relation with technology. The capacity for identifying the possibilities of alienation and disalienation represents a condition of competent use. I concluded, on the basis of the experiences shared by my respondents, that the establishment of a critical hermeneutic relation – a pointed interest in the technology as such, leading to a critical knowledge of the powers and distortions implicit in its code – represents one possible way of disalienation.

My examination of the home environment into which the Internet was introduced revealed another area of hard signifying work and struggle to define the user-technology relation. Bringing the Internet home, people had to deal with the question of exactly where the novelty belonged in terms of location, schedule and interfamily relationships. One aspect of this question referred to the symbolic ownership of the Internet connection: Did it belong equally to all family members or was there a privileged or solely entitled user? A second dimension had to do with privacy of use: would the person using the Internet at any particular time be allowed (or encouraged) to face the medium one-to-one, withdrawing from the ongoing life of the family collectivity or, on the contrary, would other family members be present and allowed to intervene? Finally, the place of the medium was selected with regard to the kind of activity it supported – imposed or intrinsic, work or pleasure.

The specific constellations of choices made along these three lines contributed to the emergence of different use practices and interfamily relations anchored in the medium. The Internet connection was used to demarcate zones of individual privacy within the home as well as to aid the creation of special bonds between family members and new ways of connecting to the broader social world. Gender roles with regard to the medium were renegotiated with some unexpected outcomes, such as the mother-son collaboration in mastering the technology and the leadership of women in Internet adoption motivated by perceived motherly responsibilities. Thus the function and the definition of the Internet within the individual home was negotiated with regard to the users' role in the family and the set of values established by the family group.

Certainly, these positions and values themselves had to be re-considered in the face of the new possibilities and challenges brought forth by the new medium. New responsibilities had to be added to the job characteristics of different family members. Patterns of time organization in the home had to be modified. The meaning of being at home and being together was changing and people struggled to make sense of these changes and reconcile desired new opportunities with valued old ways of life.

Suggestions for Political Practice: Grounded Visions of the Possible

Investigating the stabilized practices involving Internet use in the context of users' social-biographical situations, I discovered a multiplicity of situationally rational conceptions of the medium's usefulness and functionality. I referred to the various sets of activities growing out of these conceptions as 'use genres'. Use genres demonstrated a dual character in that they represented recurring patterns of local action undertaken by users and, at the same time, they gave the medium itself symbolic and substantive qualities that others could discover. Furthermore, these genres were related to conditions of individual existence characteristic of contemporary society and represented responses to widespread situational needs. I see these genres as a rich resource of ideas that can direct a pursuit of democratic Internet development. Democratic, in this context, means not only building a medium that is equitably accessible, but also equitably meaningful: inclusive of users' interests and goals, diverse in terms of features and supported activities, open and responsive to users' intervention and actively seeking users' involvement. The point is not to concoct utopian schemes for realizing the visions of theorists, technologists and political leaders, but rather to elaborate visions to be asserted in a technical and political process with an eye and ear turned to the unglamorous everyday initiatives of ordinary users. The political quality of users' resistance and creativity does not find expression in movements that have been conventionally and formally touted political. Rather, it lies in small gestures immersed in the current of daily life that despite their apparent triviality prove to be crucial in countering domination and instigating social change.[2] Democratic Internet development would mean bridging users' experiences with technical and political decision-making.

The agents of such a democratic Internet development would comprise a wide variety of players spanning the traditional and the non-traditional participants in socio-technical innovation. Various civic and public organizations and interest groups can establish an effective presence on the Internet by providing supportive platforms for the genres invented by users. Some of the cases I studied exemplified models for this: a web site of a local Attention Deficit Disorder parent support group, an organization of political refugees growing out of a mailing list and subsequently utilizing that list for further organizing. The cases of virtual community involvement I came across were particularly illuminating with respect to the kinds of Internet use representatives of disenfranchised groups found meaningful. Disease related associations, home care services, unemployment centres, ethnic and other civic organizations can adopt the role of equipment, service and content providers, and hubs for client-to-client or member-to-member sharing and organizing. Initiatives like that will, of course, be feasible if they receive support and funding from public bodies.

   Notable among the use genres I observed was the practice of talking back to public institutions and the mass media. I found a discrepancy between the ways these bodies framed their relationship with the prospective users of their Internet services, and the expectations of users themselves. Government and media sites were based on a traditional information-producer/provider versus client model. Users wished to be involved in a dialogue. Naïve hopes for a technologically mediated direct democracy aside, it can still be argued that there is room for more imaginative forms of two-way communication between citizens and institutions. A whole new practice of Internet-based *participatory public relations* can be imagined if citizens' interests, and not solely institutional agenda, are taken as cues. These possibilities need to be addressed imaginatively and realistically by a grassroots movement for a democratic Internet. Among the important tasks of such a movement would be the provision of non-commercial server space accessible to citizens' groups. Governments, for their part, should learn to appreciate the down-to-earth interests and projects of ordinary users and provide them with the resources they need.

   Equally suggestive were the use genres related to knowledge acquisition and application. In most of the cases I studied, users had become lay researchers willing to make informed decisions on matters of daily life and were aware, thanks to the Internet, of the wide range of alternatives available. Others were looking for intellectual challenges and/or exchange with a view to personal development. Universities and similar educational institutions had a limited assortment of offers along these lines. While the users counted on the new medium to bring knowledge spatially and humanly[3] closer to them, the response of universities, one of the central knowledge brokers in society, remained rigid and circumscribed within the old functional logic. Packaging and selling formal courses online, which is now the prevalent direction in universities' utilization of the Internet, I contend, is only one among numerous initiatives that the institutions of higher education can take in the new field of social action opening up for them. A critique of the real with the possible suggests that instead of (or parallel to) adopting market models for knowledge distribution, universities should work to transform themselves into open sources of knowledge modelled on the example of public broadcasting and adding to it a participatory component.

   Are these suggestions a product of utopian imagination? Is the critique of the real with the possible a futile enterprise that will be swept aside by the operational autonomy of the politically and economically powerful? The close investigation of users' worlds and their dealings with the Internet sustains the faith in alternative possibilities. After all, as Latour (1988) insists, the difference between the real and the possible is fragile (and that is why the critique proposed by Lefebvre's makes sense in the first place). What matters, Latour continues:

> are all the differences experienced between those that resist for long and those that do not, those that resist courageously and those that do not, those that know how to ally or isolate themselves and those that do not (p. 159).

Suggestions for Research: Critical Researchers as a Relevant Social Group

Speaking about alliances, I see the union between users and critical Internet researchers, many of whom are also ordinary users in their everyday lives, as a necessary condition for an effective critique of the real with the possible. The experience of this study confirmed my belief in the usefulness of a qualitative, ethnographically informed approach for providing a holistic, contextualized understanding of the social construction of the Internet as a technology and a communication medium. The examination of concrete human activities embedded in local situations uncovers important and previously missing aspects of this medium's social shaping. The standpoint of users proves to be a crucial vantage point towards the present and future of the Internet. The images of the medium captured from this perspective provide a healthy mixture of realism and optimism that can inform and direct its development.

Technical development and content and service creation performed by experts in specialized spheres is completed and ratified or, on the contrary, undermined and rendered inconsequential in the everyday dealings of ordinary users. The Internet can evolve into an inclusive and empowering communication medium if technical and content-related problems are defined and their solutions sought with conscious consideration of the users' perspective and, ideally, with the direct participation of everyday users. The Internet can stabilize as an oppressive, alienating technology and institution if users' perspectives and situated rationalizations are systematically ignored or counteracted by designers, developers and regulators. The important dilemma still to be tackled is, to paraphrase Lefebvre (1991), whether human beings will simply be made profitable through new high-tech mechanisms, or whether their everyday lives will be changed for the better building on the possibilities created by the new powerful technology (see p. 230). Critical communication research into the Internet is not simply a meta-enterprise of registering the resolution

195

of this dilemma, when and if it occurs. Research should be directly involved in its tackling. Internet researchers of all feathers are relevant social groups that participate in the construction of the Internet.

Therefore, a user-centred research practice, engaging researchers as user advocates should be consciously and persistently evolved. The results of such a research enterprise would be knowledge *for* users, a form of consciousness raising (see Smith's (1987) discussion of sociology for women) that explicates for users the intertwining of misery and power, of amplification and reduction in their daily transactions with the Internet. This research would produce a socio-technical literacy of action and choice.

Concrete projects to undertake within such a research paradigm would include, for example, the in-depth study of the uses of the Internet performed, attempted and imagined by people finding themselves in adverse situations: homebound, suffering from isolating illnesses, unemployed, elderly, new immigrants, delinquent youth or victims of abuse. Can the Internet help with the mastering of such situations? Through what political and design initiatives can the already unfolding creativity of such users be supported?

Multi-sited ethnographies (see Marcus, 1995) tracking the making of complex socio-technical phenomena such as Internet use genres are needed so that the diverse agencies involved in the process could be discerned. A popular web site, a virtual community, or an Internet campaign, represent perfect objects for an ethnography that looks at how such phenomena are constructed, who takes part and why, what role is played by technological design, policy and culture. The answers to these questions could broaden the field of awareness and choice open to the human beings evoking and continuously modifying these use genres in their daily practice.

Governments and civic groups can benefit from user-centred research that explicates the everyday problems and activities leading users to their web sites or other Internet-based services. The new dialogic practices that can grow around a democratic Internet would need a heavy research investment in order to take off and stabilize as a routine form of communication between organizations and their members and clients.

Insights gained from research are also required for the development of flexible learning forms and forums hosted by universities but driven by the situated agendas of particular communities and categories of learners.

Groupware designs and the experiences of people who build and participate in various forms of virtual togetherness presents another set of pressing research issues. Will togetherness on the Internet be as 'natural' to achieve as consumption? Can research help online groups with their sometimes painful search for appropriate models of communication?

To contribute to the realization of a 'community-oriented', participatory model of the Internet, research should examine social life online by looking at and beyond the screen. Both the systematic knowledge of designers and the situated knowledges of diverse categories of users are essential to this project.

Consumption through the Internet (online buying) was a theme that did not resonate deeply with the experiences of the users I interviewed at the early stage of e-commerce development when my study took place. Only a few of them had bought a limited number of commercial products online. However, there were clear signs of a desire in users to employ the Internet in making rational consumer choices – to compare prices and to avoid falling for advertisement and in-store manipulation. User-centred research on e-commerce could seek to identify possibilities for user empowerment in the face of the online commercial schemes, possibly by means of consumer-to-consumer communication and organizing.

Final Reflections

Admittedly, many of the research questions that arose from my theoretical reflections did not find their answers in my empirical study. Similarly, many of the themes emerging from the study remained unexplored. There is much that I would have liked to have done to make this research a richer ethnography and a deeper-cutting critique. A longitudinal data collection by visiting the homes of my respondents periodically over a period of time would have shown how conceptions and practices change with experience and perhaps how initial mobilization turns into unreflective routine. An examination of household budgets would have given me a better idea of the economic standing of the people I interviewed and whether anything had to be sacrificed in exchange for the latest gadgets of technical progress, as Lefebvre (1991) had predicted. Interviewing all the family members in all the participating households would have unearthed more of the values, hier-archies and struggles underlying the Internet use arrangements in the home. More thorough digging into the layers of electronic artefacts in the memory of users' computers and more precise documenting of the findings would have uncovered the structures of the interpersonal networks sus-tained through electronic communication. It would have revealed the nature of the information resources on which users drew and would have gained insight into the emerging new sources of authoritative discourse in society. These additional data would have provided for better substantiated analysis, evaluation and critique of domestic Internet use.

My project, like every research project in the real world, was bound by my own and my respondents' time limitations. Lack of funding forced me to keep down the size of my respondent group. Interestingly, there was a bright side to these limitations as well. I ended up working with a group of volunteers who were intrinsically motivated to share their experiences as Internet users. I did all the interviewing, transcription and analysis myself, which made me live through the narrative of each respondent, hold it in my head in its entirety and make sense of the different themes with regard to the whole story. Finally, the fact that nobody was financing my research freed me to pursue my own interests and the paths suggested by my respondents. It also allowed me to be open and sincere with the people I interviewed, as there were no foreign agendas behind the questions I was asking them. This provided for authentic and enjoyable (at least to me) human communication.

But it wasn't before I approached the end of the process that I realized there was more to my relationship with the people I studied. As I step out of their stories, I find myself immersed in a swarm of voices. The unanswered e-mail messages of my friends and colleagues from overseas ring in my head as loud and clear as the voice of my son over my shoulder demanding computer time so that he could play 'The Age of Empire' with a schoolmate over the Internet. The music that my husband downloaded from Napster creeps into the room. In the back of my mind I still feel guilty for not responding to that unknown student from Algeria who asked me for help with his project a few days ago. So I stop to think. Am I empowered or oppressed? Is there a single message in this cacophony and what is its meaning? Where do I stand? What should I do? And as I am turning my research questions to myself, I know: everything is still at stake.

Notes

[1]I have come across a number of quantitative surveys asking users to indicate which activities out of a suggested list they perform on the Internet. 'Surfing' always accounts for a high percentage of the answers. This observation has left me wondering what sense different people put in this word that has come to be associated with Internet use in a trite manner.

[2]Harding (1991) draws attention to a similar argument made by Aptheker (1989) with regard to the unrecognized political contribution of women (see pp. 129–30).

[3]I have borrowed some of the language and inspiration for this claim from Benjamin's (1968) 'The work of art in the age of mechanical reproduction.'

Appendix Respondent Description

Name	Age	Occupation	Education	Household members	Originally from	Income (Canadian dollars)	ISP	Computer	Home Internet for n years
Myra*	28	Doctoral student/physicist	MA PhD courses	Fiancé	Albania	20–50K	VCN University	PC 486	
Vera	34	Freelance writer	BA	Daughter 6 Son 4	Los Angeles	35–50K	Compu Serve	Pentium; Power book	5
Sandy	35	Part-time telemarketer	Undergrad courses	Daughter 5	Canada	20–50K	Major local	Power Mac	1.5
Jane	35	Homemaker	College courses	Husband Sons 14, 12 Daughter 9	Vancouver	20–50K	VCN	Old Mac	1
Sophie	35	Part-time nutrition consultant	College courses	Husband Sons 13, 11	Vancouver	35–50K	Small local	PC 486	2
Dana	36	Operations manager	BA + Diploma	None	Vancouver	35–50K	Small local	PC 486	
Martha	41	Meat-wrapper On disability	College 4 years Univ. 1 year	Son 16	Canada	20–50K	VCN Small local	Pentium	4
Dorris	46	Nurse	College	None	Canada	35–50K	College	Pentium	4

(Continued)

Appendix (Continued)

Name	Age	Occupation	Education	Household members	Originally from	Income (Canadian dollars)	ISP	Computer	Home Internet for n years
Carol	47	Marketing director quit job	MA	Husband Sons 14, 11	Canada	60–100K	AOL	Pentium	3
Ellen	49	Editor on disability	MA	None	Britain	under 20K	VCN	Old Mac	2
Rita	49	Accountant	University courses	Husband **Son 9** **Daughter 13**	Jamaica	over 100K	ASDL Major local	4 home computers; LAN Pentium	2
Larry	22	Student part-time work	College courses	Mother father 2 sisters	China	20–50K	VCN College	PC	2
Patrick	33	Technician	BS	**Fiancé**	Eastern Europe	20–50K	VCN	PC 486	1.5
Norris	35	Teaching assistant	BA Economics	Mother	Tanzania	20–50K	VCN AOL	Pentium	1.5
Alex	36	Jewellry designer	Art college	**Wife** Son 6	Bulgaria	20–50K	Sprynet	Mac 6200	4
Matthew**	37	ISP customer support person	BA Communication	**Wife** Sons 15, 7 Daughters 13, 4	Britain	20–50K	Small local	Power Mac	5
Radul	40	Auto body technician	Technical college	**Wife** Son 14	Romania	60–70K	Major local	Pentium	2

Appendix *(Continued)*

Name	Age	Occupation	Education	Household members	Originally from	Income (Canadian dollars)	ISP	Computer	Home Internet for n years
Theodore	45	Parking patroller	BA	Wife Son 8	Ethiopia	60–100K	VCN	PC 386	4
Merlin	58	Unemployed mechanical engineer	BS	Wife	USA	under 20K	VCN	PC 386	10
Don	60	Self-employed psychologist/ counsellor	MA	Wife Sons 22, 18	Los Angeles	20–50K	Small local	Pentium	3
Reiner	62	Retired mech.eng. technician	Technical college	**Wife**	Germany	20–50K	Cable Major local	PC 486	4
Garry	67	Retired naval radio-operator	College equivalent	None	Britain	20–50K	VCN	PC 486	1.5
John	73	Retired mechanical engineer	BS equivalent	**Wife**	Britain	20–50K	VCN	PC 386	4

Note: The bold font style indicates that the respective household member has been interviewed.

*Myra was an academic, a PhD student in theoretical physics, and in this way did not strictly match the definition of a non-professional user I was working with. Her story however was inextricably intertwined with that of Patrick, her fiancé, who in fact responded to my call for participation. She actively participated in the interview along with Patrick. Their home computer on which I performed my tour was used mainly by Patrick.

**Matthew was not a simple customer in the strict sense as he was providing services on the Web. His story was interesting to me because it demonstrated the evolution of a user into active provider of Internet-based content and services. The mailing list that Matthew moderated represented a case of a virtual community initiated by a user.

References

Abbate, Janet E. (1994) *From Arpanet to Internet: A History of ARPA-sponsored computer networks, 1966–1988*. Unpublished PhD, University of Pennsylvania, Philadelphia.

Akrich, Madeleine (1992) The de-scription of technical objects. In Wiebe E. Bijker, and John Law, (Eds), *Shaping technology/building society: studies in sociotechnical change* (pp. 205–244). Cambridge, MA, London: MIT Press.

Akrich, Madeleine, and Latour Bruno (1992) A summary of a convenient vocabulary for the semiotics of human and nonhuman assemblies. In Wiebe Bijker, and John Law, (Eds), *Shaping technology/building society: studies in sociotechnical change* (pp. 259–265). Cambridge, MA: MIT Press.

Anderson, Benedict (1983) *Imagined communities: reflections on the origin and spread of nationalism*. London: Verso.

Ang, Ien (1991) *Desperately seeking the audience*. London: Routledge.

Aptheker, Bettina (1989) *Tapestries of life: women's work, women's consciousness and the meaning of daily life*. Amherst: University of Massachusetts Press.

Aune, Margrethe (1996) The computer in everyday life: Patterns of domestication of a new technology. In Marette Lie and Knut H. Sorensen (Eds), *Making technology our own? Domesticating technology into everyday life* (pp. 91–120). Oslo, Stockholm, Copenhagen, Oxford, Boston: Scandinavian University Press.

Bakardjieva, Maria and Smith, Richard (2001) The internet in everyday life: computer networking from the standpoint of the domestic user. *New Media & Society*, 3 (1): 67–83.

Bakhtin, Mikhail M. (1981) *The dialogic imagination: four essays*. Translated by Caryl Emerson and Michael Holquist. Edited by Michael Holquist. Austin: University of Texas Press.

Bakhtin, Mikhail (1984) *Rabelais and his world*. Bloomington: Indiana University Press.

Bakhtin, Mikhail (1986) *Speech genres and other late essays*. Translated by Vern W. McGee. Edited by Caryl Emerson and Michael Holquist. Austin: University of Texas Press.

Baym, Nancy K. (1995) The emergence of community in computer-mediated communication. In Steven G. Jones (Ed.), *Cybersociety: computer-mediated communication and community* (pp. 138–163). Thousand Oaks: Sage.

Becker, Howard S. (1953) Becoming a marijuana user. *American Journal of Sociology, 59*, 235–242.

Becker, Howard S. (1963) *Outsiders: studies in the sociology of deviance.* London: Free Press.

Benjamin, Walter (1968) The work of art in the age of mechanical reproduction. In *Illuminations* (pp. 219–253). New York: Harcourt, Brace and World.

Benston, Margaret L. (1988) Women's voices/men's voices: technology as language. In Cheris Kramarae (Ed.), *Technology and women's voices: keeping in touch* (pp. 15–28). London: Routledge & Kegan Paul.

Berg, Anne J., and Lie, Marette (1995) Do artefacts have gender? Feminism and the domestication of technical artifacts. *Science, Technology & Human Values, 20* (3), 332–351.

Bijker, Wiebe E. (1993) Do not despair: there is life after constructivism. *Science, Technology & Human Values, 18*, 113–138.

Bijker, Wiebe E. (1995) *Of bicycles, bakelites, and bulbs: toward a theory of sociotechnical change.* Cambridge, MA: MIT Press.

Bijker, Wiebe E. (2001) Technology, social construction of. In Neil J. Smelser and Paul B. Baltes (Eds), *International encyclopedia of the social and behavioral sciences*, 1st ed. Amsterdam, New York: Elsevier.

Bijker, Wiebe E. and Law, John (Eds) (1992) *Shaping technology/building society: studies in socio-technical change.* Cambridge, MA: MIT Press.

Borgmann, Albert (1992) *Crossing the postmodern divide.* Chicago: University of Chicago Press.

Braverman, Harry (1975) *Labor and monopoly capital: the degradation of work in the twentieth century.* New York: Monthly Review Press.

Bruner, Jerome (1987) Life as a narrative. *Social Research, 51*, 11–32.

Callon, Michele (1987) Society in the making: The study of technology as a tool for sociological analysis. In Wiebe E. Bijker, Thomas P. Hughes, and Trevor J. Pinch (Eds), *The Social conctruction of technological systems: new directions in the sociology and history of technology* (pp. 83–103). Cambridge, MA, London: The MIT Press.

Carey, James W. (1989) *Communication as culture: essays on media and society.* Boston: Unwin Hyman.

Castells, Manuel (1996) *The rise of the network society* (*Information Age*, Vol.1). Cambridge, MA: Blackwell Publishers.

Castells, Manuel (1997) *The power of identity* (*Information Age*, Vol.2). Malden, MA, Oxford: Blackwell.

Castells, Manuel (1998) *End of millennium* (*Information Age*, Vol.3). Malden, MA, Oxford: Blackwell.

Castells, Manuel (2001) *The Internet galaxy: reflections on the Internet, business and society.* Oxford: Oxford University Press.

Center for Media Education (1996) *Web of deception: threats to children from online marketing* [Online]. Available: http://tap.epn.org/cme/cmwdecov.html [1999, 20 November].

Certeau, Michel de (1984) *The practice of everyday life.* Berkley and Los Angeles: University of California Press.

Certeau, Michel de; Giard, Luce, and Mayol, Pierre (1998) *The practice of everyday life*, vol. 2. Minneapolis, MN: University of Minnesota Press.

Clark, Katerina, and Holquist, Michael (1984) *Mikhail Bakhtin*. Cambridge, MA: Belknap Press of Harvard University Press.

Cockburn, Cynthia (1992) The circuit of technology: Gender, identity and power. In Roger Silverstone and Eric Hirsch (Eds), *Consuming technologies: media and information in domestic space*. London: Routledge.

Cockburn, Cynthia (1993) Feminism/constructivism in technology studies: notes on genealogy and recent developments. Paper presented at the conference on European Theoretical Perspectives on New Technology: feminism, Constructivism and Utility, CRICT, Brunel University, 16–17 September.

Cohen, Lizabeth (1990) *Making a new deal: industrial workers in Chicago, 1919–1939*. Cambridge, New York: Cambridge University Press.

Correll, Shelley (1995) The ethnography of an electronic bar: the lesbian café. *Journal of Contemporary Ethnography*, *24* (3), 270–298.

Cowan, Ruth Schwartz (1983) *More work for mother: the ironies of household technology from the open hearth to the microwave*. New York: Basic Books.

Cowan, Ruth Schwartz (1987) The consumption junction: a proposal for research strategies in the sociology of technology. In Wiebe E. Bijker, Thomas P. Hughes, and Trevor J. Pinch (Eds), *The Social conctruction of technological systems: new directions in the sociology and history of technology* (pp. 261–280). Cambridge, MA, London: The MIT Press.

Cummings, Jonathon, and Kraut, Robert (2002) Domesticating computers and the Internet. *Information Society, 18* (3), 221–232.

Czikszentmihaly, Michali, and Rochberg-Halton, Eugene (1981) *The meaning of things: domestic symbols and the self*. Cambridge: Cambridge University Press.

Dreyfus, Hubert L. (1998) *Kierkegaard on the Internet: anonymity vs. commitment in the present age* [Online]. Available: http://ist-socrates.berkeley.edu/~hdreyfus/html/paper_kierkegaard.html [2003, January 8].

Drucker, Susan J.; Tentokali, Vana, and Gumpert, Gary (1997) Time and space in domestic life. In Susan J. Drucker and Gary Gumpert (Eds), *Voices in the street: explorations in gender, media, and public space* (pp. 43–58). Cresskill, NJ: Hampton Press.

Dutton, William H. (1996) Network rules of order: regulating speech in public electronic fora. *Media Culture & Society, 18*, 269–290.

Feenberg, Andrew (1991) *The critical theory of technology*. New York: Oxford University Press.

Feenberg, Andrew (1993a) Subversive rationalization: technology, power and democracy. *Inquiry, 35*, 301–322.

Feenberg, Andrew (1993b) The technocracy thesis revisited: on the critique of power. *Inquiry, 37*, 85–102.

Feenberg, Andrew (1995) *Alternative modernity: the technical turn in philosophy and social theory*. Los Angeles: University of California Press.

Feenberg, Andrew (1996) Four lectures on technique and modernity (unpublished manuscript). Paris: Ecole des Hautes Etudes en Sciences Sociales.

Feenberg, Andrew (1999) *Questioning technology*. Unpublished manuscript.

Foucault, Michel (1980) *Power/knowledge*. Edited by Colin Gordon. New York: Pantheon.

Garfinkel, Harold (1967) *Studies in ethnomethodology*. Englewood Cliffs, NJ: Prentice-Hall.

Gibson, James J. (1979) *The ecological approach to visual perception*. Hillside, NJ: Lawrence Erlbaum Associates, Inc.

Gibson, William (1984) *Neuromancer*. New York: Ace Books.

Giddens, Anthony (1984) *The constitution of society: outline of the theory of structuration*. Berkeley and Los Angeles: University of California Press.

Gill, Rosalind, and Grint, Keith (1995) The gender-technology relation: contemporary theory and research. In Keith Grint and Rosalind Gill (Eds), *The gender-technology relation: contemporary theory and research* (pp. 1–28). London; Bristol, PA: Taylor and Francis.

Gillespie, Marie (1995) *Television, ethnicity and cultural change*. London, New York: Routledge.

Goffman, Erving (1959) *The presentation of self in everyday life*. Garden City, NY: Doubleday Anchor Books.

Gray, Ann (1992) *Video playtime: the gendering of a leisure technology*. London, New York: Routledge.

Grint, Keith, and Woolgar, Steve (1997) *The machine at work: technology, work and organization*. Cambridge: Polity Press.

Habermas, Jurgen (1984) *The theory of communicative action* (Vol.2). Translated by Thomas McCarthy. Boston: Beacon Press.

Haddon, Leslie (1991) Researching gender and home computers. In Knut Sorensen and Anne-Jorun Berg (Eds), *Technology and everyday life: trajectories and transformations*. Report No. 5. Oslo: NAVF-NTNF-NORAS.

Haddon, Leslie (1992) Explaining ICT consumption: the case of the home computer. In Roger Silverstone and Eric Hirsch (Eds), *Consuming technologies: media and information in domestic spaces* (pp. 82–96). London: Routledge.

Hall, Stuart (1973) Encoding and decoding in the television discourse. *CCCS Stencilled Paper, 7*. University of Birmingham.

Hakken, David (1999) *Cyborg@cyberspace: an ethnographer looks at the future*. New York, London: Routledge.

Haraway, Donna (1995) Situated knowledges: the science question in feminism and the privilege of partial perspective. In Andrew Feenberg and Alastair Hannay (Eds), *Technology and the politics of knowledge* (pp. 175–193). Bloomington: Indiana University Press.

Harding, Sandra (1991) *Whose science? whose knowledge? thinking from women's lives*. Ithaca, NY: Cornell University Press.

Havel, Václav, and Keane, John (Eds) (1985) *The power of the powerless: citizens against the state in central-eastern Europe*. Armonk, NY: M.E. Sharpe.

Heller, Agnes (1984) *Everyday life*. London, Boston: Routledge and Kegan Paul.

Henwood, Flis; Kennedy, Helen, and Miller, Nod (2001) *Cyborg lives? women's technobiographies*. York: Raw Nerve Books Limited.

Highmore, Ben (2002) *Everyday life and cultural theory: an introduction*. London, New York: Routledge.

Hiltz, Roxanne, and Turoff, Murray (1978) *The network nation: human communication via computer*. London, Amsterdam, Don Mills, Ontario, Sydney, Tokyo: Addison Wesley.

Hine, Christine (1998) Virtual ethnography. [Online]. Paper presented at the IRISS '98, Bristol, UK. Available: http://www.sosig.ac.uk/iriss/papers/paper16.htm [1999, June 9].

Hine, Christine (2000) *Virtual ethnography*. London, Thousand Oaks, New Delhi: Sage.

Hobson, Dorothy (1982) *'Crossroads': The drama of a soap opera*. London: Methuen.

Holstein, James, A., and Gubrium, Jaber, F. (1995) *The active interview*. Thousand Oaks, CA: Sage.

HomeNet (1999) *Overview* [Online]. Available: http://homenet.hcii.cs.cmu.edu/progress/index.html [2003, January 8].

hooks, bell (1990) *Yearning*. Boston, MA: South End Press.

Hughes, Thomas P. (1987) The evolution of large technological systems. In Wiebe E. Bijker, Thomas P. Hughes, and Trevor J. Pinch (Eds), *The social conctruction of technological systems: new directions in the sociology and history of technology* (pp. 51–82). Cambridge, MA; London, England: The MIT Press.

Ihde, Don (1990) *Technology and the lifeworld: from garden to earth*. Indiana Bloomington and Indianapolis: University Press.

Industry Canada, Task Force on Electronic Commerce (26 August 1999a). *Canadian Internet commerce statistics summary sheet* [Online]. Available: http://strategis.ic.gc.ca/virtual_hosts/e-com/using/en/e-comstats.pdf [2000, January 20].

Industry Canada (July 1999) *Information and communication technologies: economic and statistical information* [Online]. Available: http://strategis.ic.gc.ca/pics/sf/sld001.htm [2000, 20 January].

Jones, Steven G. (Ed.) (1995) *Cybersociety: computer-mediated communication and community*. Thousand Oaks, CA: Sage.

Jones, Steven G. (Ed.) (1997) *Virtual culture: identity and communication in cybersociety*. London; Thousand Oaks, CA: Sage.

Katz, Elihu, and Lazarsfeld, Paul F. (1964) *Personal influence: the part played by people in the flow of mass communications*. New York: Free Press.

Kollock, Peter, and Smith, Marc (1999) Communities in cyberspace. In Marc Smith and Peter Kollock (Eds), *Communities in cyberspace* (pp. 1–22). London, New York: Routledge.

Kraut, Robert and Cummings, Jonathon N. (2002) Domesticating computers and the Internet. *The Information Society, 18* (3), pp. 221–232.

Kraut, Robert, and Kiesler, Sara (2003) The social impact of internet use. *Psychological Science Agenda, 16* (3), 8–10.

Kraut, Robert; Patterson, Michael; Lundmark, Vicki; Kiesler, Sara; Mukophadhyay, Tridas, and Scherlis, William (1998) Internet paradox: a social technology that reduces social involvement and psychological well-being? *American Psychologist, 53* (9), 1017–1031.

Kumar, Krishan (1995) *From post-industrial to post-modern society: New theories of the contemporary world*. Cambridge, MA: Blackwell Publishers.

Latour, Bruno (1987) *Science in action: how to follow scientists and engineers through society*. Milton Keynes: Open University Press.

Latour, Bruno (1988) *The pasteurization of France*. Cambridge, MA; London: Harvard University Press.

Latour, Bruno (1992) Where are the missing masses? the sociology of a few mundane artifacts. In Wiebe E. Bijker and John Law (Eds), *Shaping technology/building society: studies in socio-technical change*. Cambridge, MA: MIT Press.

Latour, Bruno (1993) *We have never been modern*. New York, London, Toronto, Sydney, Tokyo, Singapore: Harvester Wheatsheaf.

Latour, Bruno (1998) *Thought experiments in social science: From the social contract to virtual society* [Online]. Available: www.brunel.ac.uk/reseafch/virtsoc/text/latour2.htm [2000, January 30].

Lally, Elaine (2002) *At home with computers*. Oxford, New York: Berg.

Law, John (1987) Technology and heterogeneous engineering: the case of Portugese expansion. In Wiebe E. Bijker, Thomas P. Hughes, and Trevor J. Pinch (Eds), *The social construction of technological systems* (pp. 111–134). Cambridge, MA: MIT Press.

Law, John, and Callon, Michel (1992) The life and death of an artifact: a Network analysis of technical change. In Wiebe E. Bijker and John Law (Eds), *Shaping technology/building society: studies in socio-technical change*. Cambridge, MA: MIT Press.

Law, John, and Hassard, John (Eds) (1999) *Actor network theory and after*. Oxford, Malden, MA: Blackwell.

Lazarsfeld, Paul F.; Berelson, Bernard, and Gaude, Hazel (1948) *The people's choice: how the voter makes up his mind in a presidential campaign*. New York: Columbia University Press.

Lefebvre, Henri (1971) *Everyday life in the modern world*. New York, Evanston, San Francisco, London: Harper & Row.

Lefebvre, Henri (1991) *Critique of everyday life. Vol.1: introduction*. London, New York: Verso.

Leiner, Barry K.; Cerf, Vinton G.; Clark, David D.; Khan, Robert; Kleinrock, Leonard; Lynch, Daniel C.; Postel, Jon; Roberts, Larry G. and Wolff, Stephen (1997) *A brief history of the Internet* (Version 3.1) [Online]. Available: http://isoc.org/internethistory/ [February 20].

Leiss, William (1990) *Under technology's thumb*. Montreal: McGill-Queen's University Press.

Leont'ev, Aleksei (1978) *Activity, consciousness, and personality*. Translated by M.J. Hall. Englewood Cliffs, NJ: Prentice-Hall.

Licklider J.C.R., and Taylor, Robert W. (1968) The computer as a communication device. *Science & Technology, 76*, 21–31.

Lie, Marette, and Sorensen, Knut H. (1996) Making technology our own? domesticating technology into everyday life. In Marette Lie and Knut H. Sorensen

(Eds), *Making technology our own? domesticating technology into everyday life.* (pp. 1–30). Oslo, Stockholm, Copenhagen, Oxford, Boston: Scandinavian University Press.

Lukács, George (1971) *History and class consciousness.* Translated by R. Livingstone. Cambridge, MA: MIT Press.

Mackay, Hugh (1997) *Consumption in everyday life.* London, Thousand Oaks, New Delhi: Sage.

Mackay, Hughie, and Gillespie, Gareth (1992) Extending the social shaping of technology approach: ideology and appropriation. *Social Studies of Science, 22,* 685–716.

Marcus, George E. (1995) Ethnography in/of the world system: the emergence of multi-sited ethnography. *Annual Review of Anthropology, 24,* 95–117.

Marcus, George E., and Fischer, Michael, M.J. (1986) *Anthropology as cultural critique: an experimental moment in the human sciences.* Chicago; London: University of Chicago Press.

Marcuse, Herbert (1964) *One-dimensional man.* Boston: Beacon Press.

Markham, Anette (1998) *Life online. Researching real experience in virtual space.* Walnut Creek: Sage, AltaMira Press.

Marvin, Carolyn (1988) *When old technologies were new: thinking about electric communication in the late nineteenth century.* New York: Oxford University Press.

Mauss, Marcel (1967) *The gift: forms and functions of exchange in archaic societies.* Translated by Ian Cunninson. New York: W.W. Norton.

McLuhan, Marshall (1964) *Understanding media: the extensions of man.* New York: McGraw-Hill.

Melucci, Alberto (1989) *Nomads of the present: social movements and individual needs in contemporary society.* London; Victoria; Australia, Auckland: Hutchinson Radius.

Miller, Carolyn R. (1994) Genre as social action. In Aviva Freedman, and Peter Medway (Eds), *Genre and the new rhetoric* (pp. 23–42). London: Taylor and Francis.

Miller, Daniel, and Slater, Don (2000) *The internet: an ethnographic approach.* Oxford, New York: Berg.

Mishler, George E. (1986) *Research interviewing: context and narrative.* Cambridge, MA: Harvard University Press.

Moores, Shaun (1993) *Interpreting audiences: ethnography of media consumption.* London, Thousand Oaks, New Delhi: Sage.

Moores, Shaun (1996) *Sattelite television and everyday life: articulating technology.* Luton: University of Luton Press.

Morley, David (1986) *Family television: cultural power and domestic leisure.* London: Comedia.

Morley, David (1992) *Television, audiences, and cultural studies.* London, New York: Routledge.

Morley, David (1994) Between the public and the private: the domestic uses of information and communications technologies. In Jon Cruz and Justin Lewis (Eds), *Viewing, reading, listening: audiences and cultural reception* (pp. 101–121). Boulder, Colorado: Westview Press.

Morley, David (2000) *Home territories: media, mobility and identity*. London and New York: Routledge.

Moyal, Ann (1992) The gendered use of the telephone: an Australian case study. *Media, Culture & Society, 14* (1), 51–72.

Munro, Moira, and Madigan, Ruth (1999) Negotiating space in the family home. In Irene Cieraad (Ed.), *At home: an anthropology of domestic space* (pp. 107–117). Syracuse, New York: Syracuse University Press.

Mynatt, Elizabeth; O'Day, Vicki; Adler, Anette and Ito, Mizuko (1998) Network communities: Something old, something new, something borrowed. *Computer Supported Cooperative Work: The Journal of Cooperative Computing, 7*, 123–156.

National Statistics Online (2004) Internet access [Online]. Available: http://www.statistics.gov.uk/cci/nugget.asp?id=8 [2004, May 31].

Nightingale, Virginia (1989) What is 'ethnographic' about ethnographic audience research? *Australian Journal of Communication, 16*, 51–63.

Nikolchina, Miglena (2002) The seminar: *Mode d'emploi* Impure spaces in the light of late totalitarianism. *A Journal of Feminist Cultural Studies 13.1*, 96–127.

Noble, David F. (1984) *Forces of production: a social history of industrial automation*. New York: Knopf.

Oudshoorn, Nelly, and Pinch, Trevor (2003) How users and non-users matter. In Nelly Oudshoorn, and Trevor Pinch (Eds), *How users matter: the co-construction of users and technologies*. Cambridge, MA: MIT Press.

Pinch, Trevor, and Bijker, Wiebe E. (1987) The social construction of facts and artifacts. In Wiebe E. Bijker, Thomas P. Hughes, and Trevor J. Pinch (Eds), *The social construction of technological systems* (pp. 17–50). Cambridge, MA: MIT Press.

Postman, Neil (1992) *Technopoly: the surrender of culture to technology*. New York: Knopf.

Propp, Vladimir I. (1928/1968) *Morphology of the folktale*. Austin: University of Texas Press.

Rakow, Lana (1992) *Gender on the line: women, the telephone and community life*. Urbana: University of Illinois Press.

Reid, Elizabeth M. (1991) Electropolis: communication and community on Internet Relay Chat. Unpublished MA thesis, University of Melbourne.

Reid, Elizabeth M. (1995) Virtual worlds: culture and imagination. In Steven G. Jones (Ed.), *Cybersociety: computer-mediated communication and community* (pp. 164–183). Thousand Oaks, London, New Delhi: Sage.

Rheingold, Howard (1993) *The virtual community: homesteading on the electronic frontier*. Reading, MA: Addison-Wesley.

Robins, Kevin, and Webster, Frank (1999) *Times of the technoculture: from the information society to the virtual life*. London, New York: Routledge.

Rosenzweig, Roy (1998) Wizards, bureaucrats, warriors & hackers: writing the history of the Internet. *American Historical Review, 103* (5), 1530–1552.

Schrøder, Kim C. (1999) The best of both worlds? media audience research between rival paradigms. In Pertti Alasuutari (Ed.), *Rethinking the media audience: the new agenda* (pp. 38–68). London, Thousand Oaks, New Delhi: Sage.

Schuler, Douglas, and Namioka, Aki (1993) *Participatory design: principles and practices.* Hillsdale, NJ: Lawrence Erlbaum Associates.

Schutz, Alfred (1964) *Collected papers II: studies in social theory.* The Hague: Martinus Nijhoff.

Schutz, Alfred (1970) *On phenomenology and social relations.* Selected writings, edited and with an introduction by Helmut R. Wagner. Chicago and London: The University of Chicago Press.

Schutz, Alfred (1964) The homecomer. *Collected Papers II* (pp. 106–119). The Hague: Martinus Nijhoff.

Schutz, Alfred, and Luckmann, Thomas (1973) *The structures of the life-world.* Evanston, IL: North-Western University Press.

Seiter, Ellen (1999) *Television and new media audiences.* Oxford: Clarendon Press.

Sharp, Joanne P. (1996) Gendering nationhood: a feminist engagement with national identity. In Nancy Duncan (Ed.), *Body space: destabilizing geographies of gender and sexuality* (pp. 97–108). New York: Routledge.

Shields, Rob (2001) Henri Lefebvre: Philosopher of everyday life. In Anthony Elliott and Bryan Turner (Eds), *Profiles in contemporary social theory.* London, Thousand Oaks, CA: Sage.

Silverstone, Roger (1994) *Television and everyday life.* London and New York: Routledge.

Silverstone, Roger, and Haddon, Leslie (1996) Design and the domestication of information and communication technologies: technical change and everyday life. In Robin Mansell and Roger Silverstone (Eds), *Communication by design: The politics of information and communication technologies* (pp. 44–74). Oxford, New York: Oxford University Press.

Silverstone, Roger; Hirsch, Eric and Morley, David (1992) Information and communication technologies and the moral economy of the household. In Roger Silverstone and Eric Hirsch (Eds), *Consuming technologies: media and information in domestic spaces* (pp. 15–31). London: Routledge.

Slack, Jennifer Daryl (1984) *Communication technologies and society: conceptions of causality and the politics of technological intervention.* Norwood, NJ: Ablex.

Slater, Don (2002) Social relationships and identity, online and offline. In Leah Lievrouw and Sonia Livingstone (Eds), *Handbook of new media: social shaping and consequences of ICTs* (pp. 533–546). London: Sage.

Slouka, Mark (1995) *War of the worlds: cyberspace and the high-tech assault on reality.* New York: Basic Books.

Smith, Dorothy (1987) *The everyday world as problematic: a feminist sociology.* Toronto: University of Toronto Press.

Smith, Dorothy (1999) *Writing the social.* Toronto, Buffalo, London: University of Toronto Press.

Smith, Marc, and Kollock, Peter (1999) *Communities in cyberspace.* London, New York: Routledge.

Spigel, Lynn (1992) *Make room for TV: television and the family ideal in postwar America.* Chicago and London: The University of Chicago Press.

Statistics, Canada (1999) *Canadian Statistics: selected dwelling characteristics and household equipment*, [Online]. Available: http://www.statcan.ca/english/Pgdb/People/Families/famil09c.htm [2000, January 20].

Statistics, Canada (2000) Household Internet Use. *The Daily*, Friday, May 19 [Online]. Available http://www.statcan.ca/Daily/English/000519/d000519b.htm [2004, January 8].

Statistics, Canada (2004) *Canadian Statistics: selected dwelling characteristics and household equipment*, [Online]. Available: http://www.statcan.ca/english/Pgdb/famil09c.htm [2004, November 5].

Stone, Rosanne (1995) *The war of desire and technology at the close of the mechanical age*. Cambridge, MA: MIT Press.

Suchman, Lucy A. (1987) *Plans and situated actions: the problem of human-machine communication*. Cambridge; New York: Cambridge University Press.

Tomlinson, Alan (1990) Home fixtures: doing it yourself in a privatized world. In Alan Tomlinson (Ed.), *Consumption, identity, and style: marketing, meanings, and the packaging of pleasure* (pp. 57–76). London, New York: Routledge.

Turkle, Sherry (1984) *The second self: computers and the human spirit*. New York: Simon & Schuster.

Turkle, Sherry (1988) Computational reticence: why women fear the intimate machine. In Cheris Kramarae (Ed.), *Technology and women's voices: keeping in touch* (pp. 41–61). London: Routlege & Kegan Paul.

Turkle, Sherry (1995) *Life on the screen: identity in the age of the internet*. New York: Simon & Schuster.

US Department of Commerce and National, Telecommunications and Information Administration (July 1995). *Falling through the Net: a survey of the 'have-nots' in rural and urban America* [Online]. Available: http://www.ntia.doc.gov/ntiahome/ [2000, January 20].

US Department of Commerce, National Telecommunications and Information and Administration (July 1998) *Falling through the Net II: new data on the digital divide* [Online]. Available: http://www.ntia.doc.gov/ntiahome/ [2000, 20 January].

US Department of Commerce, National Telecommunications and Information Administration (July 1999) *Falling through the net: defining the digital divide* [Online]. Available: http://www.ntia.doc.gov/ntiahome/fttn99/contents.html [2000, 20 January].

Voloshinov, Valentin N. (1929/1986) *Marxism and the philosophy of language*. Translated by L. Matejka and I.R. Tutnik. Cambridge, MA, London: Harvard University Press.

Vygotsky, Lev S. (1978) *Mind in society: the development of higher psychological processes*. Edited by Michael Cole, Vera John-Steiner, Sylvia Scribner and Ellen Souberman. Cambridge, MA: Harvard University Press.

Waites, Bernard (1989) Everyday life and the dynamics of technological change. In Colin Chant (Ed.), *Science, technology and everyday life 1870–1950* (pp. 9–20). London, New York: Routledge in association with The Open University.

Watson, Nessim (1997) Why we argue about virtual community: a Case study of the phish.net fan community. In Steven G. Jones (Ed.), *Virtual culture: identity and communication in cybersociety*. London, Thousand Oaks, New Delhi: Sage.

Weintraub, Jeff (1997) The theory and politics of the public/private distinction (pp. 1–42). In Jeff Weintraub, and Krishan Kumar (Eds), *Public and private in thought and practice: perspectives on a grand dichotomy*. Chicago, London: University of Chicago Press.

Weisman, Leslie (1992) *Discrimination by design: a feminist critique of the man-made environment*. Urbana: University of Illinois Press.

Wellman, Barry (2001) Computer networks as social networks. *Science, 293*, 14 September, 2031–2034.

Wellman, Barry (1999) The network community: an Introduction. In Barry Wellman (Ed.), *Networks in the global village: life in contemporary communities* (pp. 1–48). Boulder, CO, Oxford: Westview Press.

Wellman, Barry (1988) The community question re-evaluated. In Michael P. Smith (Ed.), *Power, community and the city*. New Brunswick, NJ: Transaction Books.

Wellman, Barry (1979) The community question: The intimate networks of East Yorkers. *American Journal of Sociology, 84* (5), 1201–1229.

Wellman, Barry, and Haythornthwaite, Caroline (2002) Th*e internet in everyday life*. Oxford, Malden, MA: Blackwell Publishers.

Wellman, Barry, and Gulia, Milena (1999) Net-surfers don't ride alone: virtual communities as communities. In Barry Wellman (Ed.), *Networks in the global village: life in contemporary communities* (pp. 331–366). Boulder, CO, Oxford: Westview Press.

Werry, Chris (1999) Imagined electronic community: representations of virtual community in contemporary business discourse. Paper presented at Exploring Cyber Society, Newcastle, UK.

Wertsch, James V. (1998) *Mind as action*. New York: Oxford University Press.

Wertsch, James V. (1991) *Voices of the mind: a sociocultural approach to mediated action*. Cambridge, MA: Harvard University Press.

Wertsch, James V., del Río, Pablo, and Alvarez, Amelia (1995) Sociocultural studies: history, action, and mediation. In James V. Wertsch, Pablo del Rio, and Amelia Alvarez (Eds), *Sociocultural studies of mind*. Cambridge, New York: Cambridge University Press.

Williams, Raymond (1974) *Television: technology and cultural form*. London: Fontana.

Williams, Raymond (1985) *Keywords: a vocabulary of culture and society*. New York: Oxford University Press.

Winner, Langdon (1977) *Autonomous technology: technics-out-of-control as a theme in political thought*. Cambridge, MA: MIT Press.

Winner, Langdon (1993) Upon opening the black box and finding it empty: social constructivism and the philosophy of technology. *Science, Technology & Human Values, 18* (3), 362–378.

Winston, Brian (1998) *Media technology and society: a history: from the telegraph to the internet*. London, New York: Routledge, 1998.

Wittgenstein, Ludwig (1958) *Philosophical investigations*. Translated by G.E.M. Anscombe. Oxford: Basil Blackwell.

Woolgar, Steve (1991) Configuring the user: the case of usability trials. In John Law (Ed.), *The Sociology of monsters: essays on power, technology and domination* (pp. 57–102). London, New York: Routledge.

Woolgar, Steve (1996) Technologies as cultural artifacts. In William Dutton, (Ed.) *Information and communication technologies: visions and realities* (pp. 87–102). Oxford: Oxford University Press.

Zuboff, Shoshana (1988) *In the age of the smart machine: the future of work and power.* New York: Basic Books.

Index